FOCUS
ON
GRAMMAR

AN INTEGRATED SKILLS APPROACH

FOCUS
ON
GRAMMAR

AN INTEGRATED SKILLS APPROACH

THIRD EDITION

MARJORIE FUCHS
MARGARET BONNER

PEARSON
Longman

To the memory of my parents, Edith and Joseph Fuchs—MF

To my parents, Marie and Joseph Maus, and to my son, Luke Frances—MB

FOCUS ON GRAMMAR 4: An Integrated Skills Approach

Pearson Education, 10 Bank Street, White Plains, NY 10606

Vice president, multimedia and skills: Sherry Preiss
Executive editor: Laura Le Dréan
Senior development editor: Andrea Bryant
Production supervisor: Christine Edmonds
Marketing manager, higher education: Timothy P. Benell
Senior production editor: Kathleen Silloway
Art director: Ann France
Manufacturing manager: Nancy Flaggman
Photo research: Aerin Csigay
Cover design: Rhea Banker
Cover images: Large shell, background, Nick Koudis, RF; large shell, center image, Kaz Chiba;
    background, Comstock Images, RF
Text design: Quorum Creative Services, Rhea Banker
Text composition: ElectraGraphics, Inc.
Text font: 11/13 Sabon, 10/13 Myriad Roman
Illustrators: Steve Attoe pp. 108, 201; Burmar Technical Corporation pp. 320, 379; Ron Chironna pp.
    162, 336, 337; Chris Gash pp. 170, 373, 413; David Klug, pp. 52, 53, 396; Suzanne Mogensen, pp.
    41, 130; Andy Myer pp. 168, 240, 342, 346; Dusan Petricic pp. 246, 294; Steven Schulman p. 304;
    Susan Scott pp. 17, 256; Meryl Treatner pp. 72, 114; PC&F 59, 62.
Text credits: **p. 191**, based on information from Margaret Mead and Rhoda Metraux, *A Way of
    Seeing* (New York: McCall, 1970); **p. 210**, Eva Hoffman, *Lost in Translation: A Life in a New
    Language* (New York: Penguin, 1989); **p. 239**, based on information from *Psychology Today*,
    October 1979; **p. 286**, based on information from Judith Stone, "It's a Small World after All,"
    Discover (February 1992), pp. 23–25.
Photo credits: see p. x.

Library of Congress Cataloging-in-Publication Data

Focus on grammar. An integrated skills approach — 3rd ed.
    p. cm.
    ISBN 0-13-147466-9 (v. 1 : student book : alk. paper) — ISBN 0-13-189971-6 (v. 2 :
student book : alk. paper) — ISBN 0-13-189984-8 (v. 3 : student book : alk. paper) — ISBN
0-13-190008-0 (v. 4 : student book : alk. paper) — ISBN 0-13-191273-9 (v. 5 : student book
: alk. paper)
    1. English language—Textbooks for foreign speakers. 2. English language—Grammar—
Problems, exercises, etc.
PE1128.F555 2005
428.2'4—dc22

                                                                              2005007655

ISBNs: 0-13-191241-0 (Student Book B)
        0-13-193922-X (Student Book B with Audio CD)

LONGMAN ON THE **WEB**

Longman.com offers online resources for
teachers and students. Access our Companion
Websites, our online catalog, and our local
offices around the world.

Visit us at **longman.com**.

Printed in the United States of America

1 2 3 4 5 6 7 8 9 10—WC—12 11 10 09 08 07 06 05

CONTENTS

APPENDICES

ABOUT THE AUTHORS

Marjorie Fuchs has taught ESL at New York City Technical College and LaGuardia Community College of the City University of New York and EFL at the Sprach Studio Lingua Nova in Munich, Germany. She has a master's degree in Applied English Linguistics and a Certificate in TESOL from the University of Wisconsin–Madison. She has authored and co-authored many widely used books and multimedia materials, notably *Crossroads, Top Twenty ESL Word Games: Beginning Vocabulary Development, Families: Ten Card Games for Language Learners, Focus on Grammar 3: An Integrated Skills Approach, Focus on Grammar 3 CD-ROM, Focus on Grammar 4 CD-ROM, Longman English Interactive 3* and *4, Grammar Express Basic, Grammar Express Basic CD-ROM, Grammar Express Intermediate,* and the workbooks to the *Longman Dictionary of American English, the Longman Photo Dictionary, The Oxford Picture Dictionary, Focus on Grammar 3* and *4,* and *Grammar Express Basic.*

Margaret Bonner has taught ESL at Hunter College and the Borough of Manhattan Community College of the City University of New York, at Taiwan National University in Taipei, and at Virginia Commonwealth University in Richmond. She holds a master's degree in Library Science from Columbia University; and she has done work toward a Ph.D. in English Literature at the Graduate Center of the City University of New York. She has authored and co-authored numerous ESL and EFL print and multimedia materials, including textbooks for the national school system of Oman, *Step into Writing: A Basic Writing Text, Focus on Grammar 3: An Integrated Skills Approach, Focus on Grammar 4 Workbook, Grammar Express Basic, Grammar Express Basic CD-ROM, Grammar Express Basic Workbook, Grammar Express Intermediate, Focus on Grammar 3 CD-ROM, Focus on Grammar 4 CD-ROM, Longman English Interactive 4,* and *The Oxford Picture Dictionary Intermediate Workbook.*

CREDITS

INTRODUCTION

The *Focus on Grammar* series

Written by ESL/EFL professionals, *Focus on Grammar: An Integrated Skills Approach* helps students to understand and practice English grammar. The primary aim of the course is for students to gain confidence in their ability to speak and write English accurately and fluently.

The **third edition** retains this popular series' focus on English grammar through lively listening, speaking, reading, and writing activities. The new *Focus on Grammar* also maintains the same five-level progression as the second edition:

- Level 1 (Beginning, formerly Introductory)
- Level 2 (High-Beginning, formerly Basic)
- Level 3 (Intermediate)
- Level 4 (High-Intermediate)
- Level 5 (Advanced)

What is the *Focus on Grammar* methodology?

Both controlled and communicative practice

While students expect and need to learn the formal rules of a language, it is crucial that they also practice new structures in a variety of contexts in order to internalize and master them. To this end, *Focus on Grammar* provides an abundance of both controlled and communicative exercises so that students can bridge the gap between knowing grammatical structures and using them. The many communicative activities in each Student Book unit provide opportunity for critical thinking while enabling students to personalize what they have learned in order to talk to one another with ease about hundreds of everyday issues.

A unique four-step approach

The series follows a four-step approach:

Step 1: Grammar in Context shows the new structures in natural contexts, such as articles and conversations.

Step 2: Grammar Presentation presents the structures in clear and accessible grammar charts, notes, and examples.

Step 3: Focused Practice of both form and meaning of the new structures is provided in numerous and varied controlled exercises.

Step 4: Communication Practice allows students to use the new structures freely and creatively in motivating, open-ended activities.

Thorough recycling

Underpinning the scope and sequence of the *Focus on Grammar* series is the belief that students need to use target structures many times, in different contexts, and at increasing levels of difficulty. For this reason, new grammar is constantly recycled throughout the book so that students have maximum exposure to the target forms and become comfortable using them in speech and in writing.

A complete classroom text and reference guide

A major goal in the development of *Focus on Grammar* has been to provide students with books that serve not only as vehicles for classroom instruction but also as resources for reference and self-study. In each Student Book, the combination of grammar charts, grammar notes, a glossary of grammar terms, and extensive appendices provides a complete and invaluable reference guide for students.

Ongoing assessment

Review Tests at the end of each part of the Student Book allow for continual self-assessment. In addition, the tests in the new *Focus on Grammar* Assessment Package provide teachers with a valid, reliable, and practical means of determining students' appropriate levels of placement in the course and of assessing students' achievement throughout the course. At Levels 4 (High-Intermediate) and 5 (Advanced), Proficiency Tests give teachers an overview of their students' general grammar knowledge.

 ## What are the components of each level of *Focus on Grammar*?

Student Book

The Student Book is divided into eight or more parts, depending on the level. Each part contains grammatically related units, with each unit focusing on specific grammatical structures; where appropriate, units present contrasting forms. The exercises in each unit are thematically related to one another, and all units have the same clear, easy-to-follow format.

Teacher's Manual

The Teacher's Manual contains a variety of suggestions and information to enrich the material in the Student Book. It includes general teaching suggestions for each section of a typical unit, answers to frequently asked questions, unit-by-unit teaching tips with ideas for further communicative practice, and a supplementary activity section. Answers to the Student Book exercises and audioscripts of the listening activities are found at the back of the Teacher's Manual. Also included in the Teacher's Manual is a CD-ROM of teaching tools, including PowerPoint presentations that offer alternative ways of presenting selected grammar structures.

Workbook

The Workbook accompanying each level of *Focus on Grammar* provides additional exercises appropriate for self-study of the target grammar for each Student Book unit. Tests included in each Workbook provide students with additional opportunities for self-assessment.

Audio Program

All of the listening exercises from the Student Book, as well as the Grammar in Context passages and other appropriate exercises, are included on the program's CDs. In the book, the symbol ⌒ appears next to the listening exercises. Another symbol ⌒, indicating that listening is optional, appears next to the Grammar in Context passages and some exercises. All of these scripts appear in the Teacher's Manual and may be used as an alternative way of presenting the activities.

Some Student Books are packaged with a separate Student Audio CD. This CD includes the listening exercise from each unit.

CD-ROM

The *Focus on Grammar* CD-ROM provides students with individualized practice and immediate feedback. Fully contextualized and interactive, the activities broaden and extend practice of the grammatical structures in the reading, writing, speaking, and listening skills areas. The CD-ROM includes grammar review, review tests, score-based remedial practice, games, and all relevant reference material from the Student Book. It can also be used in conjunction with the *Longman Interactive American Dictionary* CD-ROM.

Assessment Package (NEW)

An extensive, comprehensive Assessment Package has been developed for each level of the third edition of *Focus on Grammar*. The components of the Assessment Package are:

1. **Placement, Diagnostic, and Achievement Tests**

   - a Placement Test to screen students and place them into the correct level
   - Diagnostic Tests for each part of the Student Book
   - Unit Achievement Tests for each unit of the Student Book
   - Part Achievement Tests for each part of the Student Book

2. **General Proficiency Tests**

   - two Proficiency Tests at Level 4 (High-Intermediate)
   - two Proficiency Tests at Level 5 (Advanced)

   These tests can be administered at any point in the course.

3. **Audio CD**

   The listening portions of the Placement, Diagnostic, and Achievement Tests are recorded on CDs. The scripts appear in the Assessment Package.

4. **Test-Generating Software**

   The test-bank software provides thousands of questions from which teachers can create class-appropriate tests. All items are labeled according to the grammar structure they are testing, so teachers can easily select relevant items; they can also design their own items to add to the tests.

Transparencies (NEW)

Transparencies of all the grammar charts in the Student Book are also available. These transparencies are a classroom visual aid that will help instructors point out important patterns and structures of grammar.

Companion Website

The companion website contains a wealth of information and activities for both teachers and students. In addition to general information about the course pedagogy, the website provides extensive practice exercises for the classroom, a language lab, or at home.

What's new in the third edition of the Student Book?

In response to users' requests, this edition has:

- a new four-color design
- easy-to-read color coding for the four steps
- new and updated reading texts for Grammar in Context
- post-reading activities (in addition to the pre-reading questions)
- more exercise items
- an editing (error analysis) exercise in each unit
- an Internet activity in each unit
- a Glossary of Grammar Terms
- expanded Appendices

References

Alexander, L. G. (1988). *Longman English Grammar.* White Plains: Longman.

Biber, D., S. Conrad, E. Finegan, S. Johansson, and G. Leech (1999). *Longman Grammar of Spoken and Written English.* White Plains: Longman.

Celce-Murcia, M., and D. Freeman (1999). *The Grammar Book.* Boston: Heinle and Heinle.

Celce-Murcia, M., and S. Hilles (1988). *Techniques and Resources in Teaching Grammar.* New York: Oxford University Press.

Firsten, R. (2002). *The ELT Grammar Book.* Burlingame, CA: Alta Book Center Publishers.

Garner, B. (2003). *Garner's Modern American Usage.* New York: Oxford University Press.

Greenbaum, S. (1996). *The Oxford English Grammar.* New York: Oxford University Press.

Leech, G. (2004). *Meaning and the English Verb.* Harlow, UK: Pearson.

Lewis, M. (1997). *Implementing the Lexical Approach.* Hove East Sussex, UK: Language Teaching Publications.

Longman (2002). *Longman Dictionary of English Language and Culture.* Harlow, UK: Longman.

Willis, D. (2003). *Rules, Patterns and Words.* New York: Cambridge University Press.

TOUR OF A UNIT

Each unit in the *Focus on Grammar* series presents a specific grammar structure (or two, in case of a contrast) and develops a major theme, which is set by the opening text. All units follow the same unique **four-step approach**.

Step 1: Grammar in Context

The **conversation** or **reading** in this section shows the grammar structure in a natural context. The high-interest text presents authentic language in a variety of real-life formats: magazine articles, web pages, questionnaires, and more. Students can listen to the text on an audio CD to get accustomed to the sound of the grammar structure in a natural context.

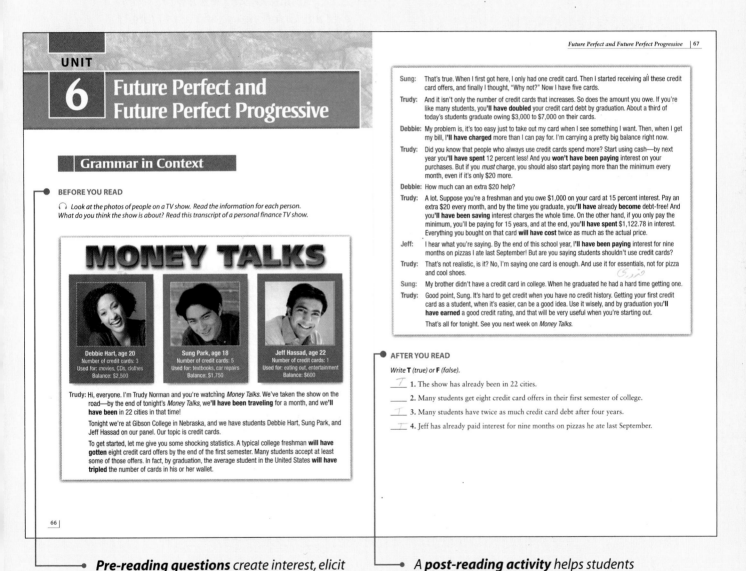

Pre-reading questions *create interest, elicit students' knowledge about the topic, and lead students to make predictions about the text.*

*A **post-reading activity** helps students understand the text and focus on the grammar structure.*

Step 2: Grammar Presentation

This section is made up of grammar charts, notes, and examples. The **grammar charts** focus on the forms of the grammar structure. The **grammar notes** and **examples** focus on the meanings and uses of the structure.

*Clear and easy-to-read **grammar charts** present the grammar structure in all its forms and combinations.*

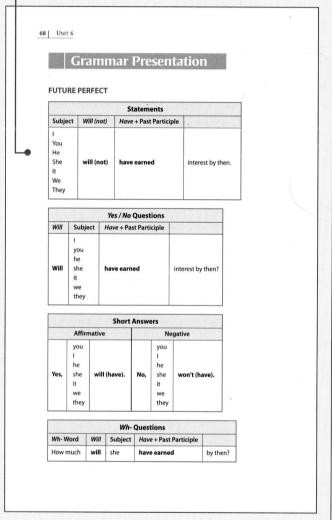

*Each **grammar note** gives a short, simple explanation of one use of the structure. The accompanying **examples** ensure students' understanding of the point.*

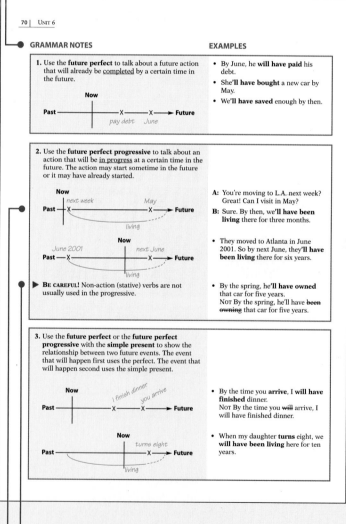

__Be careful! notes__ alert students to common errors made by students of English.

__Time lines__ clarify the meaning of verb forms and their relationship to one another.

Step 3: Focused Practice

This section provides students with a variety of contextualized **controlled exercises** to practice both the forms and the uses of the grammar structure.

*Focused Practice always begins with a "for recognition only" exercise called **Discover the Grammar**.*

Focused Practice

1 DISCOVER THE GRAMMAR

Read this magazine article about lying on the job. Circle the reporting verbs. Underline the examples of direct speech once. Underline the examples of indirect speech twice.

"Lying during a job interview is risky business," (says) Martha Toledo, director of the management consulting firm Maxwell. "The truth has a funny way of coming out." Toledo tells the story of one woman applying for a job as an office manager. The woman told the interviewer that she had a B.A. degree. Actually, she was eight credits short. She also said that she had made $50,000 at her last job. The truth was $10,000 less. "Many firms really do check facts," warns Toledo. In this case, a call to the applicant's company revealed the discrepancies.

Toledo relates a story about another job applicant, George. During an interview, George reported that he had quit his last job. George landed the new job and was doing well until the company hired another employee, Pete. George and Pete had worked at the same company. Pete eventually told his boss that his old company had fired George.

2 CONFESSIONS
Grammar Notes 3, 6–7

Complete the student's essay with the correct words.

Once when I was a teenager, I went to my Aunt Leah's house. Aunt Leah collected pottery, and as soon as I got there, she ___told___ me she ___wanted___ to show me
   1. (said / told)   2. (wants / wanted)
___her___ new bowl. She ___said___ she ___had___ just bought it.
   3. (my / her)   4. (said / told)   5. (has / had)
It was beautiful. When Aunt Leah went to answer the door, I picked up the bowl to examine it. It slipped from my hands and smashed to pieces on the floor. As Aunt Leah walked back into the room, I screamed and ___said___ that the cat had just broken ___her___ new
   6. (said / told)   7. (her / your)
bowl. Aunt Leah got this funny look on her face and ___told___ me that it really
   8. (said / told)
___wasn't___ very important.
   9. (isn't / wasn't)
I didn't sleep at all that night, and the next morning I called my aunt and ___told___
   10. (said / told)
her that I had broken ___her___ bowl. She said ___she___ 'd known that all
   11. (her / your)   12. (I / she)
along. We still laugh about the story today.

*Exercises are **cross-referenced** to the appropriate grammar notes to provide a quick review.*

---

*A **variety of exercise types** guide students from recognition to accurate production of the grammar structure.*

4 TIME LINE
Grammar Notes 3–5

*This time line shows some important events in Monique's life. Use the time line and the cues below to write sentences about her. Use **when** or **while**.*

born in Canada	moves to Australia	meets Paul	starts medical school	marries	gets medical degree	gets first job	starts practice at Lenox Hospital	has son; starts book	finishes book; does TV interview	book becomes a success; quits job
1973	1988	1989	1995	1996	1999	2000	2002	2003	2004	2005

1. moves to Australia / meets Paul   *She met Paul when she moved to Australia.*
2. gets married / studies medicine   *She got married while she was studying medicine.*
3. lives in Australia / gets married   *she was in australia*
4. receives medical degree / gets her first job   *after she got her first job when she*
5. practices medicine at Lenox Hospital / has a son   _____
6. writes a book / works at Lenox Hospital   *she was working at lenox when she wrote*
7. does a TV interview / finishes her book   *she did a TV _____ when she finished*
8. leaves job / her book becomes a success   *her book becomes a success when she left her job*

5 EDITING

Read Monique's letter to a friend. There are eleven mistakes in the use of the simple past and the past progressive. The first mistake is already corrected. Find and correct ten more.

Dear Crystal,

    I was writing chapter two of my new book when I ~~was thinking~~ *thought* of you. The last time I saw you, you walked down the aisle to marry Dave. That was more than two years ago. How are you? How is married life?

    A lot has happened in my life since that time. While I ~~worked~~ *was working* at Lenox Hospital, I began writing. In 2004, I was ~~publishing~~ *published* a book on women's health issues. It was quite successful here in Australia. I even got interviewed on TV. When I was getting a contract to write a second book, I decided to quit my hospital job to write full-time. That's what I'm doing now. Paul, too, has had a career change. While I ~~was writing~~ *was thinking*, he was attending law school. He ~~was getting~~ *got* his degree last summer.

    Oh, the reason I thought of you while I wrote was because the chapter was about rashes. Remember the time you were getting that terrible rash? We rode our bikes ~~when~~ *were riding* you were falling into a patch of poison ivy. And that's how you met Dave! When you were falling off the bike, he offered to give us a ride home. Life's funny, isn't it?

    Well, please write soon, and send my love to Dave. I miss you!

        Monique

*Focused Practice always ends with an **editing** exercise to teach students to find and correct typical mistakes.*

Step 4: Communication Practice

This section provides open-ended **communicative activities** giving students the opportunity to use the grammar structure appropriately and fluently.

---

*A **listening** activity gives students the opportunity to check their aural comprehension.*

*Many exercises and activities are **art based** to provide visual cues and an interesting context and springboard for meaningful conversations.*

---

*A **writing** activity allows students to use the grammar structure in a variety of formats.*

10 | LET'S GET TOGETHER

Complete the schedule below. Write in all your plans for next week. Then work with a partner. Without showing each other your schedules, find a time to get together by asking and answering questions using the future progressive.

Example: **A:** What will you be doing at 11:00 on Tuesday?
B: I'll be taking a history test.

	MONDAY	TUESDAY	WEDNESDAY	THURSDAY	FRIDAY
9:00					
11:00					
1:00					
3:00					
5:00					
7:00					

11 | WRITING

Write a paragraph about your life 10 years from now. What will you be doing for a living? What kind of family life will you have? What hobbies will you be enjoying? What will you do to achieve these things? Use the future and future progressive.

Example: In 10 years, I will be working for the space program. I am going to be planning the first colony on Mars. First I will have to graduate from college.

12 | ON THE INTERNET

Do a search on space activities. Find information about what will be happening during the 21st century. For example, will tourists be traveling to the moon or Mars? Will scientists "terraform" Mars (make the Martian atmosphere safe for people from Earth)? Are there going to be farms and factories in space?

Work with a small group. Find your own organization or look at information from these:

SEDS (Students for the Exploration and Development of Space)
The Mars Society
The Planetary Society
Space.com

Present your predictions to the class.

Example: A lot of different countries are going to be developing space. China will probably be sending people to the moon. The European countries and Japan will work together to explore the planet Mercury . . .

*An **Internet** activity gives students the opportunity to expand on the content of the unit and interact with their classmates creatively and fluently.*

TOUR BEYOND THE UNIT

In the *Focus on Grammar* series, the grammatically related units are grouped into parts, and each part concludes with a section called **From Grammar to Writing** and a **Review Test** section.

From Grammar to Writing

This section presents a point which applies specifically to writing, for example, avoiding sentence fragments. Students are guided to practice the point in a **piece of extended writing**.

An **introduction** relates the grammar point to the writing focus.

Students practice **pre-writing strategies** such as brainstorming, word-mapping, and outlining.

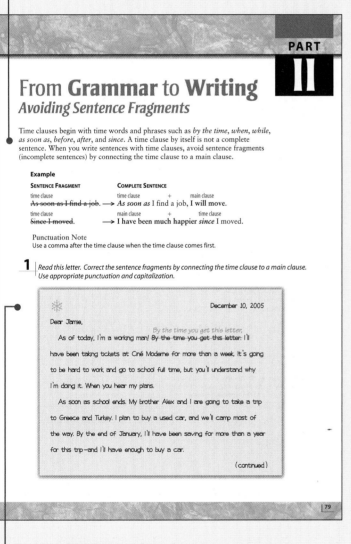

PART II

From **Grammar** to **Writing**
Avoiding Sentence Fragments

Time clauses begin with time words and phrases such as *by the time*, *when*, *while*, *as soon as*, *before*, *after*, and *since*. A time clause by itself is not a complete sentence. When you write sentences with time clauses, avoid sentence fragments (incomplete sentences) by connecting the time clause to a main clause.

Example

SENTENCE FRAGMENT	COMPLETE SENTENCE
time clause	time clause + main clause
As soon as I find a job. →	*As soon as* I find a job, **I will move.**
time clause	main clause + time clause
Since I moved. →	**I have been much happier** *since* I moved.

Punctuation Note
Use a comma after the time clause when the time clause comes first.

1 Read this letter. Correct the sentence fragments by connecting the time clause to a main clause. Use appropriate punctuation and capitalization.

> ❄   December 10, 2005
>
> Dear Jamie,
>   ~~By the time you get this letter,~~
>   As of today, I'm a working man! ~~By the time you get this letter.~~ I'll
> have been taking tickets at Ciné Moderne for more than a week. It's going
> to be hard to work and go to school full time, but you'll understand why
> I'm doing it. When you hear my plans.
>   As soon as school ends. My brother Alex and I are going to take a trip
> to Greece and Turkey. I plan to buy a used car, and we'll camp most of
> the way. By the end of January, I'll have been saving for more than a year
> for this trip—and I'll have enough to buy a car.
>
>   (continued)

| 79

From Grammar to Writing | 117

2 Before writing the essay in Exercise 1, the student made a Venn diagram showing the things that Brasília and Washington, D.C. have in common, and the things that are different. Complete the student's diagram.

Brasília   Washington, D.C.

in South America national capital in North America

3 Before you write . . .

1. Work with a partner. Agree on a topic for an essay of comparison and contrast. For example, you can compare two places, two people, two types of food, or two TV programs.
2. Brainstorm ideas and complete a Venn diagram like the one in Exercise 2.

4 Write an essay of comparison and contrast using your diagram in Exercise 3.

5 Exchange essays with a different partner. Underline once all the additions that show similarity. Underline twice the additions that show difference. Write a question mark (?) above the places where something seems wrong. Then answer the following questions.

	Yes	No
1. Did the writer use the correct auxiliary verbs in the additions?	☐	☐
2. Did the writer use correct word order?	☐	☐
3. Do the examples show important similarities and differences?	☐	☐

4. What are some details you would like to know about the two things the writer compared? _____

_____

6 Work with your partner. Discuss each other's editing questions from Exercise 5. Then rewrite your own paragraph and make any necessary corrections.

Writing formats include business letters, personal letters, notes, instructions, paragraphs, reports, and essays.

The section includes **peer review** and **editing** of the students' writing.

Review Test

This review section, covering all the grammar structures presented in the part, can be used as a test. An **Answer Key** is provided at the back of the book.

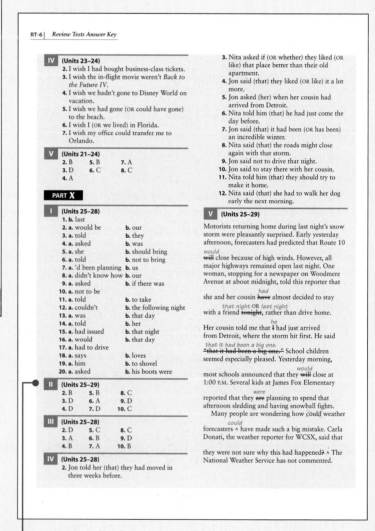

PART IX

Review Test

I *Circle the letter of the correct word(s) to complete each sentence.*

1. I _____ late for work if the bus doesn't arrive soon.   A B Ⓒ D
   - (A) am
   - (B) was
   - (C) 'll be
   - (D) 've been

2. I _____ a flight attendant if I didn't get airsick.   A B C D
   - (A) would become
   - (B) became
   - (C) become
   - (D) had become

3. What do you do when your bus _____ late?   A B C D
   - (A) were
   - (B) is
   - (C) would be
   - (D) had been

4. If the teacher cancels class today, I _____ you.   A B C D
   - (A) have joined
   - (B) could have joined
   - (C) 'll join
   - (D) join

5. This flight is full. _____ someone gives up a seat, you won't get on this flight today.   A B C D
   - (A) If
   - (B) Unless
   - (C) When
   - (D) Where

6. If you _____ early enough, we can't save a seat for you.   A B C D
   - (A) 'll check in
   - (B) check in
   - (C) don't check in
   - (D) have checked in

7. If I hadn't been fascinated with flying, I _____ a pilot.   A B C D
   - (A) would become
   - (B) became
   - (C) won't become
   - (D) wouldn't have become

8. I'm going to Gerry's for Thanksgiving, but I can't stand to eat turkey. What _____ if that happened to you?   A B C D
   - (A) would you do
   - (B) did you do
   - (C) do you do
   - (D) will you do

(continued)

361

> The Review Tests *include* **multiple-choice questions** *in standardized test formats, giving students practice in test taking.*

IV **(Units 23–24)**
2. I wish I had bought business-class tickets.
3. I wish the in-flight movie weren't *Back to the Future IV.*
4. I wish we hadn't gone to Disney World on vacation.
5. I wish we had gone (OR could have gone) to the beach.
6. I wish I (OR we lived) in Florida.
7. I wish my office could transfer me to Orlando.

V **(Units 21–24)**
2. B	5. B	7. A
3. D	6. C	8. C
4. A		

PART X

I **(Units 25–28)**
1. b. last

2. a. would be	b. our
3. a. told	b. they
4. a. asked	b. was
5. a. she	b. should bring
6. a. told	b. not to bring
7. a. 'd been planning	b. us
8. a. didn't know how	b. our
9. a. asked	b. if there was
10. a. not to be	
11. a. told	b. to take
12. a. couldn't	b. the following night
13. a. was	b. that day
14. a. told	b. her
15. a. had issued	b. that night
16. a. would	b. that day
17. a. had to drive	
18. a. says	b. loves
19. a. him	b. to shovel
20. a. asked	b. his boots were

II **(Units 25–29)**
2. B	5. B	8. C
3. D	6. A	9. D
4. D	7. D	10. C

III **(Units 25–28)**
2. D	5. C	8. C
3. A	6. B	9. D
4. B	7. A	10. B

IV **(Units 25–28)**
2. Jon told her (that) they had moved in three weeks before.

3. Nita asked if (OR whether) they liked (OR like) that place better than their old apartment.
4. Jon said (that) they liked (OR like) it a lot more.
5. Jon asked (her) when her cousin had arrived from Detroit.
6. Nita told him (that) he had just come the day before.
7. Jon said (that) it had been (OR has been) an incredible winter.
8. Nita said (that) the roads might close again with that storm.
9. Jon said not to drive that night.
10. Jon said to stay there with her cousin.
11. Nita told him (that) they should try to make it home.
12. Nita said (that) she had to walk her dog early the next morning.

V **(Units 25–29)**

Motorists returning home during last night's snow storm were pleasantly surprised. Early yesterday afternoon, forecasters had predicted that Route 10 ~~will~~ *would* close because of high winds. However, all major highways remained open last night. One woman, stopping for a newspaper on Woodmere Avenue at about midnight, told this reporter that she and her cousin ~~have~~ *had* almost decided to stay with a friend ~~tonight~~ *that night OR last night*, rather than drive home.

Her cousin told me that ~~I~~ *he* had just arrived from Detroit, where the storm hit first. He said *that it had been a big one.* ~~"that it had been a big one."~~ School children seemed especially pleased. Yesterday morning, most schools announced that they ~~will~~ *would* close at 1:00 P.M. Several kids at James Fox Elementary reported that they ~~are~~ *were* planning to spend that afternoon sledding and having snowball fights.

Many people are wondering how ~~could~~ weather forecasters ^ *could* have made such a big mistake. Carla Donati, the weather reporter for WCSX, said that they were not sure why this had happened? ^ The National Weather Service has not commented.

> The Review Tests Answer Key *provides* **cross-references** *to the appropriate unit(s) for easy review.*

ACKNOWLEDGMENTS

Before acknowledging the many people who have contributed to the third edition of *Focus on Grammar*, we wish to express our gratitude to those who worked on the first and second editions and whose influence is still present in the new work.

Our continuing thanks to:

- Joanne Dresner, who initiated the project and helped conceptualize the general approach of *Focus on Grammar*.

- Joan Saslow, our editor for the first edition, and Françoise Leffler, our editor for the second edition, for helping to bring the books to fruition.

- Sharon Hilles, our grammar consultant, for her insight and advice on the first edition.

In the third edition, *Focus on Grammar* has continued to evolve as we update materials and respond to the valuable feedback from teachers and students who have been using the series. We are grateful to the following editors and colleagues:

- Laura Le Dréan, Executive Editor, for her dedication and commitment. In spite of an incredibly full schedule, she looked at every page of manuscript and offered excellent suggestions. In addition, she was always available and responsive to authors' concerns.

- Andrea Bryant, Senior Development Editor, for her enthusiasm and energy and her excellent ear for natural language. Her sense of contemporary culture helped us to reflect the spirit of the new millennium.

- Kathleen Silloway, Senior Production Editor, for piloting the book through its many stages of production and for always giving us a heads up when more *FOG* was about to roll in.

- Irene Schoenberg, for generously sharing her experience in teaching our first two editions and for her enthusiastic support.

Finally, we are grateful, as always, to Rick Smith and Luke Frances for their helpful input and for standing by and supporting us as we navigated our way through our third *FOG*.

We also wish to acknowledge the many reviewers for reading the manuscript and offering many useful suggestions.

Elizabeth Ackerman, California State University at Los Angeles, Los Angeles, CA; **Mary Ann Archbold,** South Bay Adult School, Redondo Beach, CA; **Larisa Álvarez Ávila,** Centro Educativo Renacimiento, Mérida, Yucatán, Mexico; **Vahania Carvajal García,** Instituto Cultural Regina Teresiano, Hermosillo, Sonora, Mexico; **Marilyn De Liro Álvarez,** Instituto "Las Brisas" Nuevo León, Mexico; **Amelia Chávez Ruiz,** Lake Forest School Mexico State, Mexico; **Elizabeth Clemente,** Instituto Tecnológico de Estudios Superiores de Monterrey, Atizapan, Mexico State, Mexico; **Stephen M. Drinane,** Rockland Community College, Suffern, NY; **Susanna Eguren,** Instituto Cultural Peruano Norteamericano, Lima, Peru; **Barbara Fields,** Beverly Hills Adult School,

Beverly Hills, CA; **Carolyn Flores,** University of Texas–Pan American, Edinburg, TX; **Leon Geyer,** Bell Language School, Brooklyn, NY; **Anthony Halderman,** Cuesta College, San Luis Obispo, CA; **M. Martha Hall,** The New England School of English, Cambridge, MA; **Heather Hein,** University of Denver, Denver, CO; **Mary Hill,** North Shore Community College, Danvers, MA; **Angela Hughes,** Instituto Tecnológico de Estudios Superiores de Monterrey, Atizapan, Mexico State, Mexico; **Peggy Hull,** Dodge City Community College, Dodge City, KS; **Silvia Icela Espinoza Galvez,** Colegio Lux, Hermosillo, Sonora, Mexico; **Alice Jarvis,** Glendale Community College, Glendale, CA; **Jennifer Johnston,** Southwest Missouri State University, Springfield, MO; **Melanie Joy,** Roxbury Community College, Roxbury Crossing, MA; **Lisa Krol,** University of Saskatchewan, Saskatoon, Saskatchewan, Canada; **Jeanne Lachowski,** University of Salt Lake City, Salt Lake City, UT; **David Lane,** Puente Learning Center, Los Angeles, CA; **Elena Lattarulo,** Cuesta College, San Luis Obispo, CA; **Anik Low,** Collège Jean-de-Brébeuf, Montreal, Québec, Canada; **Craig Machado,** Norwalk Community College, Norwalk, CT; **Vanessa Marín de Cervantes,** Ladies' World, Guadalajara, Jalisco, Mexico; **Javier Martínez García,** Instituto Las Américas, Mexico City, D.F., Mexico; **Louis Mavalankar,** Truman College–Chicago, Chicago, IL; **Sheryl Meyer,** University of Denver, Denver, CO; **Irina Morgunova,** Roxbury Community College, Roxbury Crossing, MA; **Georgina Orozco,** Instituto Cumbre, Ciudad Obregón, Sonora, Mexico; **Kathleen Pierce,** Bell Language School, Brooklyn, NY; **Melissa Powers Lee,** University of Texas at Austin, Austin, TX; **Kate Price,** University of Denver, Denver, CO; **Rachel Robbins,** Red River College, Winnipeg, Manitoba, Canada; **Maria Roche,** Housatonic Community College, Bridgeport, CT; **Ernesto Romo,** Lake Forest School, Mexico State, Mexico; **Karen Roth,** University of British Columbia, Vancouver, B.C., Canada; **Fernando Rujeles,** Centro Colombo Americano, Bogotá, Colombia; **René Sandoval,** Martin Luther King, Jr. School, Guadalajara, Jalisco, Mexico; **Anne-Marie Schlender,** Austin Community College, Austin, TX; **Rusten Seven,** Dokuz Eylul University School of Languages, Izmir, Turkey; **Judy Tanka,** American Language Center–University of California, Los Angeles, Los Angeles, CA; **Modesto L. Tollison,** Tarrant County College, Fort Worth, TX; **Jacqueline Torres Ramírez,** Instituto Horland Johnson, Guadalajara, Jalisco, Mexico; **María Elena Vera de la Rosa,** Lake Forest School, Mexico State, Mexico; **Magneli Villanueva Morales,** Universidad Regiomontana, Monterrey, Nuevo León, Mexico; **Essio Zamora,** Instituto Carlos Gracido, Oaxaca, Mexico; **Ian Zapp,** Colegio México Irlandés, Guadalajara, Jalisco, Mexico.

Modals:
Review and Expansion

15 Modals and Similar Expressions: Review

Grammar in Context

BEFORE YOU READ

🎧 *Do you like to watch reality TV? Which shows do you enjoy? Can you learn something from these shows or are they just entertaining? Read this article about reality TV.*

Josh Souza

REALITY TV

"Everyone Should Have an Audience"
—*Josh Souza, contestant,* Big Brother 2, *USA*

"I know reality TV is not really reality."
—*Ikaika Kaho'ano, contestant,* Making the Band, *United States*

The situations in reality TV **may** not always **be** realistic, but those contestants on the screen are really laughing, crying, and plotting against each other. Viewers continue to be fascinated.

Although some **might think** a show is cruel or embarrassing and they **ought to stop** watching, they simply **can't change** the channel. With everyone at school or work talking about last night's episode, a lot of people **may watch** reality TV just to keep up with the conversations. But the secret thrill of many viewers **has got to be** the thought, "The next celebrity **could be** me!"

"Reality is the best business model for TV."
—*Shuman Ghosemajumder, media expert, www.shumans.com*

Reality TV started in Europe at a time when local TV networks **weren't able to afford** to buy foreign shows. And because writers and actors were expensive, they also **couldn't develop** shows of their own. Then Bob Geldof of the British television company Planet 24 had the bright idea of filming ordinary people in out-of-the-ordinary situations. Geldof knew that people love seeing themselves on TV, so he thought there **had to be** a lot of people willing to try it. Why **should** producers **pay** for actors and writers when they **could use** real people with real emotions?

"I didn't know we actually had to survive."
—Martin Melin, first winner, Expedition Robinson, *Sweden*

Expedition Robinson was Geldof's brainchild. A group of contestants and a television crew go to a desert island. The contestants **have to figure out** how to survive, and the television audience **can watch** their struggle. Geldof **couldn't sell** his idea in England, but an adventurous Swedish producer bought it. It just **might work**, she thought. Filming started in 1997.

Everyone struggled that first season. The contestants and the crew were on a tropical island, and technicians thought the equipment **might not work** in the heat. The winner, Martin Melin, was shocked that his group **had to find** their own food. The TV crew was equally shocked when the group wanted to explore the island. "You **can't go** into the jungle!" they yelled. But the group went—and the crew **was able to follow** with cameras. To everyone's surprise, it all worked, and the show was a smash hit. Now known as *Survivor*, it has become popular all over the world.

Tribes compete on Survivor Africa

"I can't act, I can't sing, I can't dance—but people don't care."
—Brian Dowling, winner, Big Brother 2, *UK*

Big Brother, first produced in the Netherlands in 1999, was another surprise hit. In this show, a group of strangers **had to stay** in a house for 100 days. They **couldn't go out** or **talk** to anyone outside the group. Intense feelings developed in this situation, and cameras and microphones recorded everything that happened. Viewers were glued to their television screens, and the show's website got 100 million hits during that first season. Today, *Big Brother* is the most successful reality show in the world, with versions in North and South America, Europe, and Africa.

Contestants on Big Brother 4 *react to new housemates*

". . . viewers often prefer homegrown shows that better reflect local tastes, cultures, and historical events."
—Suzanne Kapner, New York Times, *January 2, 2003*

Reality shows around the world reflect different cultural values. Japanese viewers, for example, love to watch contestants who **are able to face** difficulty and not complain. Italian audiences, on the other hand, enjoy seeing big emotional reactions. Some cultures don't like fierce competition between individuals. On one Chinese show, for example, relatives win prizes for each other, reflecting the idea that people **should win** for their families, not only themselves. In Europe, contestants **might not have** perfect teeth or figures, but in the United States, even the losers **have got to be** gorgeous.

Reality shows come in different flavors for different audiences, but in one way, they're all the same. All over the world, it's clear that ordinary people like to be on TV—and viewers love to watch them. That **must be** why they're tuning in by the millions!

AFTER YOU READ

*Write **T** (true) or **F** (false).*

_____ **1.** Some people believe that it's wrong to watch cruel reality shows.

_____ **2.** Bob Geldof believed there were many people willing to be on reality shows.

_____ **3.** In the first *Expedition Robinson*, the crew was required to find food for everyone.

_____ **4.** The first *Big Brother* contestants were allowed to call their families.

_____ **5.** Some contestants on European shows are not beautiful or handsome.

Grammar Presentation

MODALS AND SIMILAR EXPRESSIONS: REVIEW

Ability: *Can* and *Could*			
Subject	Modal	Base Form of Verb	
She	**can (not)**	**act.**	
	could (not)	**act**	last year.

Ability: *Be able to**				
Subject	*Be able to*		Base Form of Verb	
She	**is (not)**	**able to**	**act.**	
	was (not)		**act**	last year.

Advice: *Should, Ought to, Had better*			
Subject	Modal	Base Form of Verb	
You	**should (not)** **ought to** **had better (not)**	**watch**	this TV show.

Necessity: *Must* and *Can't*		
Subject	Modal	Base Form of Verb
You	**must (not)** **can't**	**go.**

Necessity: *Have (got) to**		
Subject	*Have (got) to*	Base Form of Verb
They	**(don't) have to**	**go.**
He	**has (got) to**	

*Unlike modals, which have one form, *be* in *be able to* and *have* in *have (got) to* change for different subjects.

Assumptions: *May, Might, Could, Must, Can't*			
Subject	Modal	Base Form of Verb	
They	may (not) might (not) could (not) must (not) can't	be	actors.

Assumptions: *Have (got) to**			
Subject	*Have (got) to*	Base Form of Verb	
They	have (got) to	be	actors.
He	has (got) to		an actor.

*Unlike modals, which have one form, *have* in *have (got) to* changes for different subjects.

Future Possibility: *May, Might, Could*			
Subject	Modal	Base Form of Verb	
It	may (not) might (not) could	start	at 8:00.

GRAMMAR NOTES

EXAMPLES

1. Modals are auxiliary ("helping") verbs. They express:

  a. social functions such as giving advice.

  b. logical possibilities such as making assumptions.

  REMEMBER: Modals have <u>only one form</u>. They do not have *-s* in the third person singular. Always use **modal + base form** of the verb.

- You **should watch** this program.
- It **could be** the best of the season.

- She **might record** it.
  NOT She ~~mights~~ record it.
  NOT She might ~~to record~~ it.

2. Use *can* or *be able to* to describe **present ability**.

  USAGE NOTE: *Can* is more common than *be able to* in the present.

  Use *could* or *was / were able to* for **past ability**.

  REMEMBER: Use the correct form of *be able to* for all other verb forms.

- She **can sing**, but she **can't dance**.
- We **aren't able to get** Channel 11.

- Before she took lessons, she **could sing**, but she **wasn't able to dance** very well.

- Since her lessons, she **has been able to get** good roles on TV.

(continued)

3. Use *should* and *ought to* to give **advice**.

USAGE NOTE: *Should* is more formal than *ought to*.

Use *had better* for **urgent advice**—when you believe that something bad will happen if the person does not follow the advice.

Use *should* to **ask for advice**.

Use *shouldn't* and *had better not* for negative statements.

- You **should watch** *Survivor* tonight.
- Terri **ought to watch** it too.

- You**'d better stop** watching so much TV or your grades will suffer.

- **Should** I **buy** a new TV set?

- You **shouldn't get** your old TV repaired.
- You**'d better not stay up** too late.

---

4. Use *have to*, *have got to*, and *must* to express **necessity**.

USAGE NOTES

a. We usually use *have to* in conversation and informal writing.

b. We also use *have got to* in conversation and informal writing to express a strong feeling.

c. *Must* expresses necessity in <u>writing</u>, including official forms, signs, and manuals.

When *must* is used in <u>spoken</u> English, the speaker

- is usually in a position of power.

- is expressing urgent necessity.

Use *must* and *have got to* for the present or future.

REMEMBER: Use the correct form of *have to* for all other verb forms.

▶ BE CAREFUL! The meanings of *must not* and *don't have to* are very different.

Use *must not* to express **prohibition**.

Use *don't have to* to express that something is **not necessary**.

USAGE NOTE: We often use *can't* to express prohibition in spoken English.

- You **have to press** *Start* to begin recording.

- You**'ve got to see** this! It's really funny!

- You **must put** it on Channel 3 to record. *(VCR instruction manual)*

- You **must go** to bed right now, Tommy! *(mother talking to her young son)*
- You **must see** a doctor about that cough. *(friend talking to a friend)*

- You **must go** to bed now.
- You**'ve got to get up** early tomorrow.

- He **had to go** to bed early last night.
- She **has had to miss** her favorite program since she enrolled in that class.

- They **must not leave** the house. *(They are not allowed to leave.)*
- They **don't have to leave** the house. *(It isn't necessary for them to leave.)*

- He **can't leave**.

5. Use modals to make **assumptions** ("best guesses"). These modals show how certain we are about something.

100% certain

AFFIRMATIVE	NEGATIVE
must	can't, couldn't
have (got) to	must not
may	may not
might, could	might not

0% certain

a. Use *must*, *have to*, and *have got to* when you are almost **100% certain** that something is true.

- It **must be** 10:00. *Mystery Time* just came on.

- This **has to be** a rerun. I'm sure I've seen it before.

Use *may*, *might*, and *could* when you are **less certain**.

- He **may be** the murderer. He looks guilty.

- He **could be** home now. The lights are on.

b. Use *can't* and *couldn't* when you are almost 100% certain that something is **impossible**.

- They **can't be** guilty. They weren't even in the city when the crime occurred.

- They **couldn't own** a gun. They hate violence.

Use *must not* when you are **slightly less certain**.

- You **must not know** them very well. You've only met them twice.

Use *may not* and *might not* when you are **even less certain**.

- We **may not have** enough evidence. No one saw the suspect.

6. Use *may*, *might*, and *could* to talk about **future possibility**.

- The show **may start** at 10:00. I'm not sure.
- It **might be** very good.
- Josh **could win** the contest tonight.

Use *may not* and *might not* to say that something **possibly will not happen**.

- It **may not make** people laugh.
- It **might not be** good.

▶ BE CAREFUL! *Couldn't* means that something is **impossible**.

- It **couldn't start** at 10:00. *Mystery Time* is on then.

USAGE NOTE: We usually do not begin questions about possibility with *may*, *might*, or *could*. Instead we use *will* or *be going to* and phrases such as *Do you think . . .?* or *Is it possible that . . .?*

A: *Do you think* Midge *will find* the murderer?
B: She **might**. She's a good detective.

However, we often use *may*, *might*, or *could* in **short answers** to these questions.

A: *Is* she *going to be* in the show next year?
B: She **may**. She hasn't decided yet.

Focused Practice

1 DISCOVER THE GRAMMAR

A *Read the FAQ (Frequently Asked Questions) from a reality TV website. Underline the modals and similar expressions. Also underline the verbs that follow.*

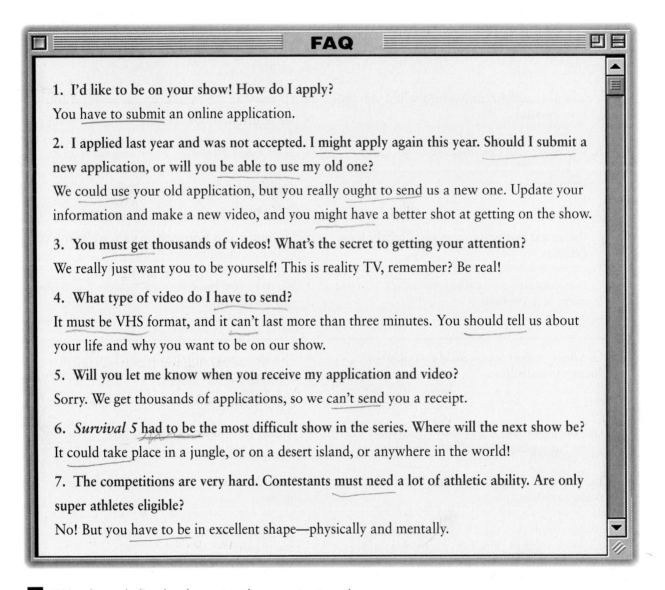

FAQ

1. I'd like to be on your show! How do I apply?

You have to submit an online application.

2. I applied last year and was not accepted. I might apply again this year. Should I submit a new application, or will you be able to use my old one?

We could use your old application, but you really ought to send us a new one. Update your information and make a new video, and you might have a better shot at getting on the show.

3. You must get thousands of videos! What's the secret to getting your attention?

We really just want you to be yourself! This is reality TV, remember? Be real!

4. What type of video do I have to send?

It must be VHS format, and it can't last more than three minutes. You should tell us about your life and why you want to be on our show.

5. Will you let me know when you receive my application and video?

Sorry. We get thousands of applications, so we can't send you a receipt.

6. *Survival 5* had to be the most difficult show in the series. Where will the next show be?

It could take place in a jungle, or on a desert island, or anywhere in the world!

7. The competitions are very hard. Contestants must need a lot of athletic ability. Are only super athletes eligible?

No! But you have to be in excellent shape—physically and mentally.

B *Write the underlined verbs next to the correct categories.*

Ability: *will be able to use – can't send*

Advice: *should I submit – ought to send – should tell*

Necessity: have to submit *have to send – must be VHS format – must need have to be*

Future Possibility: *might apply*

Assumptions: _____

2 | A NIGHT OF TV

Circle the correct words to complete these conversations.

1. **A:** What do you feel like watching?

   B: It's 8:00. We could / shouldn't watch *Survivor*. It's just starting now.

2. **A:** Do you think Josh is still the most unpopular guy on the island?
   nobody likes everybody knows

   B: He can't / must be. He's been lying to everybody, and now they know it.

3. **A:** This show is really exciting, but I may / 've got to leave now, or I'll be late.

   B: No problem. I can / should tape the rest of the show for you.

4. **A:** There's a two-hour mystery on at 9:00.

   B: If we watch that, we won't be able to / have to watch *Big Brother* at 9:00.

   A: That's what VCRs are for. We could / 'd better not watch one show and tape the other.

5. **A:** This mystery is good! I think the law clerk is the killer.

   B: The clerk doesn't have to / couldn't be the killer. She was on a plane to Barbados at the time.

6. **A:** Is it OK if I turn the volume up? I shouldn't / can't hear what they're saying.

   B: Sure. But you 're not able to / 'd better not make it too loud, or you'll wake the baby.

7. **A:** What's the matter with Chet on *Fear Factor*? He's acting kind of strange.

   B: He must / 'd better be sick. He had to / should eat that disgusting food, remember?

8. **A:** I'm going to see what's on Channel 13. I love their nature shows.
   advise

   B: Look at that cheetah run! They have got to / ought to be the fastest animals in the world!

9. **A:** Do you think Tara's team can / has to win the race tonight?

   B: Oh, they might / couldn't win. They're too far behind.

10. **A:** Poor Rob is leaving *Big Brother*. It must / might be awful to get kicked out of the house.
    very strong

    B: Don't worry. He's famous now. I'm sure he might / 'll be able to find a job on TV.

11. **A:** How can / should you watch those horror movies? They give me the creeps.

    B: You 've got to / don't have to remember that it's all special effects.

12. **A:** I just heard the weather forecast. It's going to clear up this afternoon.

    B: Oh, good. That means I don't have to / must not take my umbrella.

3 | THAT COULD BE ME!

Complete this Entertainment Today *interview with reality-show producer Chris Barrett.*
Rewrite the phrases in parentheses. Use modals.

ENTERTAINMENT TODAY

ET: People _____*can't stop*_____ talking about reality TV. Why is it so popular?
  1. (do not have the ability to stop)

CB: I _____*can tell*_____ you why TV producers love it. They
  2. (have the ability to tell)

don't have to
_____*may not hire*_____ writers or actors. That means they
  3. (it isn't necessary that they hire)

are able to
_____*can make*_____ reality shows very cheaply.
  4. (have the ability to make)

ET: That _____*can't be*_____ the reason for the huge audiences, though.
  5. (I'm almost 100% certain that isn't)

CB: We _____*might never*~~*could never*~~ *know* all the reasons, but viewers
  6. (it's possible we will never know)

have to love
_____*may love*_____ watching ordinary people like themselves. They
  7. (almost certainly love)

might look
_____*may look*_____ at a winner and think, "That
  8. (it's possible that they look)

_____*could be*_____ me someday!"
  9. (it's possible that will be)

don't have may not
ET: But we _____*can't to love*~~*can't*~~_____ all the contestants on these shows, do we?
  10. (it's not necessary for us to love)

have got to feel
CB: No, but we _____*could feel*_____ strongly about the contestants—love *or*
  11. (it's urgent that we feel)

hate them.

must
ET: It _____*could be*_____ hard to find the right contestants. What do you
  12. (I'm certain that it is)

look for?

CB: They _____*shouldn't have*_____ problems talking about personal stuff.
  13. (it's advisable that they not have)

can
We like it when they _____*are able to cry*_____ in front of a camera.
  14. (have the ability to cry)

should
ET: Maybe we _____*ought to talk*_____ about what's next for you.
  15. (it's advisable that we talk)

may
CB: Next season, I _____*might to do*_____ a drama about 12 people shipwrecked
  16. (it's possible that I will do)

on an island.
  had better
ET: No more reality TV? You _____*have got to start*_____ looking for writers and actors!
  17. (it's urgent that you start)

4 | EDITING

Read these posts to a reality TV message board. There are thirteen mistakes in the use of modals. The first mistake is already corrected. Find and correct twelve more.

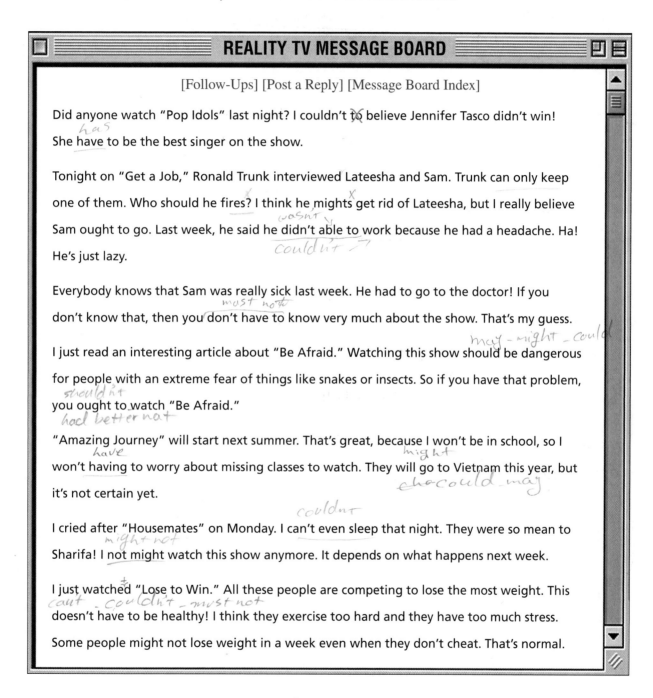

REALITY TV MESSAGE BOARD

[Follow-Ups] [Post a Reply] [Message Board Index]

Did anyone watch "Pop Idols" last night? I couldn't to believe Jennifer Tasco didn't win!

She ~~have~~ *has* to be the best singer on the show.

Tonight on "Get a Job," Ronald Trunk interviewed Lateesha and Sam. Trunk can only keep

one of them. Who should he ~~fires~~? I think he ~~mights~~ *might* get rid of Lateesha, but I really believe

Sam ought to go. Last week, he said he didn't able to work because he had a headache. Ha!

He's just lazy.

Everybody knows that Sam was really sick last week. He had to go to the doctor! If you

don't know that, then you don't have to know very much about the show. That's my guess.

I just read an interesting article about "Be Afraid." Watching this show should be dangerous

for people with an extreme fear of things like snakes or insects. So if you have that problem,

you ought to watch "Be Afraid."

"Amazing Journey" will start next summer. That's great, because I won't be in school, so I

won't having to worry about missing classes to watch. They will go to Vietnam this year, but

it's not certain yet.

I cried after "Housemates" on Monday. I can't even sleep that night. They were so mean to

Sharifa! I not might watch this show anymore. It depends on what happens next week.

I just watched "Lose to Win." All these people are competing to lose the most weight. This

doesn't have to be healthy! I think they exercise too hard and they have too much stress.

Some people might not lose weight in a week even when they don't cheat. That's normal.

Communication Practice

5 | LISTENING

🎧 *Listen to these two contestants in a reality TV show. Then listen again and complete their conversation with the modals that you hear. Listen a third time to check your answers.*

JOSH: We ___'ve got to___ climb the hill today. I ___should___ go first.
  1.   2.

TARA: OK, Josh, but you ___had better not___ mess up this time.
  3.

JOSH: Why is everybody so mad at me? They ___must___ know I'm really a nice guy.
  4.

TARA: Very funny. Well, we ___have to___ work together today, and they know it.
  5.

JOSH: Are you worried? That hill ___couldn't___ be very hard to climb.
  6.

TARA: We have to go down the other side. It's almost straight down to the water. Pete

  ___might not___ be able to do it.
  7.

JOSH: You ___ought to___ help him climb down.
  8.

TARA: Oh, really? You ___must not___ know what he's been saying about me.
  9.

JOSH: I know, but let's face it—Pete ___'ll be able___ help us in the next challenge.
  10.

TARA: Hmmm. We ___have got to___ find our team's flag in the water near the rocks.
  11.

JOSH: It ___'s got to be___ very deep out there.
  12.

TARA: So I ___shouldn't___ let Pete know that *I* know that he's been plotting against me?
  13.

JOSH: You know you ___can___ do it. And tonight I'll get him voted off the island.
  14.

TARA: I don't know about that. He ___has got to___ be the most popular guy here.
  15.

JOSH: And everybody hates me. Never mind. I ___can___ make it happen.
  16.

*Now read the statements and decide if they are true (**T**) or false (**F**).*

___T___ **1.** Josh thinks it's a good idea for him to go first.

_____ **2.** Josh thinks it will be hard to climb the hill.

_____ **3.** Tara believes it's possible that Pete won't be able to climb down the hill.

_____ **4.** Pete can't help them find the flag.

_____ **5.** Josh isn't sure he can get Pete voted off the island.

quissing   *who watches*

6 | SPECULATING SPECTATORS

Work with a partner. Look at the TV listings. Discuss the types of programs you think they are.

versus
=
against

	8:00	8:30	9:00	9:30	10:00	10:30	11:00	11:30
SATURDAY 8 P.M.–MIDNIGHT								
Channel 1	Around the World in 18 Days		The Dark Glove ('98) Roy Collins				Live at 11	Johnny!
2	Great Performances: Vivaldi, Mozart, Stravinsky				Garden World			Nighttime
3	To Mars and Back		King of the Jungle		The Joke's on You	How to Boil Water	The Hulk vs. Bad Boy	Pet Heroes
4	Judge Jim	Detective Ramsey	The Long Goodbye ('96) Vera Garcia, Antonio Serrano				Top Ten	Volcano
5	Argentina vs. Spain				The Week that Was		The Civil War	
6	Elvis Presley: A Portrait of a Singer's Life		Recipes for Life	Ask Dr. Anne	Shadows in the Sand ('99) Crystal Powers (Part 2)			
7	Rita's World	You Guessed It!	Money Week	October Sky ('99) Laura Dern, Jake Gyllenhaal			A Laugh a Minute	

Example: A: *Around the World in 18 Days.* What type of show do you think that is?
B: It could be a travel show.
A: Or it might be a news show with international reports.
C: With a name like that, it's got to be a reality show.

7 | INTERNATIONAL TV

As a class, talk about TV in a country that you know. Discuss these questions:

- How many channels can you watch?

- How late can you watch?

- What programs do you recommend? What programs don't you recommend?

- Which reality shows can you watch?

- Do you have to pay a tax or government fee for using a TV?

- Do you have to have any special equipment, such as a satellite dish?

- Can you watch programs from other countries?

- Should foreign shows have subtitles, or should they be dubbed?

8 | DESERT ISLAND

Work in small groups. You are going to be on a reality TV show called Desert Island. *Your group will be on the island for five weeks and can take only three of the following items. As a group, decide on the three items. Compare your choices with the choices of the other groups.*

matches	a battery-operated CD player	a knife
a solar-powered computer	a book (your choice)	a flashlight
a toothbrush	a pen and paper	chocolate

Example: **A:** We have to take matches. With matches we can start a fire . . .
B: I agree. And with a fire, we could cook.

Now add one more item (not from the list) to take with you.

Example: **A:** I think we should take a blanket.

9 | WRITING

Write a transcript of a conversation between two reality show contestants. They have to choose three things to bring with them to a desert island. Use modals and similar expressions. You can use Exercise 5 and Exercise 8 for ideas.

Example: DINO: I've got to have some chocolate.
TRISH: Be real! You can't make a fire with chocolate.

10 | ON THE INTERNET

🌐 *Do a search on* **Survivor**, **Big Brother**, *or another reality show that you like. What do you have to do to be on the show? Check their websites for "eligibility requirements" or "application." Make a list. Then work in a group and compare information about different shows.*

Example: **A:** For *Big Brother* you have to send a video of yourself, but it can't be more than two minutes long.
B: You have to send a video for *Survivor* too. But it doesn't have to be only two minutes. It can be three minutes.

Advisability in the Past

(handwritten: should have on the past)

(handwritten: negative | should (not) / could / might] no negative / ought (not) to / for regret)

Grammar in Context

BEFORE YOU READ

🎧 *What are some examples of typical regrets that people have? Why do you think the article is called "Useless Regrets"? Read this article from a popular psychology magazine.*

(handwritten: sorry)

Useless Regrets ▶▶▶▶▶▶▶▶▶▶▶▶

(handwritten: destroy / broke)

"It **might have been**." These are not only the saddest words, but perhaps the most destructive. According to recent ideas in psychology, our feelings are mainly the result of the way we *think* about reality, not reality itself.

According to Nathan S. Kline, M.D., it's not unusual to feel deep regret about things in the past that you think you **should have done** and did not do—or the opposite, about things you did and feel you **should not have done**. In fact, we learn by thinking about past mistakes. For example, a student who fails a test learns that he or she **should have studied** more and can improve on the next test.

(handwritten: so scared / unable to / move)

However, thinking too much about past mistakes and missed opportunities can create such bad feelings that people become paralyzed and can't move on with their lives. Arthur Freeman, Ph.D., and Rose DeWolf have labeled this process "woulda/coulda/shoulda thinking," and they have written an entire book about this type of disorder.

(continued)

For all sad words of tongue or pen
*The saddest are these: "It **might have been**."*
—John Greenleaf Whittier

I **should have been** rich and famous by now.

I **ought to have applied** to college.

I **could have become** a doctor.

My parents **shouldn't have discouraged** me.

Useless Regrets ▶▶▶▶▶▶▶▶▶▶▶▶▶▶▶▶▶▶▶▶▶▶▶▶▶

In *Woulda/Coulda/Shoulda: Overcoming Regrets, Mistakes, and Missed Opportunities,* Freeman and DeWolf suggest challenging regrets with specifics. "Instead of saying, 'I **should have done** better,'" they suggest, "Write down an example of a way in which you **might have done** better. Exactly what **should** you **have done** to produce the desired result? Did you have the skills, money, experience, etc. at the time?" In the case of the student who **should have studied** more, perhaps on that occasion it was not really possible.

When people examine their feelings of regret about the past, they often find that many of them are simply not based in fact. A mother regrets missing a football game in which her son's leg was injured. She blames herself and the officials. "I **should have gone,**" she keeps telling herself. "I **could have prevented** the injury. They **might** at least **have telephoned** me as soon as it happened." Did she *really*

have the power to prevent her son's injury? **Should** the officials **have called** her *before* looking at the injury? Probably not.

Once people realize how unrealistic their feelings of regret are, they are more ready to let go of them. Cognitive psychologist David Burns, M.D., suggests specific strategies for dealing with useless feelings of regret and getting on with the present. One amusing technique is to spend 10 minutes a day writing down all the things you regret. Then say them all aloud (better yet, record them), and listen to yourself.

After you recognize how foolish most feelings of regret sound, the next step is to let go of them and to start dealing with the problems you face right now.

I **shouldn't have told** that joke in the office. My career is ruined.

I **ought to have cleaned** the house instead of going out this weekend. My mother's right. I'm just lazy.

My boyfriend **could have told** me he was going out of town this weekend. He's an inconsiderate jerk. I **should** never **have started** going out with him.

AFTER YOU READ

*Look at the photo on page 239. Then read the following statements. Write **T** (true) or **F** (false).*

___F___ **1.** The woman is rich and famous.

___F___ **2.** She is a doctor.

___F___ **3.** She applied to college.

___T___ **4.** Her parents didn't encourage her.

Grammar Presentation

ADVISABILITY IN THE PAST:
SHOULD HAVE, OUGHT TO HAVE, COULD HAVE, MIGHT HAVE

	Statements			
Subject	Modal*	*Have*	Past Participle	
He	should (not) ought (not) to could might	have	told	her.

Contractions		
should have	=	**should've**
could have	=	**could've**
might have	=	**might've**
should not have	=	**shouldn't have**

Should, *ought to*, *could*, and *might* are modals. Modals have only one form. They do not have *-s* in the third person singular.

Yes / No Questions				
Should	Subject	*Have*	Past Participle	
Should	he	**have**	told	her?

Short Answers							
Affirmative				Negative			
Yes,	he	**should**	have.	**No,**	he	**shouldn't**	have.

Wh- Questions					
Wh- Word	*Should*	Subject	*Have*	Past Participle	
When	**should**	he	**have**	told	her?

(continued)

GRAMMAR NOTES

EXAMPLES

1. Use the modals *should have*, *ought to have*, *could have*, and *might have* to talk about actions and states that were **advisable** (good ideas) in the past, **but did not happen**. These modals often communicate a sense of regret or blame.

- I **should've applied** to college.
  (I didn't apply to college, and now I'm sorry.)
- I **ought to have taken** that job.
  (I didn't take the job. That was a big mistake.)
- She **could've gone** to a much better school.
  (She didn't go to a better school. Now she regrets her choice.)
- You **might've told** me.
  (You didn't tell me. That was wrong.)

2. USAGE NOTE: ***Should not have*** and ***ought not to have*** are the only forms used in **negative** statements about advisability in the past. *Should not have* is more common.

Should have is the most common form used in **questions**.

- He **shouldn't have missed** the math exam.
- He **ought not to have missed** the math exam.
- **Should** he **have called** the teacher?

3. PRONUNCIATION NOTES:

  a. In informal speech, ***have*** in modal phrases is often pronounced like the word *of*.

  ▶ **BE CAREFUL!** Do not write *of* instead of *have* with past modals.

  b. In informal speech, ***to*** in *ought to* is pronounced like the word *a*.

  ▶ **BE CAREFUL!** Do not write *a* instead of *to* with *ought*.

- **could have** ("could of")

- I **should** *have* **gone**.
  NOT I ~~should of~~ gone.

- **ought to** ("oughta")

- I **ought** *to* **have gone**.
  NOT I ~~ought a~~ have gone.

Reference Note
For information about *could have* and *might have* to express **speculations about the past**, see Unit 17, pages 252–253.

Razi

Focused Practice

1 | DISCOVER THE GRAMMAR

Read the first sentence in each item. Circle the letter of the sentence that is closest in meaning.

1. I shouldn't have called him.
   a. I called him.
   b. I didn't call him.

2. My parents ought to have moved away from that neighborhood.
   a. They're going to move, but they're not sure when.
   b. Moving was a good idea, but they didn't do it.

3. I should have told them what I thought.
   a. I didn't tell them, and now I regret it.
   b. I told them, and that was a big mistake.

4. He might have warned us about the traffic.
   a. He didn't know, so he couldn't tell us.
   b. He knew, but he didn't tell us.

5. Felicia could have been a vice president by now.
   a. Felicia didn't become a vice president.
   b. Felicia is a vice president.

6. They shouldn't have lent him their car.
   a. They refused to lend him their car.
   b. They lent him their car.

7. I ought not to have bought that sweater.
   a. I bought the sweater.
   b. I didn't buy the sweater.

2 | ETHICS DISCUSSION
Grammar Notes 1–3

A class is discussing an ethical problem. Complete the discussion with the correct form of the verbs in parentheses or with short answers. Choose between affirmative and negative.

PROBLEM: Greg, a college student, worked successfully for a clothing store for a year. He spent most of his salary on books and tuition. One week he wanted some extra money to buy a sweater to wear to a party. He asked for a raise but his boss refused. The same week, Greg discovered an extra sweater in a shipment he was unpacking. It was very stylish and just his size. Greg "borrowed" it for the weekend and then brought it back. His boss found out and fired him.

(continued)

TEACHER: _____Should_____ Greg's boss _____have given_____ him a raise?
1. (Should / give)

STUDENT A: Yes, he _____should have_____. After all, Greg had worked there for a whole
2.

year. His boss _____shouldn't have refused_____ at that point.
3. (should / refuse)

STUDENT B: But maybe his boss couldn't afford a raise. Anyway, Greg still

_____shouldn't have taken_____ the sweater. It wasn't his.
4. (should / take)

TEACHER: What _____should_____ he _____have done_____ instead?
5. (should / do)

STUDENT C: He _____might have asked_____ his boss to sell him the sweater. Then he
6. (might / ask)
_____could have payed_____ for it slowly, out of his salary.
7. (could / pay)

STUDENT A: He _____ought to have woren_____ his old clothes to the party. A new sweater just
8. (ought to / wear)
wasn't worth all this trouble.

TEACHER: Well, _____should_____ Greg's boss _____have fired_____ him?
9. (should / fire)

STUDENT B: No, he _____shouldn't have_____. Greg had been a good employee for a year.
10.
And he brought the sweater back.

TEACHER: How _____should_____ his boss _____have handled_____ the situation?
11. (should / handle)

STUDENT C: He _____ought to have warned_____ him. He _____shouldn't have_____ just
12. (ought to / warn)
_____fired_____ him without any warning.
13. (should / fire)

3 | GRETA REGRETS

Grammar Notes 1–3

Complete Greta's regrets or complaints about the past using the modals in parentheses.
Choose between affirmative and negative.

1. I didn't go to college. Now I'm unhappy with my job.

   (should) _I should have gone to college._

2. My brother quit a good job, and now he's sorry. I knew it was a mistake, but I didn't warn him. How inconsiderate of me.

   (might) _I might have to warned him not to quit a job_

3. I feel sick. I ate all the chocolate.

   (should) _I shouldn't have eatten all the choc_

[handwritten at top: I couldn't go to the party last week.]

4. Christina didn't come over. She didn't even call.

(might) _she might have called._

5. I didn't have enough money to buy the shirt. Why didn't Ed offer to lend me some?

(could) _He could have offered me to lend me some money._

6. I jogged five miles yesterday, and now I'm exhausted.

(should) _I shouldn't have jogged so much._

7. The supermarket charged me for the plastic bag. They used to be free.

(should) _they shouldn't have charged me._

8. I didn't do the laundry yesterday, so I don't have any clean socks. Everyone else gets their laundry done on time. Why can't I?

(ought to) _I ought to have done the laundry on time. [yesterday]_

9. I didn't invite Cynthia to the party. Now she's angry at me.

(should) _I should have invited her to the party._

10. Yesterday was my birthday, and my brother didn't send me a card. I'm hurt.

(might) _He might to have sent me a birthday card._ *[stronger — should]*

4 | EDITING

Read this journal entry. There are six mistakes in the use of modals. The first mistake is already corrected. Find and correct five more.

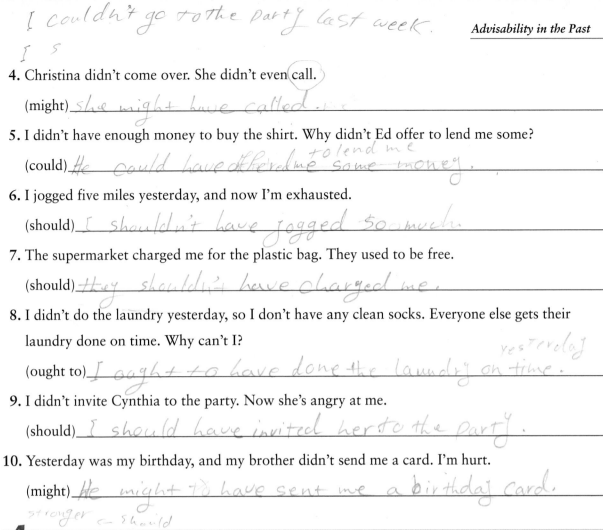

December 15

About a week ago, Jennifer was late for work again, and Doug, our boss, told me he
wanted to fire her. I was really upset. Of course, Jennifer shouldn't ~~had~~ *have* been late so
often, but he might ~~has~~ *have* talked to her about the problem before he decided to let her
go. Then he told me to make her job difficult for her so that she would quit. I just
pretended I didn't hear him. What a mistake! I ought ~~a~~ *to* have confronted him right
away. Or I could at least *have* warned Jennifer. Anyway, Jennifer is still here, but now
I'm worried about my own job. Should I ~~of~~ *have* told Doug's boss? I wonder. Maybe I should
handle*d* things differently last week. The company should never ~~has~~ *have* hired this guy.

Communication Practice

5 | LISTENING

🎧 *Jennifer is taking Dr. David Burns's advice by recording all the things she regrets at the end of the day. Listen to her recording. Then listen again and check the things she did.*

> ### TO DO
>
> ☑ Homework   ☑ Call Aunt Rose
> ☑ Walk to work   ☑ Call Ron
> ☐ Make $100 bank deposit   ☐ Go to supermarket
> ☑ Buy coat   ☐ Finish David Burns's book

6 | WHAT A MESS!

Work with a partner. Look at the picture of Jennifer's apartment. What should she have done? What shouldn't she have done? Write as many sentences as you can in five minutes. When you are done, compare your answers with those of your classmates.

Example: She should have paid the electric bill.

7 | S.O.S.

A sense of obligation is a feeling that you should do or should have done something. How strong is your sense of obligation? Take this test and find out.

Sense of Obligation Survey (S.O.S.)

INSTRUCTIONS: Read each situation. Circle the letter of your most likely response.

1. You want to lose 10 pounds, but you just ate a large dish of ice cream.
   a. I shouldn't have eaten the ice cream. I have no willpower.
   b. I deserve to enjoy things once in a while. I'll do better tomorrow.

2. Your friend quit her job. Now she's unemployed.
   a. Maybe she was really unhappy at work. It's better that she left.
   b. She shouldn't have quit until she found another job.

3. You had an appointment with your doctor. You arrived on time but had to wait more than an hour.
   a. My doctor should have scheduled better. My time is valuable too.
   b. Maybe there was an emergency. I'm sure it's not my doctor's fault.

4. You bought a coat for $140. A day later you saw it at another store for just $100.
   a. That was really bad luck.
   b. I should have looked around before I bought the coat.

5. Your brother didn't send you a birthday card.
   a. He could have at least called. He only cares about himself.
   b. Maybe he forgot. He's really been busy lately.

6. You just got back an English test. Your grade was 60 percent.
   a. That was a really difficult test.
   b. I should have studied harder.

7. You just found out that an electrician overcharged you.
   a. I should have known that was too much money.
   b. How could I have known? I'm not an expert.

8. You forgot to do some household chores that you had promised to do. Now the person you live with is angry.
   a. I shouldn't have forgotten. I'm irresponsible.
   b. I'm only human. I make mistakes.

9. You got a ticket for driving five miles per hour above the speed limit.
   a. I ought to have obeyed the speed limit.
   b. The police officer could've overlooked it and not given me the ticket. It was only five miles over the speed limit.

10. You went to the movies but couldn't get a ticket because it was sold out.
    a. I should've gone earlier.
    b. Wow! This movie is really popular!

SCORING
Give yourself one point for each of these answers:

1. **a**	6. **b**
2. **b**	7. **a**
3. **a**	8. **a**
4. **b**	9. **a**
5. **a**	10. **a**

The higher your score, the stronger your sense of obligation.

Now compare your survey results with those of a classmate.

Example: **A:** What was your answer to Question 1?
B: I said I shouldn't have eaten the ice cream. What about you?

choose between to things

8 | DILEMMAS

Work with a group. Read and discuss each case. Did the people act properly or should they have done things differently?

Case 1: Sheila was in her last year of college when she decided to run for student council president. During her campaign, a school newspaper reporter asked her about something he had discovered about her past. In high school, Sheila had once been caught cheating on a test. She had admitted her mistake and repeated the course. She never cheated again. Sheila felt that the incident was over, and she refused to answer the reporter's questions. The reporter wrote the story without telling Sheila's side, and Sheila lost the election.

> **Example:** A: Should Sheila have refused to answer questions about her past?
> B: I don't think so. She should've told her side of the story.

Case 2: Mustafa is a social worker who cares deeply about his clients. Recently, there was a fire in his office building. After the fire, the fire department declared the building unsafe and wouldn't allow anyone to go back in. Mustafa worried because all his clients' records were in the building. He needed their names, telephone numbers, and other information in order to help them. He decided to take the risk, and he entered the building to get the records. His supervisor found out and fired him.

Case 3: Pierre's wife has been sick for a long time. One day, the doctor told Pierre about a new medicine that might save her life. He warned Pierre that the medicine was still experimental, so Pierre's insurance would not pay for it. At the pharmacy, Pierre discovered that the medicine was so expensive that he didn't have enough money to pay for it. The pharmacist refused to let Pierre pay for it later. Pierre took extra work on nights and weekends to pay for the medicine. Now he can't take care of his wife as well as he had before.

9 | WRITING

Write about a dilemma that you have faced. Discuss what you and others should have, might have, or could have done in the situation. Use Exercise 4 as a model. When you finish writing, exchange paragraphs with another student and discuss your ideas.

10 | ON THE INTERNET

🇨 *It's important to avoid blunders (unnecessary mistakes) in an interview. Do a search on* **interview blunders** *for a list of mistakes. With a partner, role-play an interview in which the person interviewed makes some of these blunders. Then act it out for a group. Discuss the mistakes with your group.*

> **Example:** A: He shouldn't have talked so much. He should have let the interviewer ask more questions.
> B: She shouldn't have said bad things about her previous employer. She might have just said, "I'm ready to take on more responsibility now."

Speculations and Conclusions About the Past

Grammar in Context

BEFORE YOU READ

🎧 *The great achievements of ancient cultures fascinate modern people. Look at the photo below. What do you think the design represents? Who do you think made it? When? Read one writer's theories.*

meeting

CLOSE ENCOUNTERS

In 1927, Toribio Mexta Xesspe of Peru **must have been** very surprised to see lines in the shapes of huge animals and geometric forms on the ground below his airplane. Created by the ancient Nazca culture, these beautiful forms (over 13,000 of them) are too big to recognize from the ground. However, from about 600 feet in the air, the giant forms take shape. Xesspe **may have been** the first human in almost a thousand years to recognize the designs.

Since their discovery, many people have speculated about the Nazca lines. Without airplanes, how **could** an ancient culture **have made** these amazing pictures? What purpose **could** they **have had**?

One writer, Erich von Däniken, has a theory as amazing as the Nazca lines themselves. According to von Däniken, visitors from other planets brought their civilization to the Earth thousands of years ago. When these astronauts visited ancient cultures here on Earth, the people of those cultures **must have believed** that the visitors were gods. Since the Nazcans **could have**

(*continued*)

Nazca lines

to try to find from space
That don't believe they come from space

CLOSE ENCOUNTERS

built the lines according to instructions from an aircraft, von Däniken concludes that the drawings **might have marked** a landing strip for the spacecraft of the ancient astronauts. Von Däniken writes, "The builders of the geometrical figures **may have had** no idea what they were doing. But perhaps they knew perfectly well what the 'gods' needed in order to land."

In his book *Chariots of the Gods?* von Däniken offers many other "proofs" that ancient cultures had contact with visitors from other planets. Giant statues on Easter Island provide von Däniken with strong evidence of the astronauts' presence. Von Däniken estimates that the island **could** only **have supported** a very small population. After examining the simple tools that the islanders probably used, he concludes that even 2,000 men working day and night **could not have been** enough to carve the figures out of hard stone. In addition, he says that at least part of the population **must have worked** in the fields,

gone fishing, and **woven** cloth. "Two thousand men alone **could not have made** the gigantic statues." Von Däniken's conclusion: Space visitors **had to have built** them.

Scientists, among others, are skeptical and prefer to look for answers closer to home. However, von Däniken's theories continue to fascinate people, both believers and nonbelievers. And even nonbelievers must admit that space visitors **might have contributed** to human culture. After all, no one can prove that they didn't.

Easter Island: Statues of space visitors?

AFTER YOU READ

Read the statements about von Däniken's ideas. Look at the text again. How certain was he? Check the correct column for each statement.

	Certain	Possible	Impossible
1. The Nazca lines marked a landing strip for ancient astronauts.	☐	☐	☐
2. The Nazca people believed that the visitors were gods.	☐	☐	☐
3. There were enough people on Easter Island to carve the huge statues.	☐	☐	☐

Grammar Presentation

SPECULATIONS AND CONCLUSIONS ABOUT THE PAST: *MAY HAVE, MIGHT HAVE, COULD HAVE, MUST HAVE, HAD TO HAVE*

Statements				
Subject	Modal* / *Had to*	*Have*	Past Participle	
They	**may (not)** **might (not)** **could (not)** **must (not)** **had to**	**have**	**seen**	the statues.

Contractions		
may have	=	**may've**
might have	=	**might've**
could have	=	**could've**
must have	=	**must've**
could not	=	**couldn't**

NOTE: We usually do not contract *may not have*, *might not have*, and *must not have*.

*May, might, could, and *must* are modals. Modals have only one form. They do not have *-s* in the third person singular.

Questions			
Do / Be	Subject	Verb	
Did	they	**carve**	these statues?
Were			aliens?

Short Answers			
Subject	Modal / *Had to*	*Have*	*Been*
They	**may (not)** **might (not)** **could (not)**	**have.**	
	must (not) **had to**	**have**	**been.**

Yes / No Questions: *Could*				
Could	Subject	*Have*	Past Participle	
Could	he	**have**	**seen**	aliens?
			been	an alien?

Short Answers			
Subject	Modal / *Had to*	*Have*	*Been*
He	**may (not)** **might (not)** **could (not)**	**have.**	
	must (not) **had to**	**have**	**been.**

Wh- Questions				
Wh- Word	*Could*	*Have*	Past Participle	
Who	**could**	**have**	**built**	the statues?
What			**happened**	to these people?

[handwritten annotations in right margin:]
100
was
must have /95
could have
might have   less than /50
may have
was it
couldn't have
can't have
must not have
might not have
may not have

GRAMMAR NOTES	**EXAMPLES**
1. Use *may have*, *might have*, and *could have* to express **speculations**, or possibilities, about a past situation. These speculations are usually based on facts that we have.	**FACT** Archaeologists found pictures of creatures with wings. **SPECULATIONS** • Space beings **may have visited** that civilization. • The pictures **might have marked** a landing strip for a spacecraft. • The pictures **could have shown** mythological creatures.
2. Use *must have* and *had to have* when you are almost certain about your **conclusions**. Do not use *had to have* in negative statements to draw conclusions.	**FACT** The Easter Island statues are made of stone. **CONCLUSIONS** • The islanders **must have had** very sharp tools. • The stone **must not have been** too hard for their tools. **FACT** The statues are very big. **CONCLUSIONS** • They **had to have been** very difficult to move. • They **must not have been** very easy to move. NOT They ~~didn't have to have been~~ easy to move.
3. *Couldn't have* often expresses a feeling of disbelief or **impossibility**.	• He **couldn't have believed** space visitors helped them! It doesn't make any sense.

4. Use *could have* in questions about possibility. Do not use *may have* or *might have*.

- **Could** the Nazca people **have drawn** those lines?

---

5. Use *been* in short answers to questions that include a form of *be*.

A: **Could** Erich von Däniken **have been** wrong?

B: He certainly **could have been**. There are other explanations.

A: *Was* Xesspe surprised when he saw the Nazca lines?

B: He **must have been**. No one knew about them at that time.

Use only the **modal + *have*** in short answers to questions with other verbs.

A: **Did** archaeologists **measure** the drawings?

B: They *must have*. They studied them for years.

---

6. PRONUNCIATION NOTE:

In informal speech, *have* in modal phrases is often pronounced like the word *of*.

- **could have** ("could of")

▶ **BE CAREFUL!** Do not write *of* instead of *have* with these past modals.

- They **must *have* been** very skillful. NOT They ~~must of~~ been very skillful.

Reference Note
For information about *could have* and *might have* to express **past advisability**, see Unit 16, page 242.

{ must have
{ had to have   = Fact

couldn't have   = impossible

could have   in questions about Possibility.

Focused Practice

1 | DISCOVER THE GRAMMAR

Match the facts with the speculations and conclusions.

Facts

_e_ **1.** The original title of *Chariots of the Gods?* was *Erinnerungen an die Zukunft*.

_d_ **2.** Von Däniken visited every place he described in his book.

_h_ **3.** In 1973, he wrote *In Search of Ancient Gods*.

_c_ **4.** He doesn't have a degree in archaeology.

_f_ **5.** *Chariots of the Gods?* was published the same year as the Apollo moon landing.

_b_ **6.** In the 1900s, writer Annie Besant said beings from Venus helped develop culture on Earth.

_a_ **7.** Von Däniken's books sold millions of copies.

_g_ **8.** As soon as von Däniken published his book, scientists attacked his theories.

Speculations and Conclusions

a. He must have made a lot of money.

b. He may have known about her ideas.

c. He could have learned about the subject on his own.

d. He must have traveled a lot.

e. He must have written it in German.

f. This great event had to have increased sales of the book.

g. They must not have believed his theories.

h. He might have written other books too.

2 | ON THEIR OWN?

Grammar Notes 1–4

Circle the correct words to complete the review of von Däniken's book, Chariots of the Gods?

"Here comes another one."

Who could have make / **made** the Nazca lines?
1.
Who could have carve / **carved** the Easter Island
2.
statues? According to Erich von Däniken, ancient

achievements like these are mysteries because our

ancestors could not **have** / had created these things on
3.
their own. His solution: They **must** / couldn't have gotten
4.
help from space visitors.

Von Däniken's readers may not realize that

experiments have helped explain some of these "mysteries." Von Däniken asks: How may / **could**
5.

the Nazcans have planned the lines from the ground? Archaeologists now believe that this

civilization might have / has developed flight. They think ancient Nazcans may draw / have drawn
6.   7.

pictures of hot-air balloons on pottery. To test the theory, archaeologists built a similar balloon

with Nazcan materials. The balloon soared high enough to view the Nazca lines, showing that

Nazcans themselves could / couldn't have designed the pictures from the air.
8.

But what about the Easter Island statues? Did / Could islanders have carved the huge statues
9.

from hard rock with primitive tools? And how could only 2,000 people had / have moved them?
10.

3 | WHY NOT?   *Grammar Notes 1–4*

Now complete the rest of the review from Exercise 2. Use the verbs in parentheses.

Von Däniken and early explorers thought the island's ancient culture ___must have been___
1. (must / be)

simple. They assumed that Easter Island _must not have been_ ~~had~~ many natural resources,
2. (must not / have)

so it _couldn't have supported_ a civilization. They were wrong. Studies have shown that a
3. (couldn't / support)

large population and a complex culture _could have developed_ on the island. Large
4. (could / develop)

palm trees once grew there. Islanders _must have made_ large boats from the
5. (must / make)

trees and _must have finished_ in deep water because ancient garbage dumps are full
6. (must / fish)

of the bones of deep sea fish. Ancient islanders _must have eaten_ very well, and
7. (must / eat)

as many as 15,000 people _may have lived_ on the island. From trees, they
8. (may / live)

could have made ropes to pull their statues. In 1994, DNA tests proved that the
9. (could / make)

islanders _had to have come_ from Polynesia, where there is a tradition of ancestor
10. (had to / come)

worship. But doubts remained—in the language of Rapa Nui (Easter Island), the statues are called

the living faces of our ancestors. How _could_ the Nazca people

could have called these lifeless images "living faces"? Then Sergio Rapu, a Rapa
11. (could / call)

Nui archaeologist, realized that the statues _must have had_ coral eyes. Pieces of
12. (must / have)

coral he had found fit one of the statues perfectly, and its face seemed to come to life. Scientists

are still experimenting with ways islanders _might have moved_ the huge images.
13. (might / move)

However, now no one says, "The people of Rapa Nui _couldn't have created_ these
14. (couldn't / create)

statues."

4 | NATURE PUZZLES

Read about these puzzling events. Then rewrite the answers to the questions about their causes. Substitute a modal phrase for the underlined words.

Dinosaurs existed on the Earth for about 135 million years. Then, about 65 million years ago, these giant reptiles all died in a short period of time. What could have caused the dinosaurs to become extinct?

1. It's likely that the Earth became colder. (must)

   The Earth must have become colder.

2. Probably, dinosaurs didn't survive the cold. (must not)

   must not *have* survived

3. It's been suggested that a huge meteor hit the Earth. (might)

   It might have been suggest

4. A Bigfoot didn't kidnap Ostman—that's impossible. (couldn't)

   A Bigfoot couldn't have kidnaped

5. Ostman probably saw a bear. (must)

   Osman must have seen it saw

6. It's possible that Ostman dreamed about a Bigfoot. (could)

   Osman could have dreamed about a Bigfoot.

In 1924, Albert Ostman went camping alone in Canada. Later, he reported that a Bigfoot (a large, hairy creature that looks human) had kidnapped him and taken him home, where the Bigfoot family treated him like a pet. Ostman escaped after several days. What do you think happened? Could a Bigfoot really have kidnapped Ostman?

dreamt = dreamed

7. Most likely the man changed the photo. (have to)

   Most likely the man have to [must] = have changed

8. Perhaps the man saw a large fish. (might)

   Perhaps the man might have seen saw a large fish.

9. It's possible that the man saw a dead tree trunk. (may)

   It's possible that the man may have seen a saw dead Tr.

10. It's very unlikely that a dinosaur was in the lake. (couldn't)

    It's very unlikely that a dinosaur couldn't have been in the lake

In 1932, a man was taking a walk around Scotland's beautiful Loch Ness. Suddenly, a couple hundred feet from shore, the water bubbled up and a huge monster appeared. The man took a photo. When it was developed, the picture showed something with a long neck and a small head. Since then, many people have reported similar sightings. What do you think? Did the man really see the Loch Ness monster?

5 | ARCHAEOLOGY 101 *Grammar Note 5*

Some archaeology students are asking questions in class. Use the modals in parentheses to write short answers.

1. **A:** Were the Nazcans really able to fly?

   B: _____ They might have been _____ . There's some evidence that they had hot-air
   (might)
   balloons made of cloth.

2. **A:** Is it possible that the Nazcan lines were ancient streets?

   B: _They couldn't have been_ . Some of them just lead to the tops of mountains
   (could not)
   and then end abruptly.

3. **A:** Do you think the Nazcans used them during

   religious ceremonies?

   B: _Yes, they might have used_ . But
   (might)
   we have no proof.

4. **A:** Do you think the people on Rapa Nui built the

   giant statues themselves?

   B: _Yes, they could have built_ . They
   (could)
   had the knowledge and the tools.

5. **A:** Did the original settlers of Rapa Nui come from Polynesia?

   B: _Yes, they must have come_ . There's a lot of scientific evidence to support this.
   (must)

6. **A:** Von Däniken says that many ancient artifacts show pictures of astronauts. Could these

   pictures have illustrated anything closer to Earth?

   B: _Yes, they may have showed_ . It's possible that the pictures show people dressed
   (may)
   in local costumes.

7. **A:** Was von Däniken upset by all the criticism he received?

   B: _No, he might not have been_ . After all, it created more interest in his books.
   (might not)

8. **A:** Do you think von Däniken helped increase general interest in archaeology?

   B: _Yes, He must have helped_ . Just look at how many of you are taking
   (must)
   this class!

6 | EDITING

Read this student's essay about Easter Island. There are ten mistakes in the use of modals. The first mistake is already corrected. Find and correct nine more.

Rapa Nui (Easter Island) is a tiny island in the middle of
the Pacific. To get there, the first settlers had to ~~had~~ *have*
traveled more than 1,000 miles in open boats. Some scientists
believed only the Polynesians of the Pacific islands could
have ~~make~~ *made* the journey. Others thought that Polynesians
couldn't have carved the huge stone statues on Rapa Nui. They
believed Mayans or Egyptians maybe have traveled there. (Some
people even said that space aliens might *have* helped!) Finally, a
University of Oslo scientist was able to study the DNA from
ancient skeletons. Professor Erika Halberg announced, "These
people has to have been the descendants of Polynesians."

We now know that the islanders built the statues, but we
have also learned that they must had *have* solved even more
difficult problems. The first settlers came some time between
A.D. 400 and 700. At first, Rapa Nui must be *have been* a paradise with
its fishing, forests, and good soil. Their society may have
grown too fast for the small island, however. Botanical
studies show that by the 1600s they had cut down the last
tree. The soil must not have washed away, so they couldn't
farm. And with no wood for boats, they couldn't have *been* able to
fish. For a period of time, people starved and fought
violently, but when the Dutch discovered Rapa Nui in 1722,
they found a peaceful, healthy population growing fields of
vegetables. How the islanders could *could* have learned in this short
period of time to live peacefully with so few resources? For
our troubled world today, this might be the most important
"mystery of Easter Island."

Communication Practice

7 | LISTENING

They have to made and very old.

🎧 *Some archaeology students are discussing artifacts they have found at various sites. Look at the pictures. Then listen to the students speculate and draw conclusions about what each item is. Listen again and match the pictures with the correct conversation.*

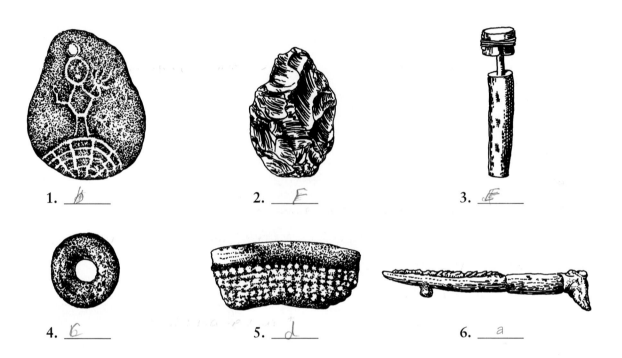

1. _b_

2. _F_

3. _E_

4. _G_

5. _d_

6. _a_

8 | USEFUL OBJECTS

Work in small groups. Look at the objects that archaeologists have found in different places. Speculate on what they are and how people might have used them. After your discussion, share your ideas with the rest of the class.

1. Archaeologists found this object in the sleeping area of an ancient Chinese house. It's about the same size as a basketball.

Example: I think people might have used this as a footstool. The floor must have been cold at night, and people could have rested their feet on it.

(continued)

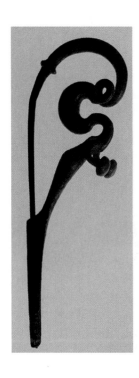

2. Archaeologists have found objects like these with men's and women's clothing. This one is about the size of a cordless telephone.

3. These artifacts were used by ancient Egyptians. The handles are each about the length of a toothbrush.

4. People in the Arctic started using these around 2,000 years ago. They used them when they were hunting or traveling. They are small enough to put in your pocket.

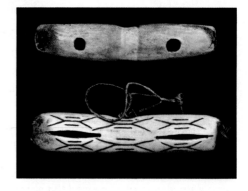

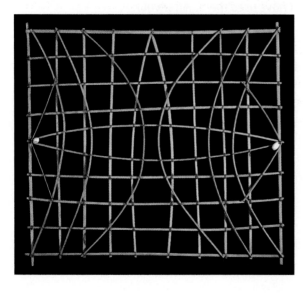

5. Polynesian people used these when they traveled. They made them with sticks, coconut fiber, and seashells. This one is about 1 foot (30.5 centimeters) wide and 1 foot long.

9 | CHARIOTS OF THE GODS?

Reread the article that begins on page 249. Then discuss your opinion about Erich von Däniken's theory with a partner. Afterward, have a class discussion. How many students think space creatures might have visited the Earth? How many think space creatures couldn't have affected human culture?

10 | ON THE INTERNET

Ⓒ *Do a search on one of these unsolved mysteries. Find several explanations. Which explanations seem more likely? Compare your information and ideas in groups.*

1. The ancient Maya once inhabited the Yucatán Peninsula in what today is Mexico and Guatemala. They had a very advanced civilization. In about A.D. 900, for no known reason, the Maya suddenly left their large and well-built cities. The jungle soon covered the entire area. Why did the Maya abandon their cities? Why did they never return?

   Example: **A:** The climate could have gotten drier. They might not have had enough water.
   B: Or they may have moved out of the cities for religious reasons.

2. On October 23, 1947, at about 7:30 A.M. in Marksville, Louisiana, a small town in the United States, it suddenly started raining fish. The town's bank director reported that hundreds of fish had fallen into his yard, and townspeople were hit by the falling fish as they walked to work. The fish were only the kinds found in local rivers and lakes, and they were all very fresh. Nothing else—no frogs, turtles, or water plants—fell that morning, only fish. How could this have happened?

3. In 1991 hikers in the Italian Alps discovered a body in some melting ice. The body, which had been in the ice for more than 5,000 years, was in almost perfect condition. The "Ice Man" had several broken ribs. He had been wearing warm winter clothing, and had been carrying a knife, an ax, dried meat, and medicines. He had been making a bow and arrows, but he had not finished them. What could have happened to him?

11 | WRITING

Write a paragraph about one of the unsolved mysteries in Exercise 10. Use modals to speculate about what caused the event. Which explanation do you think is the most likely, and why?

   Example: The Ice Man might have brought his animals into the mountains to feed. People from his time and culture often did that. Someone from another tribe could have attacked him.

From **Grammar** to **Writing**
Organizing Ideas from Freewriting

Freewriting is a way to develop ideas about a topic. To freewrite, write for a
specified length of time without stopping. Don't worry about mistakes. Then
organize the ideas in your freewriting.

> **Example:** Can't stop thinking about M's wedding in Quito last year. *(freewriting)*
> I can't stop thinking about Miguel's wedding in Quito last year. *(formal writing)*

1 | *Read Clara's freewriting about a problem she had with her cousin Miguel. Underline her ideas
about Miguel's reasons for what he did. Bracket (**[ ]**) her ideas about the appropriateness of Miguel's
and her own behavior.*

> Can't stop thinking about Miguel's wedding in Quito
> last year. Still feeling hurt and confused. Why
> didn't he invite me? Or even tell me about it? [This
> was a family reunion and he should have sent
> everyone an invitation.] He knows I'm a student, and
> <u>he must have thought I couldn't afford the airfare
> to Ecuador.</u> He could've sent me an invitation and
> let me decide for myself. On the other hand, I
> should have called him to discuss it. He might have
> even decided that I couldn't afford to send a gift.
> He shouldn't have decided for me. He couldn't have
> been angry with me! I've got to let him know how I
> feel. I should write a letter.

2 Clara decided to write a letter to Miguel. Read her outline in Exercise 3.
Write the paragraph number where Clara decides to do each of the following:

1. discuss the appropriateness of Miguel's and her own behavior ___3___

2. introduce the problem _____

3. suggest resolving the problem _____

4. speculate on reasons for Miguel's behavior _____

3 Complete Clara's letter with ideas from Exercise 1.

Dear Miguel,

I'm sorry that I haven't written for some time, but I'm still feeling hurt and confused. Miguel, why didn't you invite me to your wedding last year? You didn't even tell me about it!

Maybe your reasons for not inviting me were actually thoughtful. You know I'm a student, and ___you must have thought I couldn't afford the airfare.___

_____

_____

_____

However, I believe you should have handled the situation in a different way. This was a family reunion, and you should have sent everyone an invitation.

_____

_____

_____

We ought to solve this as soon as possible. I miss you. Please write as soon as you get this letter.

Love,

Clara

4 | *Before you write . . .*

1. Think of a problem you had with a friend or relative. Freewrite about the problem: the reasons it might have happened and what you and other people could have done differently.

2. Choose ideas and organize them.

5 | *Write a letter to the friend or relative who you had the problem with. Include ideas from your freewriting in Exercise 4. Use past modals to speculate about reasons for your problem and to express regrets and obligations.*

6 | *Exchange letters with a partner. Write a question mark (?) over anything in the letter that seems wrong. Then answer the following questions.*

	Yes	No
1. Did the writer correctly use past modals to speculate about reasons?	☐	☐
2. Did the writer correctly use past modals to express appropriateness?	☐	☐
3. Did the writer express his or her feelings and ideas clearly?	☐	☐

7 | *Work with your partner. Discuss each other's editing questions from Exercise 6. Then rewrite your letter and make any necessary corrections.*

Review Test

I *Complete this conversation by circling the correct modals.*

A: You <u>should have</u> / (must have) been up late last night. You look tired.
1.

B: I (couldn't / <u>didn't have to</u> sleep. My boss gave Joe a raise instead of me.
2.

He <u>could have</u> / <u>couldn't have</u> given me one. I've been there a whole year.
3.

A: I (can't / <u>don't have to</u> believe he did that! Well, the company <u>could</u> / <u>must not</u> have the
4.   5.

money right now.

B: Wrong. Ann got a raise and a promotion. And she('s got to / <u>should</u> be the worst
6.

employee there. By the way, your friend Amy also got a promotion.

A: Really? She <u>has to</u> / <u>may</u> be pleased about that. But, getting back to you—you
7.

(should / <u>shouldn't</u> call me when you get upset. I <u>must have</u> / <u>might have</u> been able to
8.   9.

help last night.

B: I called you at 8:00. You <u>must have</u> / <u>might not have</u> been out.
10.

A: I wasn't out. I <u>could not have</u> / <u>must not have</u> heard the phone.
11.

I <u>could have</u> / <u>ought to have</u> been in the shower.
12.

B: Well, I ended up calling Sam. What a mistake. I <u>should</u> / <u>shouldn't have</u> called him.
13.

He repeated everything to Ann.

A: That's terrible! He <u>shouldn't have</u> / <u>must not have</u> done that. I'm going to talk with him
14.

about it.

B: You <u>couldn't</u> / <u>'d better not</u>. He'll just repeat that conversation too.
15.

II *Complete this conversation with past modals. Use the correct form of the verbs in parentheses. Choose between affirmative and negative.*

A: I got a C on my math test. I ___*should have done*___ better than that.
1. (should / do)

B: Don't be so hard on yourself. It ___may *not* have been___ your fault. It just
2. (may / be)

___could have been___ a more difficult test than usual.
3. (could / be)

A: No, it ___could have *not* been___ that difficult. The rest of the class did pretty well.
4. (could / be)

I ___should have studied___ harder.
5. (should / study)

B: What ___could *not*___ you ___have done___ differently?
6. (could / do)

A: Well, for one thing, I ___should have missed___ that day of class.
7. (should / miss)

B: You missed a day? Did you get the notes?

A: No. I ___ought *not* to have *copied*___ them. Some of the problems which I got wrong
8. (ought to / copy)

___must have come___ from that day.
9. (must / come)

III *Summarize these sentences. Use the past form of the modals in parentheses. Choose between affirmative and negative.*

1. It was a mistake to stay up so late.

   (should) ___I shouldn't have stayed up so late.___

2. I regret not watching the show about Easter Island.

   (should) ___I should have watched the___

3. I'm sure it was very interesting.

   (must) ___It must have been very interesting___

4. I was surprised that the local library never bought books about Easter Island.

   (ought to) ___Local library ought to have brought books about Easter Island___

5. I'm annoyed at Sara for not reminding me about it.

   (should) ___she should have reminded me about it.___

6. I wish that John had told me about it.

   (could) ___John could have told me about it.___

7. I'm sure he didn't remember our conversation about it.

   (must) ___He must not have remembered___

   or

   forgoten

8. I feel bad that my roommate didn't invite me to the party.

(might) *My roomate might have invited* ----

9. It's possible that John didn't get an invitation.

(might) *John might not have gotten an* —

10. I'm sure he didn't forget our date.

(could) *He couldn't have forgotten* —

IV *Circle the letter of the correct word(s) to complete each sentence.*

1. There are no clean socks. I should _____ the laundry yesterday.   A B (C) D
   (**A**) did   (**C**) have done
   (**B**) do   (**D**) not have done

2. Kai wants better grades next semester. He _____ harder.   A (B) C D
   (**A**) must have studied   (**C**) must not study
   (**B**) will have to study   (**D**) shouldn't study

3. Dana didn't buy her brother a birthday card. She must _____.   (A) B C D
   (**A**) have forgotten   (**C**) forget
   (**B**) not have forgotten   (**D**) forgets

4. My wallet is missing. I _____ dropped it in the store.   A B (C) D
   (**A**) ought to have   ✓(**C**) could have
   (**B**) might   (**D**) must

5. He's going for a walk in a few minutes. He may _____ at Molly's on the way.   A B C (D)
   (**A**) have stopped   (**C**) stops
   (**B**) stopping   (**D**) stop

6. You're not coming tonight? It's already seven o'clock! You _____ let   A (B) C D
   me know sooner.
   (**A**) may   (**C**) can't
   (**B**) might have   (**D**) must have

7. You should _____ *Fear Factor* tomorrow night. I hear that it's   A B (C) D
   going to be a really exciting show.
   (**A**) have missed   (**C**) not miss
   (**B**) not have missed   (**D**) miss

(continued)

8. Mayan buildings are beautiful. The Mayans must _____ an advanced   A B C D
   civilization.
   (**A**) have   (**C**) had
   (**B**) have had   (**D**) had had

9. I don't understand this show. Clio was in Tampa on Thursday, so   A B C D
   she couldn't _____ the money from a Boston bank that day.
   (**A**) steal   (**C**) have stolen
   (**B**) had stolen   (**D**) stole

10. I'm sorry, but I _____ able to meet you for lunch tomorrow.   A B C D
    (**A**) won't be   (**C**) can't be
    (**B**) haven't been   (**D**) don't be

V | *Read this journal entry. There are nine mistakes in the use of modals. The first mistake is already corrected. Find and correct eight more.*

Friday, October 25

    What a day! I guess I'd ~~not better~~ *better not* stay up so late anymore. This morning I should of *have* gotten up much earlier. When I got to the post office, the lines were already long. I must have wait*ed* at least half an hour. My boss was furious that I was late. He might fire*d* me for lateness—even though I couldn't have worked during that time anyway. The computers were down again! We must *have* had lost four hours because of that. While the system was down, some of us were able *to* go out to lunch. Later, we all felt sick. It had to has been the food—we all ate the same thing. On the way home, I got stuck in traffic. A trip that should *have* taken twenty minutes took forty-five. Tomorrow's Saturday. I just might sleep~~ing~~ until noon.

▶ *To check your answers, go to the Answer Key on page RT-4.*

PART
VIII
The Passive

Grammar in Context

BEFORE YOU READ

🎧 *Look at the title of the article. What is geography? Have you ever studied geography in school? Did you enjoy studying geography? Is it an important subject? Why or why not? Read this article about* National Geographic, *a famous magazine.*

GEOGRAPHY

The Best Subject on Earth

Geography is the study of the Earth and its people. It sounds exciting, doesn't it? Yet for decades, students yawned just hearing the word. They **were forced** to memorize the names of capital cities, important rivers and mountains, and natural resources. They **were taught** where places were and what **was produced** there. But they **weren't shown** how our world looks and feels.

Then came *National Geographic* magazine. From the Amazon rain forests to the Sahara Desert, and from Kuala Lumpur to Great Zimbabwe—the natural and human-made wonders of our world **have been brought** to life **by** fascinating reporting and beautiful photographs, such as this one of a Russian couple, which **was taken by** Reza Deghati.

The National Geographic Society **was formed** in Washington, D.C., in 1888 **by** a group of professionals including geographers, explorers, teachers, and mapmakers. Nine months later, the first *National Geographic* magazine **was published** so that the Society could fulfill its mission—to spread the knowledge of and respect for the world, its resources, and its inhabitants.

GEOGRAPHY The Best Subject on Earth

In 1995, the first foreign-language edition of *National Geographic* magazine **was published** in Japan. Today, the magazine **is printed** in more than 20 languages and **sold** all over the world. *National Geographic* also puts out a number of special publications. *National Geographic Explorer*, for example, **has been created** for classrooms. Other publications feature travel and adventure. *National Geographic* TV programs **are watched** in over 160 million homes in 145 countries.

The study of geography has come a long way since 1888. The Society's mission **has been fulfilled**. In fact, it **has** even **been extended** to include worlds beyond Earth. From the deep seas to deep space, geography has never been more exciting!

AFTER YOU READ

Answer these questions.

1. Who memorized names of capital cities? _____children_____

2. Who took the photo of the Russian couple? _____

3. Who formed the National Geographic Society? _____

4. Who watches *National Geographic* TV? _____

Grammar Presentation

THE PASSIVE

Active	Passive
Millions of people **buy** it.	It **is bought** by millions of people.
Someone **published** it in 1888.	It **was published** in 1888.
They **have reached** their goal.	Their goal **has been reached**.

Passive Statements				
Subject	*Be (not)*	Past Participle	(*By* + Object)	
It	**is (not)**	**bought**	**by** millions of people.	
It	**was (not)**	**published**		in 1888.
Their goal	**has (not) been**	**reached**.		

(continued)

Yes / No Questions			
Be / Have	Subject	*(Been +)* Past Participle	
Is Was	it	sold	in Japan?
Has		been sold	

Short Answers					
Affirmative			Negative		
Yes,	it	is. was. has (been).	No,	it	isn't. wasn't. hasn't (been).

Wh- Questions			
Wh- Word	*Be / Have*	Subject	*(Been +)* Past Participle
Where	is was	it	sold?
	has		been sold?

GRAMMAR NOTES

EXAMPLES

1. **Active** and **passive** sentences often have similar meanings, but a **different focus**.

Active sentences focus on the **agent** (the person or thing doing the action).

Passive sentences focus on the **object** (the person or thing receiving the action).

ACTIVE
- Millions of **people read** the magazine.
  (The focus is on people.)

PASSIVE
- The **magazine is read** by millions of people.
  (The focus is on the magazine.)

2. Form the **passive** with a form of *be* + **past participle**.

► **BE CAREFUL!** Only **transitive verbs** (verbs that can have objects) have passive forms.

- It *is* **written** in more than 20 different languages.
- It *was* first **published** in 1888.
- It *has been* **sold** all over the world.

      transitive verb   object
- Ed Bly **wrote** *that article*.
- That article **was written** by Ed Bly.
  (passive form)

    intransitive verb
- It **seems** interesting.
  NOT It ~~was~~ seemed interesting.
  (no passive form)

3. Use the **passive** in the following situations:

    a. When the **agent** (the person or thing doing the action) is <u>unknown or not important</u>.

- The magazine **was started** in 1888. *(I don't know who started it.)*
- The magazine **is sold** at newsstands. *(It is not important who sells it.)*

    b. When you want to <u>avoid mentioning</u> the agent.

- Some mistakes **were made** in that article on Bolivia. *(I know who made the mistakes, but I don't want to blame the person.)*

4. Use the passive with *by* if you mention the **agent**. Only mention the agent when it is important to know who it is.

- The photographs in this article are wonderful. They were **taken** *by a famous photojournalist*.
- One of the first cameras **was invented** *by Daguerre*.

▶ **BE CAREFUL!** In most cases, you do not need to mention an agent in passive sentences. Do not include an agent unnecessarily.

- Ed Bly took a really great photo. It **was taken** last February, but it won't appear until May. NOT It was taken last February ~~by him~~ . . .

Focused Practice

1 | DISCOVER THE GRAMMAR

*Read the sentences and decide if they are active (**A**) or passive (**P**).*

___P___ **1.** The first *National Geographic* magazine was published in October 1888.

___a___ **2.** Today, millions of people read it.

___P___ **3.** The magazine is translated into many other languages.

___a___ **4.** My cousin reads it in Russian.

___P___ **5.** Most of the articles are translated from English.

___P___ **6.** Some of them are written by famous writers.

___P___ **7.** Many expeditions have been sponsored by the National Geographic Society.

agent

(continued)

_P_ 8. The results are reported in the magazine.

_P_ 9. It is known for its wonderful photography.

_P_ 10. The first underwater color photographs were taken by a *National Geographic* photographer.

_P_ 11. Photographers are sent all over the world.

_A_ 12. They take pictures of people and nature.

_P_ 13. *National Geographic* is sold at newsstands. ← *w/*

_P_ 14. It is published once a month.

Present perfect

_A_ 15. The *National Geographic* cable television channel has become very popular.

inTransitive

2 | MANY TONGUES

Grammar Notes 1–3

Look at the chart. Then complete the sentences. Some sentences will be active; some will be passive.

Language	Number of Speakers*
Arabic	197
Chinese (Cantonese and Mandarin)	1,070
English	443
Japanese	125
Korean	71
Russian	293
Spanish	341
Turkish	46

*in millions

1. Japanese _is spoken by 125 million people_ .

2. Almost 300 million people _speak Russian_ .

3. _Korean is spoken_ by 71 million people.

4. Spanish _is spoken by 341 million people._ .

5. _1070 million people speak_ Chinese.

6. _Arabic is spoken by_ 197 million people.

7. More than 400 million people _speaks English._ .

8. _Turkish is spoken by_ 46 million people.

3 | AN INTERVIEW

Grammar Note 2

🎧 *Jill Jones is interviewing a Bolivian cultural attaché for an article she's writing.*
Complete her interview with the passive form of the verbs in parentheses and short answers.

JONES: Thanks for giving me some time today. Here is my first question:

_____Was_____ the area first _____inhabited_____ by the Inca?
1. (inhabit)

ATTACHÉ: _____No it wasnt_____. Long before the Inca, a great civilization _____was created_____
2.   3. (create)

around Lake Titicaca by the Aymara. The Aymara still live in Bolivia.

JONES: Fascinating. Let's talk about agriculture. I know potatoes are an important crop in the

mountains of the Andes. _____is_____ corn _____grown_____ there as well?
4. (grow)

ATTACHÉ: _____No it isnt_____. The climate is too cold. But quinoa grows well there.
5.

JONES: Quinoa? How _____is_____ that _____spelled_____? With a *k*?
6. (spell)

ATTACHÉ: No. With a *q*—q-u-i-n-o-a. It's a traditional grain. It _____has been eaten_____ by the
7. (eat)

people of the Andes for 5,000 years.

JONES: Everyone associates llamas with Bolivia. How _____are_____ they

_____used_____?
8. (use)

ATTACHÉ: In many ways—fur, meat, transportation. But they only do well in the Andes. They

_____are not raised_____ in the lowlands of the Oriente, the eastern part of the country.
9. (not raise)

JONES: I see. I know that tin is important. Where _____is_____ it _____mined_____?
10. (mine)

ATTACHÉ: The richest deposits _____are found_____ in the Andes.
11. (find)

JONES: How about the Oriente? What _____is produced_____ there?
12. (produce)

ATTACHÉ: Oil. Petroleum _____is found_____ there. Rice and cattle are important there too.
13. (find)

JONES: What other languages _____are spoken_____ besides Spanish?
14. (speak)

ATTACHÉ: Actually, more people speak Native American

languages than Spanish.

JONES: Naturalists love Bolivia. _____are_____ jaguars

still _____seen_____ there?
15. (see)

ATTACHÉ: _____yes they are_____. And so are condors and river
16.

dolphins—many, many species.

Jaguar

4 | FREQUENTLY ASKED QUESTIONS

Grammar Note 3

Complete the FAQ (Frequently Asked Questions) about how photographers send their film to National Geographic (NG). Use the correct forms of the verbs in the boxes.

number	put	~~receive~~	send	shoot	use

National Geographic photographers on expedition have to make sure their work

_____is received_____ by NG safely and in good condition. How do they do it? Read the
1.

FAQ to find out.

Q: How _____is_____ film usually _____Sent_____ to NG headquarters?
2.

A: The film _____is put_____ into its original film can. Then very secure packaging
3.

is used
_____are shooted_____ to protect the film during shipment.
4.

Q: How do the photographers and editors know what is on each roll of film?

A: Each roll _____is numbered_____ in the order that it _____was shot_____ is. shot
5. **6.**

damage	divide	lose	pack	save

have been *have been*

Q: _____are_____ shipments ever _____damaged_____ or _____losted_____ in the mail?
7. **8.**

A: Yes, they have been, but we've learned what to do. Now big shipments _____are_____

usually _____divided_____ into two. The even-numbered rolls _____are packed_____ in one
9. **10.**

shipment, and the odd in another. That way, half the rolls _____are saved_____ if there's a
11.

problem with one shipment.

find	notify	ship	start	take	trace

Q: What other precautions _____are_____ usually _____taken_____?
12.

A: The NG office _____is notified_____ by the photographer when film _____is shipped_____.
13. **14.**

If the film does not arrive on time, it _____is traced_____ immediately. Lost shipments
15.

_____are found_____ more easily when this process _____is started_____ right away.
16. **17.**

5 | CHECKING FACTS

Read Jill Jones's article. Her editor found and circled nine factual mistakes.

A Land of Contrasts

by Jill Jones

Visitors to Bolivia are amazed by the contrasts and charmed by the beauty of this South American country's landscapes—from the breathtaking Andes in the west to the tropical lowlands in the east.

Two-thirds of Bolivia's 5 million people are concentrated in the cool western highlands, or *altiplano*. Today, as in centuries past, corn [?] and kuinoa [spelling?] are grown in the mountains. Llamas are raised only for transportation. [?] And tin, Bolivia's richest natural resource, is mined in the high Andes.

The Oriente, another name for the eastern lowlands, is mostly tropical. Rice is the major food crop, and llamas [?] are raised for meat in the lowlands. Rubber [?] is also found in this region. [not] [in the Andes] [jaguars ?]

Bolivia is home to many fascinating forms of wildlife. The colorful parrot [?] is [are] seen in the highest mountains. Boa constrictors, jaguars, and many other animals are found in the rain forests.

Hundreds of years before the Inca flourished, a great civilization was created on the shores of the Pacific, [?] probably by ancestors of Bolivia's Aymara people. Their descendants still speak the Aymara language. Today, Native American languages are still widely spoken in Bolivia. Although Portuguese [?] is spoken in the government, Quechua and Aymara are used more widely by the people. Traditional textiles are woven by machine. [?] Music is played on reed pipes whose tone resembles the sound of the wind blowing over high plains in the Andes. [around the lake] [not] [Spanish is spoken]

(continued)

Now rewrite the incorrect sentences with information from Exercise 3.

1. <u>*Corn isn't grown in the mountains. Potatoes are grown in the mountains.*</u>

2. _____

3. _____

4. _____

5. _____

6. _____

7. _____

8. _____

9. _____

6 | DID YOU KNOW?

Grammar Notes 3–4

Read Ed Bly's soccer trivia column. Complete the information with the correct form of the verbs in the first set of parentheses. If the agent (in the second set of parentheses) is necessary, include it in your answer. If not, cross it out.

⚽ Soccer is the most popular sport in the world. It <u>is played by more than 20 million people</u>.
    1. (play) (more than 20 million people)

⚽ It <u>is called</u> football _____ in 144 countries.
    2. (call) ~~(people)~~

⚽ Except for the goalie, players <u>are not allowed</u> to use their hands. Instead, the
    3. (not allow) (the rules)

ball <u>is controled by feet, the head, and the body.</u>
    4. (control) (the feet, the head, and the body)

⚽ Soccer <u>was not played</u> in the United States very much until 20 years
    5. (not play) (people)

ago. Since then, the game <u>has been made popular by</u>.
    6. (make popular) (Pelé, Beckham, and other international stars)

⚽ Forms of soccer <u>are played by different cultures</u> for thousands of years. A form of
    7. (play) (different cultures)

soccer <u>was enjoyed by chinese people</u> in China 2,000 years ago.
    8. (enjoy) (Chinese people)

⚽ It <u>was banned by King edward III of England</u> in 1365—his archers spent
    9. (ban) (King Edward III of England)

too much time playing, and too little time practicing archery.

⚽ Medieval games <u>are played by players</u> for entire days, over miles of
    10. (play) (players)

territory.

⚽ Today, the World Cup games <u>are held by the world cup</u> every four years.
    11. (hold) (The World Cup Association)

The best teams in the world compete.

7 | EDITING

Read this short biography of an internationally famous photographer whose photos have appeared in National Geographic. *(He took the photo on page 270.) There are seven mistakes in the use of the passive. The first mistake is already corrected. Find and correct six more.*

Seeing the World
by Diana Brodylo

Reza Deghati ~~is~~ *was* born in Tabriz, Iran, in 1952. When he was only 14 years old, he began teaching himself photography. At first, he took pictures of his own country—its people and its architecture. When he was 25, he ~~was~~ decided to become a professional photographer. During a demonstration he was asked by a French news agency to take photos. He only shot one and a half rolls of film (instead of the usual 20 to 40), but his photos *were* ~~was~~ published in *Paris Match* (France), *Stern* (Germany), and *Newsweek* (U.S.A).

Reza, as he is *known* ~~knew~~ professionally, has covered several wars, and he has be*en* wounded on assignment. Among all his assignments, the project dearest to his heart is photographing children, who he calls "the real victims of war." He has donated these photos to humanitarian organizations.

When he was interviewed ~~by an interviewer~~, he was asked to give advice to wannabe* photojournalists. Reza replied, "There is a curtain between the photographer and the subject unless the photographer is able to break through it. . . . Open your heart to them so they know you care."

Today Reza Deghati lives in Paris. His photos *are* ~~is~~ widely distributed in more than 50 countries around the world, and his work is published in *National Geographic* as well as many other internationally famous magazines and newspapers.

wannabe = want-to-be

15 years

Communication Practice

8 | LISTENING

🎧 *Listen to the conversations between editors at* Modern Reader. *Then listen again to each conversation and circle the letter of the sentence you hear.*

1. a. Jill hired Bob.
   b. Jill was hired by Bob.

2. **a.** I trained Minna.
   b. I was trained by Minna.

3. a. It's published just six times a year.
   b. It was published just six times a year.

4. **a.** Tony fired Jill.
   b. Tony was fired by Jill.

5. a. She interviewed Jay.
   b. She was interviewed by Jay.

6. **a.** He was laid off.
   b. Was he laid off?

9 | SAID AROUND THE WORLD

Read these proverbs from around the world. What do you think they mean? Discuss them in small groups. Are there proverbs from other cultures that mean the same thing?

- Rome wasn't built in a day. (*English*)

    Example: A: I think this means that big projects aren't finished quickly.
    B: Yes. They take a lot of time and you have to be patient.
    C: There's a proverb in French that means the same thing: "Paris wasn't built in a day."

- He who was bitten by a snake avoids tall grass. (*Chinese*)

- He ran away from the rain and was caught in a hailstorm. (*Turkish*)

- Silence was never written down. (*Italian*)

- Never promise a fish until it's caught. (*Irish*)

- Stars are not seen by sunshine. (*Spanish*)

- Write the bad things that are done to you in sand, but write the good things that happen to you on a piece of marble. (*Arab*)

- Skillful sailors weren't made by smooth seas. (*Ethiopian*)

- A good year is known by its spring. (*Portuguese*)

- Knowledge is like a garden: if it is not cultivated, it cannot be harvested. (*Guinean*)

- Great trees are envied by the wind. (*Japanese*)

- The night is dark, but the apples have been counted. (*Afghan*)

10 | INFORMATION GAP: THE PHILIPPINES

The Philippines consist of many islands. The two largest are Luzon in the north and Mindanao in the south.

Work in pairs (A and B). Student B, go to page 284 and follow the instructions there.

Student A

1. Look at the map of Luzon below. Complete the chart for Luzon. Write *Y* for yes and *N* for no.

2. Student B has the map of Mindanao. Ask Student B questions about Mindanao and complete the chart for Mindanao.

    Example: A: Is tobacco grown in Mindanao?
    B: No, it isn't.

3. Student B doesn't have the map of Luzon. Answer Student B's questions about Luzon.

    Example: B: Is tobacco grown in Luzon?
    A: Yes, it is. It's grown in the northern and central part of the island.

is grown

			Mindanao	Luzon
G R O W		tobacco	N	Y
		corn	Y	N
		bananas	Y	N
		coffee	N	Y
		pineapples	N	Y
		sugar	Y	Y
R A I S E		cattle	Y	Y
		pigs	Y	Y
M I N E		gold	Y	Y
		manganese	N	Y
P R O D U C E		cotton	N	Y
		rubber	Y	N
		lumber	Y	N

When you are done, compare charts. Are they the same?

11 | TRIVIA QUIZ

National Geographic Explorer *often has games and puzzles. Work in pairs. Complete this quiz. Then compare answers with your classmates. The answers are on page 284.*

Do you know . . . ?

1. Urdu is spoken in _____.

a. Ethiopia **b.** Pakistan **c.** Uruguay

2. Air-conditioning was invented in _____.

a. 1902 **b.** 1950 **c.** 1980

3. The X-ray was discovered by _____.

a. Thomas Edison **b.** Wilhelm Roentgen **c.** Marie Curie

4. The Petronas Towers in Kuala Lumpur were designed by _____.

a. Minoru Yamasaki **b.** Cesar Pelli **c.** I. M. Pei

5. The 2004 Olympics were held in _____.

a. Greece **b.** Japan **c.** Korea

6. A baby _____ is called a cub.

a. cat **b.** dog **c.** lion

Now, with your partner, make up your own questions with the words in parentheses. For item 10, add your own question. Ask another pair to answer your questions.

Example:

_____ Guernica _____ ____ was painted ____ by __b__ .
                              (paint)

a. ____ Monet ____ **b.** ____ Picasso ____ **c.** ____ El Greco ____

7. _____ _____ by ____.
                              (invent)

a. _____ **b.** _____ **c.** _____

8. _____ _____ by ____.
                              (compose)

a. _____ **b.** _____ **c.** _____

9. _____ _____ by ____.
                              (write)

a. _____ **b.** _____ **c.** _____

10. _____ _____ by ____.

a. _____ **b.** _____ **c.** _____

12 | WRITING

Complete the table with information about a country that you know well. Then write an essay about the country with the information you have gathered. Use the passive. You can use the article in Exercise 5 as a model.

Example: Turkey is both a European and an Asian country. European Turkey is separated from Asian Turkey by the Sea of Marmara. Citrus fruits and tobacco are grown in . . .

Name of country	
Geographical areas	
Crops grown in each area	
Animals raised in each area	
Natural resources found in each area	
Wildlife found in each area	
Languages spoken	
Art, handicrafts, or music created	

13 | ON THE INTERNET

National Geographic is famous for its photographs. Go to its website at www.nationalgeographic.com and search the photo archives. Find a photo that interests you. When and where was it taken? Who was it taken by? What does it show? What do you like about the photo? Print the photo and discuss it with your classmates.

Example: This photo was taken in Afghanistan in 1933 by Maynard Owen Williams. It shows . . .

INFORMATION GAP FOR STUDENT B

1. Look at the map of Mindanao below. Complete the chart for Mindanao. Write *Y* for yes and *N* for no.

2. Student A doesn't have the map of Mindanao. Answer Student A's questions about Mindanao.

   Example: **A:** Is tobacco grown in Mindanao?
   B: No, it isn't.

3. Student A has the map of Luzon. Ask Student A questions about Luzon and complete the chart for Luzon.

   Example: **B:** Is tobacco grown in Luzon?
   A: Yes, it is. It's grown in the northern and central part of the island.

			Mindanao	Luzon	
GROW		tobacco	N	Y	
		corn			
		bananas			Mindanao
		coffee			
		pineapples			
		sugar			
RAISE		cattle			
		pigs			
MINE		gold			
		manganese			
PRODUCE		cotton			
		rubber			
		lumber			

When you are done, compare charts. Are they the same?

Answers to Trivia Quiz Do You Know . . . ? in Exercise 11 on page 282: **1.** b, **2.** a, **3.** b, **4.** b, **5.** a, **6.** c

The Passive with Modals and Similar Expressions

Grammar in Context

BEFORE YOU READ

🎧 *What does the title of the article mean? What are some problems that can occur when people from different cultures must live and work together? Read this article about an international space project.*

not having ~~ine~~ enough room

CLOSE QUARTERS

Japanese astronauts fear that decisions **will be made** too fast, while Americans worry that in an emergency, they **might not be made** quickly enough. The French and Dutch worry that dinner **won't be taken** seriously, and Italians suspect that their privacy **may not be respected**.

The focus of all this apprehension is the International Space Station (ISS), a major international project that was launched in 1998. The finished station **will be operated** by a crew of astronauts from sixteen countries, including Brazil, Canada, Japan, Russia, and the United States, and members of the European Union. Parts of the project **have had to be delayed**, but large sections of the station have already been assembled. A crew of two or three astronauts can stay aboard for six months at a time. In addition, international scientists and even space tourists **can be transported** there for short stays. The ISS **will be completed** in 2010. The stay on the completed station **could be lengthened** to prepare for a two-year trip to Mars.

How **can** an international group of astronauts **be expected** to get along during long periods in this "trapped environment"? To find out, anthropologist Mary Lozano and engineer Clifford Wong

=scientist

(*continued*)

Astronauts in Space Station

CLOSE QUARTERS

asked astronauts from around the world about their concerns. The two scientists are hopeful that many cross-cultural problems **will be avoided** by what they have learned.

Besides the concerns already mentioned, all the astronauts worry about language. English will be the official language of the station, and, of course, a great deal of technical language **must be mastered** by everyone. However, on a social level, some members of the ISS team fear that they **might be treated** like outsiders because they won't know American slang. Another concern is food. What time **should** meals **be served**? How **should** preparation and cleanup **be handled**? **Can** religious dietary restrictions **be observed** on board?

To deal with cross-cultural differences like these, Lozano and Wong feel strongly that astronauts **should be taught** interpersonal skills as well as **given** technical and survival know-how. They have interviewed participants in each country, and they hope that what they learn from them **will be applied** in training. In the long run, they believe, cross-cultural training will not only save money but also reduce errors caused by misunderstandings, ranging from

misreading a facial expression to incorrectly interpreting data.

Often qualities like sensitivity and tolerance **can't be taught** from a textbook; they **have to be observed** and **experienced**. Lozano and Wong say that the necessary model for space station harmony **can be found** in the TV series *Star Trek*. The multicultural *Enterprise* crew has been getting along in space for eons now, and the scientists suggest that watching the show might be helpful for future astronauts. Since cross-cultural harmony **could be imagined** by the *Star Trek* creators, it **can be achieved** by the crew of the ISS. This might turn out to be the project's greatest achievement.

—LISA DOBRUS

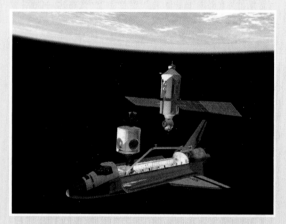

The International Space Station in space

AFTER YOU READ

*Write **T** (true), **F** (false), or **?** (the information isn't in the article).*

_____ **1.** Astronauts from 16 countries will operate the ISS.

_____ **2.** Scientists had to delay the project.

_____ **3.** The astronauts have to master technical language.

_____ **4.** Robots will serve the meals.

_____ **5.** A textbook can teach sensitivity and tolerance.

Grammar Presentation

THE PASSIVE WITH MODALS AND SIMILAR EXPRESSIONS

Statements				
Subject	**Modal***	***Be***	**Past Participle**	
The crew	**will (not)** **should (not)** **must (not)** **can (not)** **had better (not)**	**be**	**replaced**	next month.

*Modals have only one form. They do not have *-s* in the third person singular.

Statements				
Subject	***Have (got) to / Be going to****	***Be***	**Past Participle**	
The crew	**has (got) to** **doesn't have to** **is (not) going to**	**be**	**replaced**	next month.

**Unlike modals, *have* in *have (got) to* and *be* in *be going to* change for different subjects. Questions and negatives with *have (got) to* need a form of *do*.

Yes / No Questions			
Modal	**Subject**	***Be***	**Past Participle**
Will			
Should	it	be	replaced?
Must			
Can			

Short Answers					
Affirmative			**Negative**		
Yes,	it	will.	**No,**	it	won't.
		should.			shouldn't.
		must.			doesn't have to be.
		can.			can't.

Yes / No Questions				
Auxiliary Verb	**Subject**	***Have to / Going to***	***Be***	**Past Participle**
Does	it	have to	be	replaced?
Is		going to		

Short Answers					
Affirmative			**Negative**		
Yes,	it	does.	**No,**	it	doesn't.
		is.			isn't.

GRAMMAR NOTES

EXAMPLES

1. After a modal, form the passive with *be + past participle*.	• The shuttle *will* **be used** to complete the space station. • The crew *won't* **be replaced** this month. • The new menu *must* **be planned** very carefully. • Decisions *shouldn't* **be made** too quickly.
2. Use *will* or *be going to* with the passive to talk about the **future**.	• The project *will* **be completed** in five years. OR • The project *is going to* **be completed** in five years.
3. Use *can* with the passive to express **present ability**. Use *could* with the passive to express **past ability**.	• The space station *can* **be seen** from Earth. • It *could* **be seen** very clearly last year too.
4. Use *could, may, might,* and *can't* with the passive to express **future possibility** or **impossibility**.	• It *could* **be completed** very soon. • Tourists *may* **be invited**. • Plants *might* **be grown** on board. • The job *can't* **be done** by just one person.
5. Use *have (got) to, had better, should, ought to,* and *must* with the passive to express: **a. obligation** **b. advisability** **c. necessity**	 • Privacy *had better* **be respected**. • The crew *should* **be prepared** to deal with cultural differences. • Crew members *ought to* **be given** cross-cultural training. • Everyone *must* **be consulted**. • Free time *has (got) to* **be provided**.

Reference Note
For a review of **modals and similar expressions**, see Unit 15.

Focused Practice

1 | DISCOVER THE GRAMMAR

🎧 *Read this interview with scientist Dr. Bernard Kay (BK)* by Comet Magazine (CM).
Underline all the examples of the passive with modals and similar expressions.

CM: The International Space Station <u>has had to be delayed</u>. When will it be completed?

BK: It could be finished by 2010. With the shuttle* running again, work might be speeded up.

CM: What still has to be done?

BK: The new habitation module, where the astronauts eat and sleep, must be completed. When it's finished, there'll be more living space and the crew can be increased.

CM: At that point, will a separate sleeping cabin be provided for each crew member?

BK: Definitely. We feel strongly that each crew member should be given some private space.

CM: I've heard that looking out the window is the astronauts' favorite leisure activity. Maybe windows ought to be added to the cabins.

BK: Oh, they will be. A window is going to be placed in each cabin.

CM: What kind of experiments will be done on the ISS?

BK: Many kinds. But most important of all, human interactions have got to be understood better. An international crew from 16 different countries makes the ISS a wonderful laboratory for cross-cultural understanding.

CM: I guess we don't know what might be discovered, right?

BK: Right. That's what makes it so exciting.

---

*The space shuttle is a space vehicle. Like an airplane, it is flown by pilots and it can be used many times. The space shuttle has been used to bring crews, equipment, and supplies back and forth to the ISS.

2 | ZERO-G
Grammar Notes 1–5

Complete this article about zero-G (zero gravity or weightlessness) with the correct form of the words in parentheses.

Juggling oranges—it's easy in zero-G

Some tasks _____*can be accomplished*_____

1. **(can / accomplish)**

more easily in zero-G. Inside the station, astronauts

___*can be protected*___ from the

2. **(can / protect)**

deadly conditions of space—but life in almost zero-G

still _*can't be considered*_ normal.

3. **(can't / consider)**

What's it like to live on the ISS?

(continued)

*G*etting Rest: Sleeping ___can be compared___ to floating in water. It's

4. (can / compare)

relaxing, but sleeping bags ___must be attached___ to the walls of the cabins.

5. (must / attach)

Otherwise, astronauts will drift around as they sleep.

*K*eeping Clean: Showers ___can't be used___ because in zero-G, water from

6. (can't / use)

a shower flies in all directions, and sensitive equipment ___might be damaged___.

7. (might / damage)

Instead, astronauts take sponge baths. Used bath water ___have to be sucked___

8. (have to / suck)

into a container by a vacuum machine. Clothes ___could be washed___ by putting them

9. (could / wash)

into a bag with water and soap, but astronauts really ___haven't to be concerned___ with laundry.

don't

10. (not have to / concern)

They usually put dirty clothes into a trash container which ___can be sent___ back

11. (can / send)

toward Earth and ___can be burned up (or)___ in Earth's atmosphere.

12. (burn up)

burnt up

*D*ining: From the beginning, ISS planners have known that food ___should be taken___

13. (should / take)

very seriously. Unlike meals on early space missions, food on the ISS ___haven't be squeezed___

doesn't   to

14. (not have to / squeeze)

out of tubes. Frozen and dehydrated meals ___can be prepared___ in a kitchen

15. (can / prepare)

and ___can be eaten___ at a table. Regular utensils are used, but meals are

16. (eat)

packed into containers that ___must be attached___ to a tray so they don't float

17. (must / attach)

away.

*T*aking It Easy: Not surprisingly, a stressed astronaut is a grouchy astronaut. Free time

has

___have got to be provided___. Now crew members ___are going to given___

18. (have got to / provide)   be

19. (be going to / give)

pocket computers. They ___will be used___ for listening to music, looking

20. (will / use)

at photos from home, and reading e-books. Time also ___must be allowed___

21. (must / allow)

for exercise. In low-gravity environments, muscle and bone ___could be lost___

22. (could / lose)

quickly without exercise.

3 | AFTER THE SIMULATION

Grammar Notes 1–5

Some scientists who are going to join the space station have just completed a simulation of life on the station. Complete their conversations using the modals in parentheses and correct verbs from the boxes.

accept	keep	make	require	simulate	solve

CESAR: This simulation was great, but there are still some problems. I hope they

_____ *can be solved* _____ before our mission.
1. (can)

GINA: I agree. It was too warm in there. I think the temperature _____
2. (should)

at 68°.

CESAR: For me, that's still warm. Our clothing _____ of lighter material.
3. (ought to)

GINA: A space tourist _____ to join our mission. I heard they're
4. (might)

considering her application now.

CESAR: I heard that too. She _____ to take part in a simulation before she
5. (had better)

goes.

LYLE: You know, they can simulate daily life, but space walks _____
6. (can't)

very realistically.

approve	change	do	send	surprise

HANS: Did you fill in your food preference forms? They _____ to the
7. (should)

Food Systems Lab today.

HISA: I did. I'm glad the new dishes _____ by everyone. I really liked
8. (have to)

some of the Japanese and Russian meals.

HANS: Well, choose carefully. When we get to the station, the menu _____!
9. (can't)

LUIS: Shaving in zero-G is weird. The whisker dust from my beard and mustache kept flying

back into my face. I wonder if something _____ about that.
10. (could)

HANS: I have a feeling we _____ by a lot of unexpected problems.
11. (be going to)

4 | EDITING

Read an astronaut's journal notes. There are __eight__ mistakes in the use of the passive with modals and similar expressions. The first mistake is already corrected. Find and correct seven more.

October 4

October 4

6:15 A.M. I used the sleeping restraints last night, so my feet and hands didn't float around as much. I slept a lot better. I'm going to suggest some changes in the restraints, though—I think they ought to

made

be ~~make~~ more comfortable. I felt really trapped. And maybe these sleeping quarters could **be** designed

differently. They're too small.

10:45 A.M. My face is all puffy, and my eyes are red. Exercise helps a little—I'd better be **get** gotten on the

exercise bike right away. I can be misunderstanding very easily when I look like this. Sometimes

people think I've been crying. And yesterday Max thought I was angry when he turned on *Star Trek*.

Actually, I love that show.

1:00 P.M. Lunch was pretty good. Chicken teriyaki. It's nice and spicy, and the sauce can actually **be** been

tasted, even at zero gravity. They'd better fly in some more of it for us pretty soon. It's the most

popular dish in the freezer.

4:40 P.M. I'm worried about my daughter. Just before I left on this mission, she said she was planning

to quit school at the end of the semester. That's only a

month away. I want to call her and discuss it. But I worry

be

that I might get angry and yell. I might overheard by the

others. They really should figure out some way to give us

more privacy.

10:30 P.M. The view of Earth is unbelievably breathtaking!

My favorite time is spent looking out the

window—watching Earth pass below. At night a halo of

light surrounds the horizon. It's so bright that the tops of

be seen   *has*

the clouds can see. It can't be described. It simply have to

be experienced.

Communication Practice

5 | LISTENING

🎧 *Some crew members aboard the space station are watching television. Listen and read the script below. Then listen again and circle the underlined words you hear.*

PICARRO: Spaceship *Endeavor* calling Earth . . . This is Captain Picarro speaking. We've been hit by a meteorite.

EARTH: Is anyone hurt?

PICARRO: No, everyone is safe.

EARTH: You'd better start repairing the damage immediately.

PICARRO: It <u>can / can't</u> be repaired out here.
　　　　　　1.

★　★　★　★　★　★　★　★　★

PICARRO: We'll be approaching Planet CX5 of the Delta solar system in a few hours. Is their language on our computer, Dr. Sock?

SOCK: I'm checking now. . . . We don't have a language for CX5 on the computer, but we have one for CX4. Shall we try it?

PICARRO: We'd better be very careful. Our messages <u>could / should</u> be misunderstood.
　　　　　　　　　　　　　　　　　　　　　　　　　　2.

★　★　★　★　★　★　★　★　★

LON: OK. I'm ready. Let's go.

RAY: What about oxygen?

LON: Isn't the atmosphere on CX5 just like Earth's?

RAY: I think you've been in space too long. Read your manual: Oxygen <u>must / must not</u> be used on other planets.
　　　　　　　　　　　　　　　　　　　　　　　　　　　　　　　3.

★　★　★　★　★　★　★　★　★

PICARRO: I've lost contact with Lon and Ray. I hope their equipment works on CX5.

SOCK: Don't worry. They'll <u>pick up / be picked up by</u> the radar.
　　　　　　　　　　　　　4.

★　★　★　★　★　★　★　★　★

LON: Look at those plants. I want to take some back to the ship.

RAY: They <u>can / can't</u> be grown in space. We've already tried.
　　　　　　　　5.

LON: That's right. I forgot.

★　★　★　★　★　★　★　★　★

CX5: What do you want to ask us, Earthlings?

RAY: Our vehicle was hit by a meteorite. We request permission to land on your planet.

CX5: Permission granted. Our engineers will be ready for you.

RAY: Thank you. As you know, we <u>have to help / have to be helped</u> with the repairs.
　　　　　　　　　　　　　　　　　　　　　6.

6 | CLOSE QUARTERS

Work in small groups. Imagine that in preparation for a space mission, your group is going to spend a week together in a one-room apartment. Make a list of rules. Use the passive with modals and similar expressions. Compare your list with that of another group.

Some Issues to Consider

Food	Cleanliness
Clothes	Privacy
Room temperature	Language
Noise	Entertainment
Neatness	Other: _____

Example: Dinner will be served at 6:00 P.M.
The dishes must be washed after each meal.

7 | WHAT SHOULD BE DONE?

Work in groups. Look at the picture of a student lounge. You are responsible for getting it in order, but you have limited time and money. Agree on five things that should be done.

Example: **A:** The window has to be replaced.
B: No. That'll cost too much. It can just be taped.
C: That'll look terrible. It should be replaced.
D: OK. What else should be done?

8 | MONEY FOR SPACE

Sending people to the International Space Station costs millions of dollars. Should money be spent for these space projects, or could it be spent better on Earth? If so, how should it be spent? Discuss these questions with your classmates.

Example: A: I think space projects are useful. A lot of new products are going to be developed in space.

B: I don't agree. Some of that money should be spent on public housing.

9 | WRITING

Write two paragraphs about your neighborhood, your school, or your place of work. In your first paragraph, write about what might be done to improve it. In your second paragraph, write about what shouldn't be changed. Use the passive with modals and similar expressions.

Example: I enjoy attending this school, but I believe some things could be improved. First, I think that more software ought to be purchased for the language lab . . .

10 | ON THE INTERNET

Ⓒ *Do a search on* **International Space Station**. *Answer some of the questions below. Compare your information in a small group.*

1. What parts of the station are going to be assembled next?

2. How will they be used?

3. How many tourists will be permitted to travel with the crew?

4. How much money will be spent?

5. What experiments are going to be carried out?

6. When will the next mission be completed?

7. Do any problems have to be solved before the next mission?

The Passive Causative

Grammar in Context

BEFORE YOU READ

🎧 *Look at the photos. Which forms of body art do you think are attractive? Read this article from a fashion magazine.*

Body Art

ach culture has a different ideal of beauty, and throughout the ages, men and women have done amazing things to achieve the ideal. They have **had** *their hair* **shaved, cut, colored, straightened**, and **curled**; and they have **had** *their bodies* **decorated** with painting and tattoos. Here are some of today's many options:

HAIR

Getting *your hair* **done** is the easiest way to change your appearance. Today, both men and women **have** *their hair* **permed**. This chemical procedure can curl hair or just give it more body. If your hair is long, you can, of course, **get** *it* **cut**. But did you know that you can also **have** *short hair* **lengthened** with hair extensions? Of course you can **have** *your hair* **colored** and become a blonde, brunette, or redhead. But you can also **have** *it* **bleached** white or **get** *it* **dyed** blue, green, or orange!

Body Art

TATTOOS

This form of body art was created thousands of years ago. Today, tattoos have again become popular. More and more people are **having** *them* **done**. However, caution is necessary. Although you can now **get** *a tattoo* **removed** with less pain and scarring than before, **having** *one* **applied** is still a big decision.

BODY PAINT

If a tattoo is not for you, you can **have** *ornaments* **painted** on your skin instead. Some people **have** *necklaces and bracelets* **painted** on their neck and arms or **get** *a butterfly mask* **applied** to their face for a special party. Unlike a tattoo, these decorations can be washed off.

PIERCING

Pierced ears are an old favorite, but lately the practice of piercing has expanded. Many people now **are getting** *their noses, lips, or other parts of the body* **pierced** for jewelry. Piercing requires even more caution than tattooing, and aftercare is very important.

COSMETIC SURGERY

You can **get** *your nose* **shortened**, or **have** *your chin* **lengthened**. You can even **have** *the shape of your body* **changed**. There is always some risk involved, so the decision to have cosmetic surgery requires thought.

Some ways of changing your appearance may be cheap and temporary. However, others are expensive and permanent. So, think before you act, and don't let today's choice become tomorrow's regret.

—*By Debra Santana*

AFTER YOU READ

Check the correct answers.

This article discusses changes people can make to their:

☑ **1.** hair length   ☑ **5.** teeth

☑ **2.** hair color   ☐ **6.** clothing

☑ **3.** eyes   ☑ **7.** nose

☑ **4.** skin   ☑ **8.** body shape

Grammar Presentation

THE PASSIVE CAUSATIVE

			Statements		
Subject	*Have / Get*	Object	Past Participle	*(By* + Agent)	
She	**has**	*her hair*	**cut**	*by André*	every month.
He	**has had**	*his beard*	**trimmed**		before.
I	**get**	*my nails*	**done**		at André's.
They	**are going to get**	*their ears*	**pierced**.		

				Yes / No Questions		
Auxiliary Verb	Subject	*Have / Get*	Object	Past Participle	*(By* + Agent)	
Does	she	**have**	*her hair*	**cut**	*by André?*	
Has	he	**had**	*his beard*	**trimmed**		before?
Do	you	**get**	*your nails*	**done**		at André's?
Are	they	**going to get**	*their ears*	**pierced?**		

				Wh- Questions			
Wh- Word	Auxiliary Verb	Subject	*Have / Get*	Object	Past Participle	*(By* + Agent)	
How often	**does**	she	**have**	*her hair*	**cut**	*by André?*	
Where	**did**	he	**get**	*his beard*	**trimmed**		before?
When	**do**	you	**get**	*your nails*	**done**		at André's?
Why	**are**	they	**going to get**	*their ears*	**pierced?**		

GRAMMAR NOTES	EXAMPLES
1. Form the **passive causative** with the appropriate form of *have* or *get* **+ object + past participle**. *Have* and *get* have the same meaning.	• I **get** *my hair* **cut** by André. OR • I **have** *my hair* **cut** by André.

The passive causative can be used with:
  a. all verb forms
  b. modals
  c. gerunds
  d. infinitives
	• **I'll have** *the car* **washed** tomorrow.
	• You **should get** *the oil* **changed**.
	• I love **having** *my hair* **done**.
	• I want **to get** *it* **colored**.

2. Use the passive causative to talk about **services** that you arrange for someone to do for you.	• I used to color my own hair, but now I **have** *it* **colored**. • André is going to **get** *his hair salon* **remodeled** by a local architect.
▶ **BE CAREFUL!** Do not confuse the passive causative with *had* with the past perfect.	**PASSIVE CAUSATIVE WITH *HAD*** • I **had** *it* **colored** last week. *(Someone did it for me.)* **PAST PERFECT** • I **had colored** it before. *(I did it myself.)*
3. Use *by* when it is necessary to mention the **agent** (the person doing the service). Do not use *by* when it is clear who is doing the service.	• This week Lynne **is getting her hair done** *by a new stylist*. NOT: Where does Lynne get her hair done ~~by a hair stylist~~?

Reference Note
For information on when to include the **agent**, see Unit 18, page 273.

Focused Practice

1 | DISCOVER THE GRAMMAR

*Read the conversations. Decide if the statement that follows each conversation is true (**T**) or false (**F**).*

1. JAKE: Have you finished writing your article on body art?

   DEBRA: Yes. I'm going to get it copied and then take it to the post office.

   ___F___ Debra is going to copy the article herself.

2. DEBRA: I'm glad that's done. Now I can start planning for our party.

   JAKE: Me too. I'm going to get my hair cut tomorrow after work.

   _____ Jake cuts his own hair.

3. DEBRA: Speaking about hair—Amber, *your* hair's getting awfully long.

   AMBER: I know, Mom. I'm cutting it tomorrow.

   _____ Amber cuts her own hair.

4. AMBER: Mom, why didn't you get your nails done last time you went to the hairdresser?

   DEBRA: Because I did them just before my appointment.

   _____ Debra did her own nails.

5. AMBER: I was thinking of painting a butterfly on my forehead for the party.

   DEBRA: A butterfly! Well, OK. As long as it washes off.

   _____ Someone is going to paint a butterfly on Amber's forehead for her.

6. DEBRA: Jake, do you think we should get the floors waxed before the party?

   JAKE: I think they look OK. We'll get them done afterward.

   _____ Debra and Jake are going to hire someone to wax their floors after the party.

7. DEBRA: I'm going to watch some TV and then go to bed. What's on the agenda for tomorrow?

   JAKE: I have to get up early. I'm getting the car washed before work.

   _____ Jake is going to wash the car himself.

8. DEBRA: You know, I think it's time to change the oil too.

   JAKE: You're right. I'll do it this weekend.

   _____ Jake is going to change the oil himself.

2 | ESSENTIAL SERVICES

It's February 15. Look at the Santanas' calendar and write sentences about when they **had things done,** *and when they are* **going to have things done.**

FEBRUARY

SUNDAY	MONDAY	TUESDAY	WEDNESDAY	THURSDAY	FRIDAY	SATURDAY
1	2	3	4	5	6	7 Deb– hairdresser
8	9	10	11	12 Jake– barber	13 carpets	14 dog groomer
15 TODAY'S DATE	16 windows	17	18	19	20 food and drinks	21 party!! family pictures
22	23	24	25 Amber– ears pierced	26	27	28

1. The Santanas / have / family pictures / take

   The Santanas are going to have family pictures taken on the 21st.

2. Debra / get / her hair / perm

   Debra got her hair permed on 7th.

3. Amber / have / the dog / groom

   Amber had her dog groomed on 14th.

4. They / get / the windows / wash

   they are going to get the windows washed on 16th

5. They / have / the carpets / clean

   they had the carpets cleaned on the 13th.

6. Amber / have / her ears / pierce

   Amber is going to have her ears pierced on 25th

7. Jake / get / his hair / cut

   Jake got his hair cut on 12th.

8. They / have / food and drinks / deliver

   they are going to have food and drinks delivered on 20th

3 | GETTING THINGS DONE

Grammar Notes 1–3

Debra and Jake are going to have a party. Complete the conversations with the passive causative of the appropriate verbs in the box.

color	cut	develop	dry clean
paint	repair	~~shorten~~	wash

1. **AMBER:** I bought a new dress for the party, Mom. What do you think?

   DEBRA: It's pretty, but it's a little long. Why don't you _____ *get it shortened* _____?

   AMBER: OK. They do alterations at the cleaners. I'll take it in tomorrow.

2. **AMBER:** By the way, what are *you* planning to wear?

   DEBRA: My blue silk dress. I'm glad you reminded me. I'd better _*get it dry cleaned*_

   AMBER: I can drop it off at the cleaners with my dress.

3. **JAKE:** The house is ready, except for the windows. They look pretty dirty.

   DEBRA: Don't worry. We _*are going to have/get them washed*_ tomorrow.

4. **DEBRA:** Amber, your hair is getting really long. I thought you were going to cut it.

   AMBER: I decided not to do it myself this time. I _*am going to get it cut*_ by André.

5. **DEBRA:** My hair's getting a lot of gray in it. Should I _*get my hair colored*_?

   JAKE: It looks fine to me, but it's up to you.

6. **AMBER:** Mom, someone's at the door and it's only twelve o'clock!

   DEBRA: No, it's not. The clock stopped again.

   JAKE: Oh no, not again. I don't believe it! I _____ *have it* _____ already

   _____ *repaired* _____ twice this year, and it's only February!

7. **GUEST:** The house looks beautiful, Jake. I love the color. _*Did*_

   you _*have it painted*_?

   JAKE: No, actually we did it ourselves last summer.

8. **DEBRA:** I have one shot left in the camera. Come on, everyone! Say "cheese"!

   GUESTS: Cheese!

   DEBRA: Great. We took three rolls of pictures today. Maybe we can _*have it developed*_

   before Mom and Dad go back to Florida.

4 | EDITING

Read Amber's diary entry. There are seven mistakes in the use of the passive causative. The first mistake is already corrected. Find and correct six more.

> February 21: The party was tonight. It went really well! The house looked great.
>
>   *cleaned*
>
> Mom and Dad had the floors waxed and all the windows ~~clean~~ professionally so
>
>   *Printed*
>
> everything sparkled. And of course we had the whole house painted ourselves last
>
> summer. (I'll never forget *that*. It took us two weeks!) I wore my new black dress
>
>   *had*   *my hair cut*
>
> that I ~~have~~ shortened by Bo, and I ~~got cut my~~ hair by André. He did a great job.
>
>   *invited*
>
> There were a lot of guests at the party. We had ~~almost~~ 50 people invited, and they
>
> almost all showed up! The food was great too. Mom made most of the main dishes
>
>   *to have*   *d*
>
> herself, but she had the rest of the food ~~prepare~~ by a caterer. Mom and Dad hired
>
>   *had*   *taken*
>
> a professional photographer, so at the end of the party we ~~took~~ our pictures. I can't
>
> wait to see them!

Communication Practice

5 | LISTENING

🎧 *Amber has just gone to college. Listen to her conversation with Jake. Then listen again and check the correct column.*

	Amber did the job herself	Amber hired someone to do the job
1. Change the oil in her car	☐	☑
2. Change the locks	☐	☐
3. Paint the apartment	☐	☐
4. Put up bookshelves	☐	☐
5. Bring new furniture to the apartment	☐	☐
6. Paint her hands	☐	☐
7. Cut her hair	☐	☐
8. Color her hair	☐	☐

6 | MAKING PLANS

Work in groups. Imagine that you are taking a car trip together to another country. You'll be gone for several weeks. Decide where you're going. Then make a list of things you have to do and arrange before the trip. Use the ideas below and ideas of your own.

Passport and visa

Car (oil, gas, tires, brake fluid)

Home (pets, plants, mail, newspaper delivery)

Personal (clothing, hair)

Medical (teeth, eyes, prescriptions)

Other: _____

Example: A: I have to get my passport renewed.
   B: Me too. And we should apply for visas right away.

Now compare your list with that of another group. Did you forget anything?

7 | TOTAL MAKEOVER

Work in pairs. Look at the Before *and* After *pictures of a fashion model. You have five minutes to find and write down all the things she had done to change her appearance.*

Before

After

Example: She had her nose shortened.

When the five minutes are up, compare your list with that of another pair. Then look at the pictures again to check your answers.

8 | WHAT DO YOU THINK?

Work in pairs. Look at the Before *and* After *pictures in Exercise 7. Do you think the woman looks better? Why or why not?*

Example: A: I don't know why she had her nose fixed.
B: Neither do I. I think it looked fine before.

9 | BEAUTY TALK

Work in small groups. Think about other cultures. Discuss the types of things people get done in order to change their appearance. Report back to your class.

Example: In India, women get their hands painted for special occasions. I think it looks nice.

10 | WRITING

Write a short letter to someone you know. Describe your activities. Include things that you have recently done or have had done. Also talk about things you are going to do or are going to have done. Use the passive causative.

Example: Dear Sara,
I've just moved into a new apartment. I've already had it painted, but there are still so many things that I have to get done! . . .

11 | ON THE INTERNET

Do a search on a TV show or magazine that features makeovers. Use the phrase
"**Before and After + Beauty Makeover.**" *Print out some* Before *and* After *photos and discuss them with your classmates. What did the people have done? How do you feel about the results?*

Example: A: Mike had his hair colored.
B: I think he looks great as a blond. What about you?

I have to get my hair cut

I have to get my mail checked

you have to have your teeth brushed every night.

From **Grammar** to **Writing**
Changing the Focus with the Passive

In a report, you often focus on the results of an action rather than the people who performed the action. Use the passive to focus on the results.

> **Example:** Artists **carved** many wooden statues for the temple. *(active)*
> Many wooden statues **were carved** for the temple. *(passive)*

1 | *Read this report about a famous building in Korea. Underline the passive forms.*

Two Buddhist monks built Haeinsa Temple in 802 A.D. The king gave them the money to build the temple after the two monks saved his queen's life. Haeinsa burned down in 1817, but the Main Hall was rebuilt in 1818 on its original foundations. Today, Haeinsa is composed of several large, beautiful buildings. It contains many paintings and statues. Someone carved three of the statues from a single ancient tree. Behind the Main Hall is a steep flight of stone stairs that leads to the Storage Buildings. These buildings, which escaped the fire, were constructed in 1488 in order to store wooden printing blocks of Buddhist texts. It was believed that these printing blocks could protect the country against invaders. Monks carved the 81,258 wooden blocks in the 13th century. A century later, nuns carried them to Haeinsa for safekeeping. Architects designed the Storage Buildings to preserve the wooden blocks. For more than five hundred years, the blocks have been kept in perfect condition because of the design of these buildings. Haeinsa, which means *reflection on a smooth sea*, is also known as the Temple of Teaching because it houses the ancient printing blocks.

2 | *Find five sentences in Exercise 1 that would be better expressed in the passive. Rewrite them.*

1. _Haeinsa Temple was built by two Buddhist monks in A.D. 802._ _____

2. _____

3. _____

4. _____

5. _____

3 | *Answer these questions about Haeinsa Temple.*

1. When was it built?

_____

2. Who built it?

_____

3. Why was it built?

_____

4. What are some of its features?

_____

5. What is it famous for?

_____

4 | *Before you write . . .*

1. Choose a famous building to write about. Do some research in the library or on the Internet. Answer the questions in Exercise 3.

2. Work with a partner. Ask and answer questions about your topic.

5 | *Write a research report about the building you researched. Use the passive where appropriate. If possible, include a photograph or drawing of the building.*

6 | *Exchange paragraphs with a different partner. Answer the following questions.*

1. Did the writer answer all the questions in Exercise 3? _____

2. What interested you the most about the building? _____

3. What would you like to know more about? _____

4. Did the writer use the passive appropriately? _____

5. Are the past participles correct? _____

VIII

Review Test

I *Complete these conversations by circling the active or passive form of the verbs.*

LINDSAY: This is Lindsay Boyle from AL Metals. I (didn't receive) / wasn't received my airline tickets

1.

today, and I leave / 'm left for Jamaica in two days.

2.

AGENT: Let me check. Hmmm. That's strange. The tickets mailed / were mailed a week ago.

3.

You should be had / have them by now.

4.

LINDSAY: How about my hotel reservations?

AGENT: Those made / were made for you last week. They confirmed / were confirmed by the

5.   6.

Hotel Mariel today. Will you need / be needed a car when you arrive?

7.

LINDSAY: Not right away. I'll be met / meet at the airport by my client. I'll probably rent / be rented

8.   9.

a car later on. Oh, the receptionist was just handed / just handed me a note. The tickets

10.

are here. They were sent / sent to the wrong floor.

11.

AGENT: Sorry about that.

LINDSAY: Never mind. We have them now, so no harm did / was done.

12.

II *Complete these conversations with the modal and the passive form of the verbs in
parentheses.*

LINDSAY: _____Will_____ the reports _____be printed_____ by the end of next week?

1. (Will / print)

TED: Sure. In fact they _might to be delivered_ to the office by Tuesday.

2. (might / deliver)

LINDSAY: Good. I hope they turn out well. They _will be read_ by a lot of people.

3. (will / read)

TED: Don't worry. This company always does nice work. I'm sure you _will be satisfied_

4. (will / satisfy)

when you see them. _will have to be packed_

or

LINDSAY: Oh, by the way, those reports _have to be packed_ for shipment as soon as they

5. (have to / pack)

arrive. I'm taking them with me to Jamaica.

TED: I didn't know you planned to bring them. I _ought to be told_ things like
6.(ought to / tell)

that. So how long are you staying?

LINDSAY: About a week. But my stay _could be extended_. It depends on how things go.
7.(could / extend)

TED: You know, your office _should be painted_ while you're gone. And your
8.(should / paint)

computer _has to be serviced_. So maybe you should stay another week.
9.(have to / service)

LINDSAY: I think that _can be arranged_. I hear it's a pretty nice place.
10.(can / arrange)

III *Circle the letter of the correct word(s) to complete each sentence.*

1. Reggae music is _____ at Jamaica's Sunsplash Festival.   A   B (C) D
   - (**A**) perform
   - (**B**) performing
   - (**C**) performed
   - (**D**) performs

2. This wonderful festival _____ be missed.   A   B   C   D
   - (**A**) isn't
   - (**B**) wasn't
   - ✓(**C**) shouldn't
   - (**D**) hasn't

3. Music lovers from all over the world can _____ found at the festival.   A   B   C   D
   - ✓(**A**) be
   - (**B**) have
   - (**C**) been
   - (**D**) were

4. Swimmers and divers _____ Jamaica's beautiful beaches.   A   B   C   D
   - (**A**) are enjoyed
   - ✓(**B**) enjoy
   - (**C**) enjoys
   - (**D**) are enjoyed by

5. Go deep-sea fishing, and get your picture _____ with your catch.   A   B   C   D
   - ✓(**A**) taken
   - (**B**) taking
   - (**C**) took
   - (**D**) be taken

6. Jamaica _____ avoided in the fall because of dangerous storms.   A   B   C   D
   - (**A**) ought to
   - (**B**) should
   - (**C**) should have
   - ✓(**D**) ought to be

7. Jamaica was settled _____ people from Africa and Europe.   A   B   C   D
   - (**A**) at
   - ✓(**B**) by
   - (**C**) from
   - (**D**) of

(continued)

8. In the early days, many languages could _____ in Jamaica.   A B C D
   √ (**A**) be heard   (**C**) heard
   (**B**) were heard   (**D**) hear

9. Today Creole, a mixture of languages, _____ spoken widely.   A B C D
   (**A**) was   √ (**C**) is
   (**B**) were   (**D**) are

10. Tickets _____ from any travel agent or directly from the airline.   A B C D
    √ (**A**) may be purchased   (**C**) purchase
    (**B**) may purchase   (**D**) purchased

11. The last time, I _____ my ticket sent directly to my office.   A B C D
    (**A**) have   (**C**) was
    (**B**) get   √ (**D**) had

IV   *Complete this memo with the correct forms of* **have** *or* **get** *and the verbs in parentheses.*

DATE: February 17

TO: Trish

FROM: Lindsay

I'd like to _____*have*_____ some work _____*done*_____ in my office, and this seems like
                                            1. (do)

a good time for it. Please _____*have*_____ my carpet _____*cleaned*_____ while I'm gone. And
                                                        2. (clean)

while you're at it, could you _____*have*_____ my computer and printer _____*looked at*_____? It's
                                                                        3. (look at)

been quite a while since they've been serviced. Ted wants to _____*have*_____ my office

_____*painted*_____ while I'm gone. Please tell him any color is fine except pink.
4. (paint)

Last week, I _____*had*_____ some new brochures _____*designed*_____. Please call the
                                                    5. (design)

printer and _____*have*_____ them _____*delivered*_____ directly to the sales reps. And could you
                                    6. (deliver)

_____*have*_____ more business cards _____*made up*_____ too? We're almost out.
                                        7. (make up)

When I get back, it will be time to plan the holiday party. I think that we should

_____*have*_____ it _____*catered*_____ this year. While I'm gone, why don't you call around and
                    8. (cater)

get some estimates from caterers? _____*have*_____ the estimates _____*sent*_____ to Ted. See
                                                                    9. (send)

you in two weeks!

V *Complete these facts about Jamaica with the passive form of the verbs in the box. Include the agent in parentheses only where necessary.*

~~discover~~	employ	export	grow	listen to	popularize	strike

1. Jamaica _____ *was discovered by Europeans* _____ on May 4, 1494, during
   (Europeans)

   Columbus's second voyage.

2. Some of the best coffee in the world _____ *is grown* _____
   (coffee growers)

   on the slopes of Jamaica's Blue Mountains.

3. About 50,000 people _____ *are employed by the sugar industry.*
   (the sugar industry)

4. Sugar _____ *is exported* _____ to many countries.
   (sugar exporters)

5. The island _____ *is struck by haricans* _____ about once every
   (hurricanes)

   eight years, and some have caused severe damage.

6. Reggae music originated in Jamaica. It _____ *was popularized by Bob Marley*
   (Bob Marley)

   in the 1970s.

7. Now it _____ *is listend to by People* _____ everywhere.
   (people)

VI *Each sentence has four underlined words or phrases. The four underlined parts of the sentences are marked A, B, C, or D. Circle the letter of the one underlined part that is NOT CORRECT.*

1. The reports <u>were</u> <u>arrived</u> late, so I <u>had</u> <u>them sent</u> to you this morning.   **(A)** **B** **C** **D**
   A   B   C   D

2. Some mistakes <u>were</u> <u>made</u> in the brochure, but they might <u>corrected</u> *be*   **A** **B** **(C)** **D**
                  A   B   C

   before you <u>get</u> back.
             D

3. You<u>'ll see</u> a copy before they<u>'re</u> <u>printed</u> <u>by the printer.</u>   **A** **B** **C** **(D)**
        A   B   C   D

(continued)

4. A funny thing <u>was</u> happened when your <u>office</u> <u>was</u> <u>redecorated</u> yesterday.
          A   B   C   D

A B C D

5. Your office <u>was</u> almost <u>painted</u> pink, but we <u>had</u> the painters <u>used</u>
            A   B   C   D

white instead.

A B C **D**

6. An estimate from the party caterer <u>were</u> <u>left</u> on my desk, but we've
                                        was
                                        A   B

<u>got</u> <u>to wait</u> for your decision.
 C   D

A B C D

7. <u>Has</u> your stay <u>been</u> <u>extended</u>, or will you <u>be returned</u> next week?
  A   B   C   D

A B C **D**

▶ *To check your answers, go to the Answer Key on page RT-5.*

Conditionals

21 Present Real Conditionals

Grammar in Context

BEFORE YOU READ

🎧 *What is a cyber mall? Have you ever purchased something online? What are some steps people should take to shop safely online? Read this article about cyber malls.*

Pick and Click Shopping@Home
By E. Buyer

Where is the largest mall in the world? **If you think it's in Alberta, Canada, you're wrong!** It's in cyberspace! And you can get there from home on your very own computer.

Cyber shopping is fast, convenient, and often less expensive. **It doesn't matter if it's a book or a diamond necklace**—with just a click of your mouse, you can buy anything without getting up from your chair. **If you're looking for the best price, you can easily compare prices and read other buyers' reviews of products.** Shopping online can save you time and money—but you need to surf and shop safely. Here are some tips to make your trip to the cyber mall a good one:

🔒 **You are less likely to have a problem if you shop with well-known companies.**

🔒 **If you don't know the company, ask them to send you information.** What is their address? Their phone number?

🔒 **Always pay by credit card if you can. If you are unhappy with the product (or if you don't receive it), then you can dispute the charge.**

🔒 Only enter your credit card information on a secure site. **If you see a closed lock (🔒) or complete key (🔑) symbol at the bottom of your screen, the site is secure.** Also, the web address will change from http://www to https://www. This means that your credit card number will be encrypted (changed so that others can't read it). **If the site isn't secure, don't enter your credit card information.**

Pick and Click Shopping@Home

🔒 **If you have kids, don't let them give out personal information.**

🔒 **If you have any doubts about a site's security, contact the store by phone or e-mail.**

🔒 Find out the return policy. **What happens if you don't like the product?**

🔒 Print out and save a record of your purchase. **If there is a problem, the receipt gives you proof of purchase.**

🔒 **If you change your mind about an order, contact the company immediately.**

As you can see, many of these steps are similar to the ones you follow in a "store with doors." Use common sense. **If you take some basic precautions, you shouldn't have any problems.**

Internet shopping has literally brought a world of opportunity to consumers. Today we can shop 24 hours a day, 7 days a week in stores that are halfway around the globe without ever having to leave home or stand in line. As with many things in life, there are some risks. Just remember that online or off—**if an offer seems too good to be true, it probably is**. Happy cyber shopping!

"Now think long and hard Samantha. What else exactly did you purchase online with Daddy's credit card details."

AFTER YOU READ

Write **T** *(true) or* **F** *(false).*

__F__ **1.** The largest mall in the world is in Canada.

__T__ **2.** You can buy a diamond necklace online.

__T__ **3.** It's best to use a credit card when shopping online.

__F__ **4.** The author of the article thinks cyber shopping is very dangerous.

__T__ **5.** You can't trust all online offers.

in cyberspace –

dispute = اختلاف / مشاجره / جدال / دعوا / بگو مگو

Grammar Presentation

PRESENT REAL CONDITIONALS

Statements	
If Clause	Result Clause
If I **shop** online,	I **save** time.
If the mall **is** closed,	I **can shop** online.

Statements	
Result Clause	*If* Clause
I **save** time	**if** I **shop** online.
I **can shop** online	**if** the mall **is** closed.

Yes / No Questions	
Result Clause	*If* Clause
Do you **save** time	**if** you **shop** online?
Can you **shop** online	**if** the mall **is** closed?

Short Answers			
Affirmative		Negative	
Yes,	I **do**.	No,	I **don't**.
	I **can**.		I **can't**.

Wh- Questions	
Result Clause	*If* Clause
What **happens**	**if** I **don't like** it?

GRAMMAR NOTES

EXAMPLES

1. Use **present real conditional** sentences for **general truths**. The *if* clause talks about the condition, and the result clause talks about what happens if the condition occurs. Use the simple present in both clauses. USAGE NOTE: We often use *even if* when the result is <u>surprising</u>.	*if* clause result clause • **If** it**'s** a holiday, the store **is** closed. *if* clause result clause • **If** you **use** a credit card, it**'s** faster. • *Even if* it's a holiday, this store stays open.
2. You can also use **real conditional** sentences for **habits** and things that happen again and again. Use the simple present or present progressive in the *if* clause. Use the simple present in the result clause. You can often use *when* instead of *if*. This is especially true when you talk about general truths, habits, and things that happen again and again.	• **If** Bill **shops** online, he **uses** a credit card. • **If** I**'m surfing** the Web, I **use** Google. • *When* Bill **shops** online, he **uses** a credit card. • *When* I'm **surfing** the Web, I **use** Google.

3. You can use **modals** (*can, should, might, must* . . .) in the result clause.	• If you don't like the product, you *can* **return** it. • If you have children, you ***shouldn't* let** them **shop** online.

4. Use the **imperative** in the result clause to give **instructions**, **commands**, and **invitations** that depend on a certain condition. USAGE NOTE: We sometimes use ***then*** to emphasize the result in real conditional sentences with imperatives or modals.	• If you change your mind, **call** the company. • If a site isn't secure, **don't enter** your credit card information. • If you change your mind, ***then* call** the company. • If a site isn't secure, ***then* don't enter** your credit card information.

5. You can begin conditional sentences with the *if* clause or the result clause. The meaning is the same. ▶ **BE CAREFUL!** Use a comma between the two clauses only when the *if* clause comes first.	• **If I shop online,** I save time. OR • I save time **if I shop online**.

Focused Practice

1 | DISCOVER THE GRAMMAR

Read these shopping tips. In each real conditional sentence, underline the result clause once. Underline the clause that expresses the condition twice.

KNOW BEFORE YOU GO

You're shopping in a foreign city. Should you pay full price, or should you bargain? If you don't know the answer, you can pay too much or miss a fun experience. Bargaining is one of the greatest shopping pleasures if you know how to do it. The strategies are different in different places. Check out these tips before you go.

Hong Kong

Hong Kong is one of the world's greatest shopping cities. If you like to bargain, you can do it anywhere except the larger department stores. The trick is not to look too interested. If you see something you want, pick it up along with some other items and ask the prices. Then make an offer below what you are willing to pay. If the seller's offer is close to the price you want, then you should be able to reach an agreement quickly.

(continued)

Italy

Bargaining in Italy is appropriate at outdoor markets and with street vendors. In stores, you can politely ask for a discount if you want to bargain. Take your time. Make conversation if you speak Italian. Show your admiration for the object by picking it up and pointing out its wonderful features. When you hear the price, look sad. Make your own offer. End the bargaining politely if you can't agree.

Mexico

In Mexico, people truly enjoy bargaining. There are some clear rules, though. You should bargain only if you really are interested in buying the object. If the vendor's price is far more than you want to pay, then politely stop the negotiation. If you know your price is reasonable, walking away will often bring a lower offer.

Remember, bargaining is always a social interaction, not an argument. And it can still be fun even if you don't get the item you want at the price you want to pay.

---

2 | IF YOU'RE SHOPPING IN . . .   *Grammar Notes 1–4*

Read this online forum about shopping around the world. Write conditional sentences to summarize the advice.

1. Hong Kong

Q: I want to buy some traditional crafts. Any ideas?

A: You ought to visit the Western District on Hong Kong Island. It's famous for its crafts.

If you want to buy some traditional crafts, you ought to visit the Western District on Hong Kong Island.

2. Barcelona

Q: I'd like to buy some nice but inexpensive clothes. Where can I go?

A: Take the train to open air markets in towns *outside* of the city. They have great stuff.

If you would like to buy some nice but inexpensive clothes, take the train

3. Rome

Q: I'm looking for a shopping mall. Are there any in Rome?

A: You need to go away from the city center. But I think the small shops are nicer.

If you are looking for a shopping mall, you need to go away from the city center.

4. Istanbul

Q: I want to go shopping in the Grand Bazaar. Is it open on Sunday?

A: You have to go during the week. It's closed on Sunday.

If you want to go shopping in the Grand Bazar, you have to go during the week.

5. New York

  Q: I want to buy some unusual gifts. Any suggestions?

  A: Shop in Soho. The neighborhood has lots of very interesting stores.

  If you want to buy some unusual gifts, you shop in soho.

6. Bangkok

  Q: My son wants to buy computer games. Where should he go?

  A: He should try the Panthip Plaza. The selection is huge.

  If your son wants to buy computer games, he should try the Panthip Plaza.

7. Mexico City

  Q: I plan to buy some silver jewelry in Mexico. Any tips?

  A: You should be able to get something nice at a very good price. Try bargaining.

  If you plan to buy some silver jewelry in mexico, you should be able to get something nice at a very good price.

8. London

  Q: I'd like to find some nice secondhand clothing shops. Can you help me?

  A: Try the Portobello market on the weekend. Happy shopping!

  If you would like to find some nice secondhand clothing shops, try the

---

3 | FREQUENT BUYER

Grammar Notes 1–2, 5

Complete the interview with Claudia Leggett, a fashion buyer. Combine the two sentences in parentheses to make a real conditional sentence. Keep the same order and decide which clause begins with **if***. Make necessary changes in capitalization and punctuation.*

INTERVIEWER: Is understanding fashion the most important thing for a career as a buyer?

  LEGGETT: It is. *If you don't understand fashion, you don't belong in this field.*

  1. (You don't understand fashion. You don't belong in this field.)

  But buyers need other skills too.

INTERVIEWER: Such as?

  LEGGETT: *You can make better decisions If you have good business skills.*

  2. (You can make better decisions. You have good business skills.)

INTERVIEWER: "People skills" must be important too.

  LEGGETT: True. *A buyer needs great interpersonal skills if she's negotiating—*

  3. (A buyer needs great interpersonal skills. She's negotiating prices.)

(continued)

INTERVIEWER: Do you travel in your business?

LEGGETT: A lot! *There's a big international fashion fair! I'm usually there.*

4. (There's a big international fashion fair. I'm usually there.)

INTERVIEWER: Why fashion fairs?

LEGGETT: Thousands of professionals attend. *If I go to a fair, I can see hundreds of products in few days.*

5. (I go to a fair. I can see hundreds of products in a few days.)

INTERVIEWER: You just got back from the Leipzig fair, didn't you?

LEGGETT: Yes, and I went to Paris and Madrid too. *I usually stay two weeks If I travel to Europe.*

6. (I usually stay two weeks. I travel to Europe.)

INTERVIEWER: Does your family ever go with you?

LEGGETT: Often. *If my husband can come, he and our son, pietro, pietro comes to the fair with me If my...*

7. (My husband can come. He and our son, Pietro, do things together.)

8. (Pietro comes to the fair with me. My husband can't get away.)

Next week, we're all going to Hong Kong.

INTERVIEWER: What do you do when you're not at a fashion fair?

LEGGETT: *I always go shopping If I have free time.*

9. (I always go shopping. I have free time.)

---

4 | WHEN IT'S NOON IN MONTREAL . . .

Grammar Note 2

Look at the chart. Write sentences about the cities with clocks. Use the words in parentheses and **when**.
Note: The light clocks show daylight hours; the shaded clocks show evening or nighttime hours.

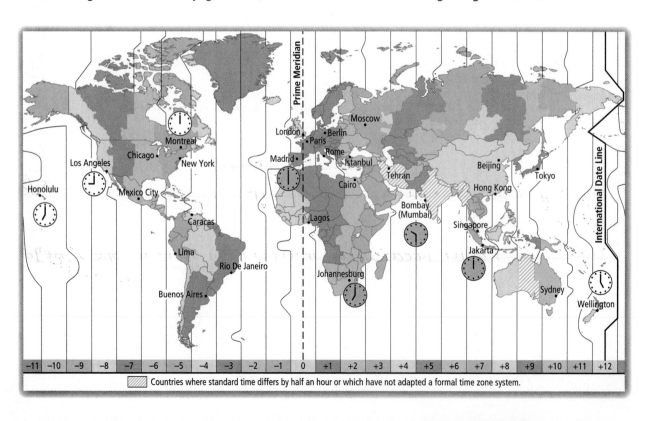

| −11 | −10 | −9 | −8 | −7 | −6 | −5 | −4 | −3 | −2 | −1 | 0 | +1 | +2 | +3 | +4 | +5 | +6 | +7 | +8 | +9 | +10 | +11 | +12 |

▨ Countries where standard time differs by half an hour or which have not adapted a formal time zone system.

1. <u>When it's noon in Montreal, it's midnight in Jakarta.</u>
   (be noon / be midnight)

2. <u>When stores are opening in Los Angeles, they're closing in Johannesburg.</u>
   (stores open / stores close)

3. when people are watching the sunrise in wellington, people are watch the sunset in madrid.
   (people watch the sun rise / people watch the sun set)

4. when it is midnight in jakarta, It is 6:00PM in madrid.
   (be midnight / be 6:00 P.M.)

5. when people are eating lunch in Montreal, people are eating dinner in johannesburg
   (people eat lunch / people eat dinner)

6. When people are getting up in Honolulu, people are going to bed in Bombai.
   (people get up / people go to bed)

7. when it is 7:AM in Honolulu, It is 7:00P.m in johannesburg.
   (be 7:00 A.M. / be 7:00 P.M.)

8. when it is 5:00AM in wellington, it is 9:00pm in losAngeless.
   (be 5:00 A.M. / be 9:00 A.M.)

5 | EDITING

Read Claudia's e-mail message. There are eight mistakes in the use of present real conditionals. The first mistake is already corrected. Find and correct seven more. Don't forget to check punctuation.

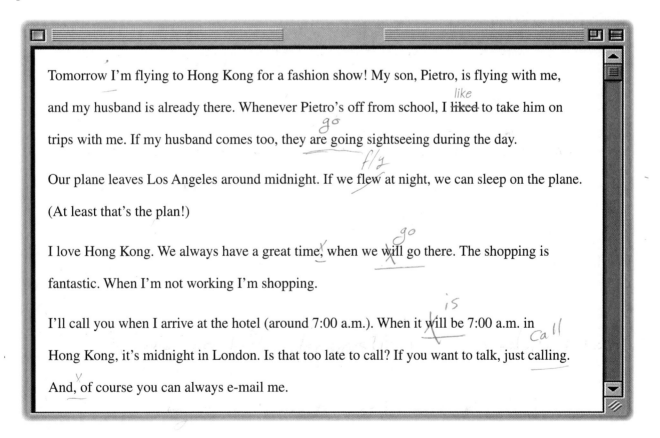

Tomorrow I'm flying to Hong Kong for a fashion show! My son, Pietro, is flying with me,

and my husband is already there. Whenever Pietro's off from school, I liked ~~like~~ to take him on

trips with me. If my husband comes too, they are going ~~go~~ sightseeing during the day.

Our plane leaves Los Angeles around midnight. If we flew ~~fly~~ at night, we can sleep on the plane.

(At least that's the plan!)

I love Hong Kong. We always have a great time, when we will go ~~go~~ there. The shopping is

fantastic. When I'm not working I'm shopping.

I'll call you when I arrive at the hotel (around 7:00 a.m.). When it will be ~~is~~ 7:00 a.m. in

Hong Kong, it's midnight in London. Is that too late to call? If you want to talk, just calling ~~call~~.

And, of course you can always e-mail me.

Communication Practice

6 | LISTENING

🎧 *Claudia and her ten-year-old son, Pietro, are flying from Los Angeles to Hong Kong by way of Taipei. First, read the situations below. Then listen to the announcements. Listen again and check the correct box.*

	True	False
1. Claudia has two pieces of carry-on luggage and Pietro has one. They can take them on the plane.	☑	☐

2. These are their boarding passes:

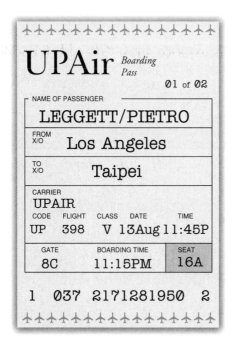

	True	False
They can board now.	☐	☑
3. Look at their boarding passes again. They can board now.	☑	☐
4. Pietro is a child. Claudia should put his oxygen mask on first.	☐	☑
5. Claudia is sitting in a left-hand window seat. She can see the lights of Tokyo.	☑	☐
6. Claudia needs information about their connecting flight. She can get this information on the plane.	☐	☑

7 | TRAVELING IN COMFORT

Work in small groups. Discuss what you do to stay comfortable when you travel. Talk about traveling by car, bus, train, and plane.

Example: A: When I travel by car, I stop every three hours.
B: I always dress comfortably when I travel by car.

8 | INFORMATION GAP: IF YOU GO . . .

Work in pairs (A and B). Student B, go to page 325 and follow the instructions there. Student A, ask Student B questions to complete the chart below. Answer Student B's questions.

	Best Time to Go	Currency	Time: When it's noon in New York . . .
Caracas, Venezuela	December–April	bolívar	
Istanbul, Turkey			8:00 P.M.
Rio de Janeiro, Brazil	April–October		2:00 P.M.
Seoul, South Korea		won	2:00 A.M.*
Vancouver, Canada	July–September		9:00 A.M.
Moscow, Russia		ruble	

*the next day

Example: A: If you travel to Caracas, what's the best time to go?
B: December through April.
What kind of currency do you need if you go there?
A: The bolívar.
When it's noon in New York, what time is it in Caracas?

When you are finished, compare charts. Are they the same?

9 | SHOPPING TIPS

Work in small groups. Discuss what you do when you want to make an important purchase (a gift, a camera, a car).

> **Example:** **A:** If I want to buy a camera, I check prices online.
> **B:** When I buy a camera, I always ask friends for recommendations.

10 | PROS AND CONS

Work in a small group. Look at the cartoon. What are some of the differences between shopping in a "store with doors" and shopping online? What are the advantages and disadvantages of each?

> **Example:** **A:** If you shop for clothes in a store, you can try them on first.
> **B:** But you have a lot more choices if you shop online.

11 | WRITING

Work in pairs. Imagine that you are preparing an information sheet for tourists about your city or town. Write a list of tips for visitors. Use present real conditional sentences. Compare your list with another pair's.

> **Example:** If you like to shop, Caterville has the biggest mall in this part of the country.
> If you enjoy swimming or boating, you should visit Ocean Park.

12 | ON THE INTERNET

Work in pairs. Decide on something you'd both like to buy (a pair of jeans, a camera, a car). Then check prices for the item at different online stores. Compare your information with your partner's.

> **Example:** **A:** If you buy the camera from Digital World, it costs $280. It's cheaper if you buy it from Gizmos.
> **B:** But you have to pay shipping if you buy it from Gizmos.

INFORMATION GAP FOR STUDENT B

Student B, answer Student A's questions. Then ask Student A questions to complete the chart below.

	Best Time to Go	Currency	Time: When it's noon in New York . . .
Caracas, Venezuela	December–April	*bolívar*	1:00 P.M.
Istanbul, Turkey	April–October	Turkish lira	
Rio de Janeiro, Brazil		real	
Seoul, South Korea	October–March		
Vancouver, Canada		Canadian dollar	
Moscow, Russia	May–September		8:00 P.M.

Example: **A:** If you travel to Caracas, what's the best time to go?
  B: December through April.
   What kind of currency do you need if you go there?
  A: The bolívar.
   When it's noon in New York, what time is it in Caracas?

When you are finished, compare charts. Are they the same?

Grammar in Context

BEFORE YOU READ

🎧 *Look at the pictures. What is a superstition? Can you give an example of one? Do you believe in any superstitions? Do you wear or carry things that make you feel lucky? Read this magazine article about superstitions.*

KNOCK ON WOOD!

If you knock on wood, you'll keep bad luck away.

You'll get a good grade on the test if you wear your shirt inside out.

You'll get a bad grade unless you use your lucky pen.

Superstitions sound silly, but millions of people all over the world believe in their power to bring good luck or prevent bad luck. Many cultures share similar superstitions:

🍀 If you break a mirror, you'll have seven years of bad luck.

🍀 If the palm of your hand itches, you're going to get some money.

🍀 If it rains when you move to a new house, you'll get rich.

All superstitions are based on a cause and effect relationship: **If X happens, then Y will also happen**. However, in superstitions, the cause is magical and unrelated to the effect. In our scientific age, why are these beliefs so powerful and widespread? The Luck Project, an online survey of superstitious behaviors, gives us some fascinating insight. Here are some of the findings:

13

Emotions can influence superstitions, especially in uncertain situations where people do not have control. **People will react more superstitiously if they are worried. They will feel less superstitious if they aren't feeling a strong need for control**.

We make our own luck. **If you believe you're lucky, you will carry out superstitions that make you feel good** (crossing your fingers for luck, for example). You probably won't fear bad luck superstitions. In contrast, **you will expect the worst if you think you're unlucky**.

More people than you might think believe in superstitions. Of the 4,000 people surveyed, 84 percent knocked on wood for good luck. Almost half feared walking under a ladder. And 15 percent of the people who studied or worked in the sciences feared the number 13.

Clearly, education doesn't "cure" superstition—college students are among the most superstitious people. Other superstitious groups are performers, athletes, gamblers, and stock traders. People in these groups often have personal good luck rituals.

Deanna McBrearty, a New York City Ballet member, has lucky hair bands. **"If I have a good performance when I'm wearing one, I'll keep wearing it,"** she says. Brett Gallagher, a stock trader, believes **he'll be more successful if he owns pet fish**. "I had fish for a while, and after they died the market didn't do so well," he points out.

Will you do better on the test if you use your lucky pen? Maybe. **If the pen makes you feel more confident, you might improve your score**. So go ahead and use it. But don't forget—**your lucky pen will be powerless unless you study**. The harder you work, the luckier you'll get.

AFTER YOU READ

Match the two parts of each sentence. Use information from the article.

__b__ 1. If you are worrying about something,   a. you'll have more good luck superstitions.

__a__ 2. If you feel you're lucky,   b. you might act more superstitious.

__d__ 3. If you study science,   c. your good luck pen won't work.

__c__ 4. If you don't study,   d. you could still be superstitious.

to be afraid (v)

frighten (ad)

fear (N)

Grammar Presentation

FUTURE REAL CONDITIONALS

Statements	
If Clause: Present	Result Clause: Future
If she **studies**,	she **won't fail** the test. she**'s going to pass** the test.
If she **doesn't study**,	she**'ll fail** the test. she **isn't going to pass** the test.

Yes / No Questions	
Result Clause: Future	*If* Clause: Present
Will she **pass** the test **Is** she **going to pass** the test	**if** she **studies**?

Short Answers			
Affirmative		Negative	
Yes,	she **will**. she **is**.	**No,**	she **won't**. she **isn't**.

Wh- Questions	
Result Clause: Future	*If* Clause: Present
What **will** she **do** What **is** she **going to do**	**if** she **passes** the test?

GRAMMAR NOTES

EXAMPLES

1. Use **future real conditional** sentences to talk about what will happen under certain conditions. The *if* clause gives the condition. The result clause gives the probable or certain result.

   Use the simple present in the *if* clause.

   Use the future with **will** or **be going to** in the result clause.

   if clause   result clause
   - **If** I **use** this pen, **I'll pass** the test.
     (It's a real possibility that I will use this pen.)
   - **If** you **feel** lucky, you**'ll expect** good things.
   - **If** you **feel** unlucky, you**'ll expect** the worst.

2. You can use **modals** (*can, should, might, must . . .*) in the result clause.

   ▶ **BE CAREFUL!** Even though the *if* clause refers to the future, use the simple present.
   - If she studies hard, she *might* **get** an A on her test.

   - **If** she **gets** an A on her test, she will stop worrying.
     NOT If she ~~will get~~ an A on her test, she will stop worrying.

3. You can begin conditional sentences with the *if* clause or the result clause. The meaning is the same.

▶ **BE CAREFUL!** Use a comma between the two clauses only when the *if* clause comes first.

- *If she uses that pen,* she'll feel lucky.

  OR

- She'll feel lucky *if she uses that pen.*

4. You can use *if* and *unless* in conditional sentences, but their meanings are very different.

Use *unless* to state a **negative condition**.

Unless often has the same meaning as *if . . . not*.

- *If* he studies, he will pass the test.

- *Unless* he studies, he will fail the test. *(If he doesn't study, he will fail the test.)*

- *Unless* you're superstitious, you won't be afraid of black cats.

  OR

- *If* you are**n't** superstitious, you won't be afraid of black cats.

Focused Practice

1 | DISCOVER THE GRAMMAR

Match the conditions with the results.

Condition

_d_ **1.** If I lend someone my baseball bat,

_e_ **2.** If it rains,

_f_ **3.** If I give my boyfriend a new pair of shoes,

_a_ **4.** If the palm of your hand itches,

_c_ **5.** If I use my lucky pen,

_b_ **6.** If you wear your sweater backwards,

Result

a. you could have an allergy.

b. people might laugh at you.

c. I'll get a good grade on the test.

d. I won't hit a home run.

e. I'm going to get wet.

f. he'll walk out of the relationship.

Now write the sentences that are superstitions.

1. *If I lend someone my baseball bat, I won't hit a home run.*

2. _____

3. _____

2 | SUPERSTITIOUS STUDENTS

Grammar Note 4

*Two students are talking about a test. Complete their conversations with **if** or **unless**.*

1. YUKI: It's midnight. _____Unless_____ we get some sleep, we won't do well tomorrow.

   EVA: But I won't be able to sleep _____unless_____ I stop worrying about the test.

   YUKI: Here's my rabbit foot. _____If_____ you put it in your pocket, you'll do fine!

2. EVA: I found my blue shirt! _____If_____ I wear my blue shirt today, I know I'll pass!

   YUKI: Great. Now _____If_____ we just clean up the room, we can leave for school.

   EVA: We can't clean up! There's a Russian superstition that says: _____If_____ you clean your

   room, you'll get a bad test grade!

3. YUKI: _____If_____ we finish the test by noon, we can go to the job fair.

   EVA: I want to get a job, but nobody is going to hire me _____unless_____ I pass this test.

4. EVA: I'm looking for my lucky pen. _____unless_____ I find it, I won't pass the test!

   YUKI: Don't worry. _____If_____ you use the same pen that you used to study with, you'll do

   great! The pen will remember the answers.

5. EVA: I was so nervous without my lucky pen. It'll be a miracle _____If_____ I pass.

   YUKI: I don't believe in miracles! _____If_____ you study, you'll do well. It's that simple.

6. EVA: Do you think Eastward will offer me a job _____If_____ I fill out an application?

   YUKI: Only _____If_____ you use your lucky pen. I'm kidding! You won't know

   _____unless_____ you try!

3 | A WORLD OF SUPERSTITIONS

Grammar Note 1

Complete the superstitions. Use the correct form of the verbs in parentheses.

- If you _____spill_____ salt at the breakfast table, you _____'ll have_____ an
      1. (spill)   2. (have)

  argument. *(Russia)*

- If a cat _____washes_____ behind its ears, it _____will rain_____. *(England)*
        3. (wash)   4. (rain)

- If you _____walk_____ under a ladder, you _____will have_____ bad
      5. (walk)   6. (have)

  luck. *(North America)*

- If you _____sweep_____ the dirt and dust out of your house through the front door, you
  7. (sweep)
  _____will sweep_____ away your family's good luck.   *(China)*
  8. (sweep)
- If your right hand _____is_____ itchy, you _____will get_____ money.
  9. (be)   10. (get)
  If your left hand _____itches_____, you _____will give_____ money.   *(Greece)*
  11. (itch)   12. (give)
- If somebody _____throws_____ away a dead mouse, the wind _____will start_____ to blow
  13. (throw)   14. (start)
  from that direction.   *(Iceland)*
- If you _____sit_____ at the corner of the table, you _____won't get_____
  15. (sit)   16. (not get)
  married.   *(Slovakia)*
- If you _____throw_____ red beans at a newly married couple, they _____will have_____ good
  17. (throw)   18. (have)
  luck.   *(Mexico)*

4 | YOU'LL BE SORRY

Grammar Notes 1 and 3

Eva is thinking of working for Eastwood. Her friend Don, who used to work there, thinks it's a terrible idea. Write his responses. Use the words in parentheses and future real conditional sentences.

1. **EVA:** If I work for Eastward, I'm going to be happy. I'm sure of it.

   DON: If you work for Eastward, you're not going to be happy. You're going to be miserable.
   (miserable)

2. **EVA:** You're such a pessimist! I'll have the chance to travel a lot if I take this job.

   DON: Not true. If you take this job, you won't leave
   (never leave the office)

3. **EVA:** But I'll get a raise every year if I stay at Eastward.

   DON: If you stay at Estward, you won't get a raise every two years. you will get a rais every two years.
   (every two years)

4. **EVA:** Well, if I join Eastward, I'm going to have wonderful health care benefits.

   DON: Stay healthy! If you join Estward, you are not going to have... you are going to have a Ter.
   (terrible health care benefits)

5. **EVA:** If I go to Eastward, I'll have helpful co-workers.

   DON: If you go to Estward, you won't have helpful co-workers. you will have un...
   (uncooperative)

6. **EVA:** I don't believe you! If I accept Eastward's offer, it will be the best career move of my life.

   DON: Believe me, If you accept Estwards offer, it wont be the best career move of
   (the worst)
   your life. it will be the worst career move of your life.

5 WHAT IF . . . *Grammar Notes 1–2*

*Yuki Tamari is not sure whether to go to law school. She made a decision tree to help her decide. In the tree, arrows connect the conditions and the results. Write future real conditional sentences about her decision. Use **may**, **might**, or **could** if the result is uncertain.*

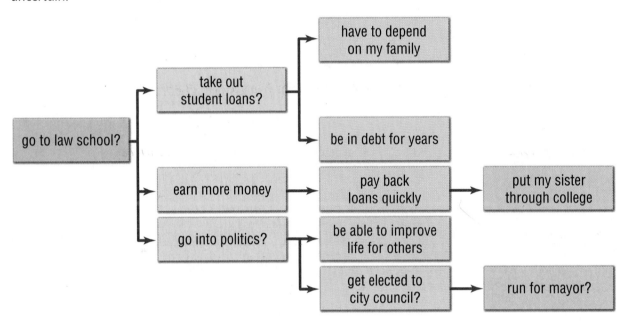

1. <u>If I go to law school, I might take out student loans.</u>

2. <u>I'll be in debt for years if I take out student loans.</u>

3. If I go to law school, I will earn more money.

4. If I earn more money, I will payback loans quickly.

5. If I take out student loans, I will have to depend on my family.

6. If I take out student loans, I will be in debt for years.

7. If I go to law school, I will take out student loans.

8. If I go into politics, I will be able to improve life for others.

9. If I payback loans quickly, I will put my sister through college.

10. If I get elected to city council, I will run for mayor.

6 | EDITING

Read Yuki's journal entry. There are seven mistakes in the use of future real conditionals. The first mistake is already corrected. Find and correct six more. Don't forget to check punctuation.

October 1

    Should I campaign for student council president? I'll have to decide
soon if I ~~wanted~~ *want* to run. If I'll be busy campaigning, I won't have much
time to study. That's a problem because I'm not going to get into law
school if I get good grades this year. On the other hand, there's so
much to do in this school, and nothing is getting done if Todd Laker
becomes president again. A lot of people know that. But will I know what
to do if I'll get the job? Never mind. I'll deal with that problem if I win.
If I become president, I cut my hair. That always brings me good luck.

(margin notes: unless I get · an · don't · will get · will · is going t get)

Communication Practice

7 | LISTENING

🎧 *Yuki is talking about her campaign platform. Listen to the interview. Then read the list of issues. Listen again and check the things that Yuki promises to work for if she is elected.*

☑ **1.** have contact with a lot of students

☐ **2.** improve the student council's newsletter

☑ **3.** publish teacher evaluations on the student council's website

☑ **4.** get the college to provide a bus service from the airport

☐ **5.** get the college to offer a major in environmental science

☐ **6.** reduce tuition costs

8 | SOLUTIONS

Work in pairs. Read these problems and discuss possible solutions. Use **if**, **if . . . not**, *or* **unless**.

1. Your neighbors are always playing music so loudly that you can't fall asleep.

   Example: If they don't stop, I'll call the police.
   Unless they stop, I'll call the landlord.
   I'll consider moving if they continue to bother me.

2. You've had a headache every day for a week. You can't concentrate.

3. You keep phoning your parents, but there is no answer. It's now midnight.

4. You like your job, but you just found out that other workers are making much more money than you are.

5. You live in an apartment building. It's winter and the building hasn't had any heat for a week. You're freezing.

6. You're 10 pounds overweight. You've been trying for months to lose weight, but so far you haven't lost a single pound.

7. You bought a radio at a local store. It doesn't work, but when you tried to return it, the salesperson refused to take it back.

8. Your roommates don't clean up after they cook. You've already reminded them several times, but they always "forget."

9. You paid for a parking space near school or work. For the past week the same car has taken your space.

9 | GOOD LUCK / BAD LUCK

Here are some superstitions about luck. Work in small groups and discuss similar superstitions that you know about.

- If you cross your fingers, you'll have good luck.

  Example: In Germany, people believe that if you press your thumbs together, you will have good luck.

- If you touch blue, your dreams will come true.

- If you break a mirror, you will have seven years of bad luck.

- If you put a piece of clothing on inside out, you will have good luck.

- If your palm itches, you're going to find some money soon.

10 | WRITING

Imagine you are running for class or school president. Write a short speech. Include five campaign promises. Use future real conditionals. In small groups, give your speeches and elect a candidate. Then hold a general class election.

Example: If I become school president, I will ask for 10 new computers . . .

11 | ON THE INTERNET

Do a search for information about superstitions in different cultures. Share your information with a group. Do different cultures have any similar superstitions?

Example: **A:** In Canada, some people believe that if a black cat walks across your path, you'll have bad luck.

B: That's a common superstition in Turkey too.

2 = unless you have a headache every day for a week, you can't concentrate.

fairy tale = cinderedla

Grammar in Context

BEFORE YOU READ

🎧 *Read the first sentence of the story and look at the picture. Is this a true story? How do fairy tales begin in your culture? Read this version of a famous fairy tale.*

The Fisherman and His Wife

Once upon a time there was a poor fisherman and his wife who lived in a pigpen near the sea. Every day the man went to fish. One day, after waiting a very long time, he caught a very big fish. To his surprise, the fish spoke and said, "Please let me live. I'm not a regular fish. **If you knew my real identity, you wouldn't kill me**. I'm an enchanted prince."

"Don't worry. I won't kill you," said the kind-hearted fisherman. With these words, he threw the fish back into the clear water, and went home to his wife.

"Husband," said the wife, "didn't you catch anything today?"

"I caught a fish, but it said it was an enchanted prince, so I let it go."

"You mean you didn't wish for anything?" asked the wife.

"No," said the fisherman. "What do I need to wish for?"

"Just look around you," said the wife. "We live in a pigpen. **I wish we had a nice little cottage. If we had a cottage, I would be a lot happier**. You saved the prince's life. Go back and ask him for it."

"I'm not going to ask for a cottage! **If I asked for a cottage, the fish might get angry**." But in the end, the fisherman was more afraid of his wife's anger.

When he got to the sea, it was all green and yellow. "**My wife wishes we had a cottage**," said the fisherman. "Just go on back," said the fish. "She already has it."

336

Famous Fairy Tales   *The Fisherman and His Wife*

When he returned home, the fisherman found his wife sitting outside a lovely little cottage. The kitchen was filled with food and all types of cooking utensils. Outside was a little garden with vegetables, fruit trees, hens, and ducks.

Things were fine for a week or two. Then the wife said, "This cottage is much too crowded. **I wish we lived in a bigger house. If we lived in a big stone castle, I would be much happier**. Go and ask the fish for it."

The fisherman didn't want to go, but he did. When he got to the sea, it was dark blue and gray. "**My wife wishes we lived in a big stone castle**," he said to the fish.

"Just go on back. She's standing in front of the door," said the fish.

When he returned home, the fisherman found his wife on the steps of a great big stone castle. The inside was filled with beautiful gold furniture, chandeliers, and carpets. There were servants everywhere.

The next morning the wife woke up and said, "**I wish I were King of all this land**."

"**What would you do if you were King?**" asked her husband. "**If I were King, I would own all this land**. Go on back and ask the fish for it."

This time, the sea was all blackish gray, and the water was rough and smelled terrible. "What does she want now?" asked the fish.

"She wants to be King," said the embarrassed fisherman.

"Just go on back. She already is."

When the fisherman returned home, he found an enormous palace. Everything inside was made of marble and pure gold,

and it was surrounded by soldiers with drums and trumpets. His wife was seated on a throne, and he said to her, "How nice for you that you are King. Now we won't need to wish for anything else."

But his wife was not satisfied. "I'm only King of *this* country," she said. "**I wish I were Emperor of the whole world. If I were Emperor, I would be the most powerful ruler on Earth**."

"Wife, now be satisfied," said the fisherman. "You're King. You can't be anything more."

The wife, however, wasn't convinced. She kept thinking and thinking about what more she could be. "**If I were Emperor, I could have anything—and you wouldn't have to ask the fish for anything more**. Go right now and tell the fish that I want to be Emperor of the world."

"Oh, no," said the fisherman. "The fish can't do that. **If I were you, I wouldn't ask for anything else**." But his wife got so furious that the poor fisherman ran back to the fish. There was a terrible storm, and the sea was pitch black with waves as high as mountains. "Well, what does she want now?" asked the fish.

"**She wishes she were Emperor of the whole world**," said the fisherman.

"Just go on back. She's sitting in the pigpen again."

And they are still sitting there today.

AFTER YOU READ

Write **T** *(true) or* **F** *(false).*

_F_ **1.** Before the man caught the fish, he and his wife lived in a nice little cottage.

_T_ **2.** At first, the fish believed that the man was going to kill him.

_T_ **3.** The man didn't want to ask for the first wish because he didn't want to make the fish angry.

_F_ **4.** The wife was satisfied with the stone castle.

_T_ **5.** The man advised his wife not to ask to be Emperor of the whole world.

Grammar Presentation

PRESENT AND FUTURE UNREAL CONDITIONALS

Statements	
If **Clause: Simple Past**	**Result Clause:** *Would* (*not*) + **Base Form**
If Mia **had** money, **If** she **were*** rich,	she **would live** in a palace. she **wouldn't live** in a cottage.
If Mia **didn't have** money, **If** she **weren't** rich,	she **wouldn't live** in a palace. she **would live** in a cottage.

*With the verb *be*, use *were* for all subjects.

Contractions		
I would	=	**I'd**
you would	=	**you'd**
he would	=	**he'd**
she would	=	**she'd**
we would	=	**we'd**
they would	=	**they'd**
would not	=	**wouldn't**

Yes / No Questions	
Result Clause	*If* **Clause**
Would she **live** here	**if** she **had** money? **if** she **were** rich?

Short Answers	
Affirmative	**Negative**
Yes, she **would**.	**No**, she **wouldn't**.

Wh- Questions	
Result Clause	*If* **Clause**
What **would** she **do**	**if** she **had** money? **if** she **were** rich?

GRAMMAR NOTES	EXAMPLES

1. Use **present and future unreal conditional** sentences to talk about unreal conditions and their results. A condition and its result may be untrue, imagined, or impossible.

The sentence can be about:

a. the **present**

OR

b. the **future**

The *if* clause gives the unreal condition, and the result clause gives the unreal result of that condition.

- *if* clause   result clause
  If I **had** more time, **I would read** fairy tales to my children.
  (But I don't have time, so I don't read fairy tales to my children.)

- *if* clause   result clause
  If I **lived** in a palace ***now***, **I would give** parties all the time.
  (But I don't live in a palace now, so I don't give parties all the time.)

- *if* clause   result clause
  If I **moved** ***next month***, **I would buy** new furniture.
  (But I'm not going to move next month, so I won't buy new furniture.)

---

2. Use the **simple past** in the *if* clause.

Use **would**, **might**, or **could + base form** of the verb in the result clause.

▶ **BE CAREFUL!**

a. The *if* clause uses the simple past, but the meaning is not past.

b. Don't use *would* in the *if* clause.

c. Use *were* for all subjects when the verb in the *if* clause is a form of *be*.

USAGE NOTE: Some people use *was* with *I*, *he*, *she*, and *it*. However, many people think this is incorrect.

- **If** they **had** a nice house, they **wouldn't want** to move.

- **If** I **had** more money ***now***, I would take a trip around the world.

- **If** she **knew** the answer, she would tell you.
  NOT If she ~~would know~~ the answer . . .

- **If** I **were** King, I would make you Prime Minister.
  NOT If I ~~was~~ King . . .

(continued)

3. Use **would** in the result clause if the result is <u>certain</u>. Do not use *will* in unreal conditional sentences.

- They love to travel. If they had time, they **would** take a trip next summer.

Use **might** or **could** in the result clause if the result is <u>not certain</u>. Do not use *may* and *can*.

- They've never been to Asia. If they took a trip, they **might** go to Japan.

OR

- If they took a trip, they **could** go to Japan.

You can also use **could** in the result clause to express <u>ability</u>.

- You don't know Japanese. If you knew Japanese, you **could** translate this article for them.

---

4. You can begin conditional sentences with the *if* clause or the result clause. The meaning is the same.

- **If I had more money,** I would move.

OR

- I would move **if I had more money**.

▶ **BE CAREFUL!** Use a comma between the two clauses only when the *if* clause comes first.

---

5. Use **If I were you, . . .** to give **advice**.

- **If I were you**, I wouldn't ask the fish for anything else. He could get angry.

---

6. Use **wish + simple past** to talk about things that you want to be true now, but that are not true.

- I **wish** I **lived** in a castle.
  (I don't live in a castle now, but I want to live in one.)
- I **wish** we **had** a yacht.
  (We don't have a yacht now, but I want one.)

Use **were** instead of *was* after *wish*.

- I **wish** I *were* a child again.
  NOT I wish I ~~was~~ a child again.

Use **could** or **would** after *wish*. Don't use *can* or *will*.

- I **wish** I *could* buy a car.
  NOT I wish I ~~can~~ buy a car.
- I **wish** she *would* call tomorrow.
  NOT I wish she ~~will~~ call tomorrow.

Focused Practice

1 | DISCOVER THE GRAMMAR

Read the numbered statements. Decide if the sentences that follow are true **(T)** *or false* **(F).**

1. If I had time, I would read fairy tales in English.

   ___F___ **a.** I have time.

   ___F___ **b.** I'm going to read fairy tales in English.

2. If it weren't so cold, I would go fishing.

   ___T___ **a.** It's cold.

   ___F___ **b.** I'm going fishing.

3. If I caught an enchanted fish, I would make three wishes.

   ___F___ **a.** I believe I'm going to catch an enchanted fish.

   ___F___ **b.** I'm going to make three wishes.

4. If I had three wishes, I wouldn't ask for a palace.

   ___F___ **a.** I have three wishes.

   ___T___ **b.** I don't want a palace.

5. If my house were too small, I would try to find a bigger one.

   ___T___ **a.** My house is big enough.

   ___T___ **b.** I'm not looking for a bigger house right now.

6. If I got a raise, I could buy a new car.

   ___F___ **a.** I recently got a raise.

   ___T___ **b.** I want a new car.

7. If we didn't earn enough money, I might train for a better job.

   ___F___ **a.** We don't earn enough money.

   ___F___ **b.** I'm training for a better job.

8. Your friend tells you, "If I were you, I wouldn't change jobs."

   ___T___ **a.** Your friend is giving you advice.

   ___T___ **b.** Your friend thinks you shouldn't change jobs.

9. I wish I were a princess.

   ___F___ **a.** I'm a princess.

   ___T___ **b.** I want to be a princess.

10. I wish I lived in a big house.

    ___T___ **a.** I want to live in a big house.

    ___T___ **b.** I don't live in a big house.

2 | ABRACADABRA?

Complete this article from a popular psychology magazine. Use the correct form of the verbs.

Marty Hijab has always wanted to invite his whole family over for the

holidays, but his apartment is small, and his family is very large.

"If I _____invited_____ them all for dinner, there
 1.(invite)

__won't be__ enough room for everyone to sit down," he
 2.(not be)

told a friend. If Marty _____were_____ a complainer, he
 3.(be)

__would moan__ about the size of his apartment and spend the
 4.(moan)

holiday at his parents' house. But Marty is a problem solver. This

year he is hosting an open house. People can drop in at different

times during the day, and there will be room for everyone.

"If life _____were_____ a fairy tale, we
 5.(be)

__could wish__ problems away," noted therapist Joel Grimes.
 6.(can / wish)

"What complainers are really saying is, 'If I _____had_____ a magical solution, I
 7.(have)

__wouldn't have to deal__ with this myself.' I wish it _____were_____ that easy," says Grimes. He
 8.(not have to deal)   **9.(be)**

gives an example of a very wealthy client who complains about his limited time for his family.

"He's waiting for a miracle to give him the time he needs. But if he __thought__ about the
                                                                        10.(think)

problem creatively, he __could find__ the time," says Grimes.
                         11.(can / find)

Even the rich have limited time, money, and space. If complainers __realized__ this,
                                                                     12.(realize)

then they __would understand__ that there will always be problems. They could then stop
          13.(understand)

complaining and look for solutions. Marty is a student. If he _____insisted_____ on a bigger
                                                               14.(insist)

apartment for his party, he __might have to wait__ for years before inviting his family over. Instead,
                            15.(may / have to wait)

he is creatively solving his problems right now.

There's an old saying: "If wishes _____were_____ horses, then beggars
                                    16.(be)

__could ride__." But wishes aren't horses. We have to learn to create our own good fortune
 17.(can / ride)

and not wait for a genie with three wishes to come along and solve our problems.

3 | MAKING EXCUSES

Grammar Notes 1–4

In his practice, psychologist Joel Grimes hears all types of excuses from his clients. Rewrite these excuses using the present unreal conditional.

1. I'm so busy. That's why I don't read bedtime stories to my little girl.

If I weren't so busy, I would read bedtime stories to my little girl.

2. My husband's not ambitious. That's why he doesn't ask for a raise.

_____

3. I'm not in shape. That's why I don't play sports.

_____

4. I don't have enough time. That's why I'm not planning to study for the exam.

_____

5. I'm too old. That's why I'm not going back to school.

_____

6. My boss doesn't explain things properly. That's why I can't do my job.

_____

7. I'm not good at math. That's why I don't balance my checkbook.

_____

8. I feel nervous all the time. That's why I can't stop smoking.

_____

9. I'm so tired. That's why I get up so late.

_____

4 | THE FISH'S WISHES

Grammar Note 6

Remember the fish from the fairy tale on pages 336–337? Read the things the fish would like to change. Then write sentences with **wish**.

1. I'm a fish. _I wish I weren't a fish._

2. I'm not a handsome prince. _I wish I were a handsome prince._

3. I live in the sea. _I wish I didn't live in the sea._

4. I don't live in a castle. _I wish I lived in a castel._

5. I have to swim all day long. _I wish I didn't have to swim all ___._

6. I am not married to a princess. _I wish I were married to a princess._

(continued)

7. The fisherman comes here every day. _I wish the fisherman didn't come here ..._

8. His wife always wants more. _I wish His wife didn't always want more._

9. She isn't satisfied. _I wish she were satisfied._

10. They don't leave me alone. _I wish They would leave me alone._

5 | WHAT IF?   *Grammar Notes 1–4*

Marty is having his open house holiday party. His nieces and nephews are playing a fantasy question game. Write questions using the present unreal conditional.

1. What / you / do / if / you / be a millionaire?

   What would you do if you were a millionaire?

2. What / you / do / if / you / be the leader of this country?

   _what would you do if you were the ___ ?_

3. How / you / feel / if / you / never need to sleep?

   How would you feel if you never needed to sleep?

4. What / you / do / if / you / have more free time?

   what would you do if you had more free time?

5. What / you / ask for / if / you / have three wishes?

   what would you ask for if you had have three wishes?

6. What / you / do / if / you / not have to work?

   what would you do if you didn't have to work?

7. Where / you / travel / if / you / have a ticket for anywhere in the world?

   _where would you Travel if you had a ticket for ___ ?_

8. If / you / can build anything / what / it / be?

   If you could build anything what would it be?

9. If / you / can meet a famous person / who / you / want to meet?

   _If you could meet a ___ who whould you want ___ ?_

10. Who / you / have dinner with / if / you can invite three famous people?

    _who would you have dinner with If you could invite ___ ?_

6 | EDITING

Read part of a book report that Marty's niece wrote. There are eight mistakes in the use of the present unreal conditional. The first mistake is already corrected. Find and correct seven more.

NAME: Laila Hijab   CLASS: English 4

The Disappearance

disappeared

What would happen to the women if all the men in the world ~~would disappear~~? What would happen to the men when there were no women? Philip Wiley's 1951 science-fiction novel, *The Disappearance*, addresses these intriguing questions. The answers show us how society has changed since the 1950s.

According to Wiley, if men and women live in different worlds, the results would be catastrophic. In Wiley's vision, men are too aggressive to survive on their own, and women are too helpless. If women didn't control them, men will start more wars. If men aren't there to pump gas and run the businesses, women wouldn't be able to manage.

If Wiley is alive today, would he write the same novel? Today, a lot of men take care of their children, and a lot of women run businesses. If Wiley were here to see these changes, he learns that men are not more warlike than women, and women are not more helpless than men.

I think if all people, both men and women, learned to cooperate more, the world will be a much better place.

Communication Practice

7 | LISTENING

🎧 *You are going to listen to a modern fairy tale about Cindy, a clever young girl, and a toad. Read the statements and listen to the story. Then listen again and write* **T** *(true) or* **F** *(false).*

_F_ **1.** Cindy wishes she had a new soccer ball.

_T_ **2.** The toad wishes Cindy would marry him.

_T_ **3.** If Cindy married the toad, he would become a prince.

_F_ **4.** Cindy wishes she could become a beautiful princess.

_F_ **5.** If Cindy became a princess, she'd have plenty of time to study science.

_T_ **6.** The toad doesn't know how to use his powers to help himself.

_T_ **7.** Cindy wants to become a scientist and help the prince.

_F_ **8.** Cindy and the prince get married and live happily ever after.

8 | JUST IMAGINE

Work in small groups. Answer the questions in Exercise 5. Discuss your answers with your classmates.

> **Example:** **A:** What would you do if you were a millionaire?
> **B:** If I were a millionaire, I would donate half my money to charity.

9 | IF I WERE YOU . . .

Work in a group. One person describes a problem. Group members give advice with **If I were you, I would / wouldn't** *. . . Use the problems below and write three more.*

1. You need $500 to pay this month's rent. You only have $300.

> **Example:** **A:** I don't know what to do! I can't pay the rent this month. I only have $300, and I need $500.
> **B:** If I were you, I'd try to borrow the money.
> **C:** If I were you, I'd call the landlord right away.

2. You are lonely. You work at home and never meet new people.

3. You never have an opportunity to practice English outside of class.

4. You have been invited to dinner. You know that the main dish is going to be shrimp. You hate shrimp.

5. _____

6. _____

7. _____

10 | JUST THREE WISHES

In fairy tales, people are often given three wishes. Imagine that you had just three wishes. What would they be? Write them down. Discuss them with a classmate.

Example: **1.** I wish I were famous.

2. I wish I spoke perfect English.

3. I wish I knew how to fly a plane.

There is an old saying: "Be careful what you wish for; it may come true." Look at your wishes again. Discuss negative results that might happen if they came true.

Example: If I were famous, I would have no free time. I wouldn't have a private life . . .

11 | WRITING

Reread the book report on page 345. Does Philip Wiley believe men and women should live in separate worlds? What are his arguments? Do you agree with him? Write two paragraphs that support your opinion. Use the present and future unreal conditional.

Example: I don't think men and women should live in separate societies, but sometimes I think that boys and girls would learn better if they went to separate schools. For example, when I was in middle school, boys and girls were embarrassed to make mistakes in front of each other . . .

12 | ON THE INTERNET

Imagine that you have just won $10,000. How would you use the money? Do a search for information about things you would do or buy. Share your information with a group.

Example: If I won $10,000, I would take my parents on a trip to Korea. If we flew Korean Airlines, the tickets would cost about $1,000 each. My brother is in college. He could come too if we went during summer vacation.

Grammar in Context

BEFORE YOU READ

🎧 *Look at the photo and the information next to it. What do you think the movie is about? What does the reviewer think of the movie? Read this online movie review.*

DVD Movie Guide 🎥

It's A Wonderful Life (1946)

Rating: ★★★★ out of ★★★★
Director: Frank Capra
Producer: Frank Capra
Screenplay: Frank Capra, Frances Goodrich,
Albert Hacket, and Jo Swerling
Stars: James Stewart, Donna Reed,
Lionel Barrymore, Thomas Mitchell, and
Henry Travers
Running Time: 129 minutes
Parental Guidelines: suitable for the
whole family

Buy this DVD

   What would have happened if you had never been born? George Bailey learns the answer in Frank Capra's great movie classic, *It's a Wonderful Life*.
   When the movie opens, George is standing on a bridge thinking about suicide. Throughout his life, he has sacrificed his dreams in order to help other people. **He could have gone to college if the family business hadn't needed him. He would have traveled around the world** instead of remaining in his hometown of Bedford Falls. Now, facing a failed business and a possible jail sentence, George decides to end his life by jumping into the river. Enter Clarence, an angel sent to help him. Clarence jumps into the water first, certain that, as always, George will put aside his own problems in order to rescue someone else.

DVD Movie Guide

Safely back on land, **George wishes he had never been born**. "I suppose **it would have been better if I had never been born at all**," he tells Clarence. "You've got your wish: You've never been born," responds his guardian angel.

Clarence then teaches George a hard lesson. In a series of painful episodes, he shows him what **life would have been like in Bedford Falls without George Bailey**. George goes back to the site of his mother's home. He finds, instead, an old, depressing boardinghouse. **If George had not supported his mother, she would have become a miserable, overworked boardinghouse owner**. George's own home is a ruin, and his wife, Mary, is living a sad and lonely life. Each scene is more disturbing than the last, until finally we end in a graveyard. We see the grave of George's little brother, Harry. **If George hadn't been alive, he couldn't have saved Harry's life. Harry would have never grown up to be a war hero**, saving the lives of hundreds of soldiers. "Harry wasn't there to save them because you weren't there to save Harry," explains Clarence. "You see, George, you really had a wonderful life."

The ending of the movie delivers a heartwarming holiday message. *It's a Wonderful Life* shows us the importance of each person's life and how each of our lives touches those of others. We see through George's eyes how **the lives of those around him would have been different if he hadn't known them**.

This movie is highly recommended for the whole family.

ancient ruins

Buy this DVD

AFTER YOU READ

Check the things that George Bailey did.

☑ **1.** helped other people

☐ **2.** went to college

☐ **3.** traveled around the world

☑ **4.** jumped into the river

☑ **5.** supported his mother

☑ **6.** got married

☑ **7.** saved his younger brother's life

☐ **8.** became a war hero

George is reunited with his family

Grammar Presentation

PAST UNREAL CONDITIONALS

Statements	
If Clause: Past Perfect	Result Clause: *Would (not) have* + Past Participle
If George **had had** money,	he **would have moved** away. he **wouldn't have stayed** home.
If he **had not stayed** home,	his father's business **would have failed**. he **wouldn't have married** Mary.

Yes / No Questions	
Result Clause	*If* Clause
Would he **have left**	**if** he **had had** money?

Short Answers	
Affirmative	Negative
Yes, he **would have**.	**No**, he **wouldn't have**.

Wh- Questions	
Result Clause	*If* Clause
What **would** he **have done**	**if** he **had had** money?

Contractions		
would have	=	**would've**
would not have	=	**wouldn't have**

GRAMMAR NOTES

1. Use **past unreal conditional** sentences to talk about past unreal conditions and their results. A condition and its result may be untrue, imagined, or impossible.

The *if* clause gives the unreal condition, and the result clause gives the unreal result of that condition.

2. Use the **past perfect** in the *if* clause. Use *would have*, *might have*, or *could have* + past participle in the result clause.

USAGE NOTE: Sometimes speakers use *would have* in the *if* clause. However, many people think this is not correct.

EXAMPLES

if clause   result clause
- **If** he **had died** young, he **wouldn't have had** children.
  (But he didn't die young, so he had children.)
- **If** George **hadn't been born**, many people's lives **would have been** worse.
  (But George was born, so people's lives were better.)

- **If** the film **had won** an Academy Award, it **would have become** famous right away.

- **If** I **had owned** a DVD player, I would have watched the movie. NOT If I ~~would have~~ owned . . .

3. Use *would have* in the result clause if the result is <u>certain</u>. Do not use *will* in unreal conditional sentences.

- If George had gone to college, he *would have* **studied** hard.

Use *might have* or *could have* in the result clause if the result is <u>not certain</u>. Do not use *may* or *can*.

- If George had gone to college, he *might have* **become** an architect.

  OR

- If George had gone to college, he *could have* **become** an architect.

You can also use *could have* in the result clause to express **ability**.

- If George had become an architect, he *could have* **designed** a bridge.

---

4. You can begin conditional sentences with the *if* clause or the result clause. The meaning is the same.

- **If he had won a million dollars,** he would have traveled around the world.

  OR

- He would have traveled around the world **if he had won a million dollars**.

▶ **BE CAREFUL!** Use a comma between the two clauses only when the *if* clause comes first.

---

5. Past unreal conditionals are often used to **express regret** about what really happened in the past.

- **If I had known** Mary lived alone, I **would have invited** her to my holiday dinner.
  (I regret that I didn't invite her.)

---

6. Use *wish* + **past perfect** to express **regret or sadness** about things in the past that you wanted to happen but didn't.

- George *wishes* he **had studied** architecture.
  (He didn't study architecture, and now he thinks that was a mistake.)

Focused Practice

1 | DISCOVER THE GRAMMAR

*Read the numbered statements. Decide if the sentences that follow are true (**T**) or false (**F**).*

1. If I had had time, I would have watched *It's a Wonderful Life.*

___T___ **a.** I didn't have time to watch *It's a Wonderful Life.*

___F___ **b.** I watched *It's a Wonderful Life.*

2. She would've watched the movie last night if she hadn't seen it before.

___F___ **a.** She watched the movie last night.

___T___ **b.** She saw the movie before.

3. I would have recorded the movie if my DVD recorder had not stopped working.

___F___ **a.** I recorded the movie.

___T___ **b.** My DVD recorder broke.

4. If George Bailey hadn't been depressed, he wouldn't have wanted to jump off the bridge.

___T___ **a.** George was depressed.

___T___ **b.** George wanted to jump off the bridge.

5. If George hadn't saved his brother's life, his brother wouldn't have become a war hero.

___F___ **a.** George didn't save his brother's life.

___T___ **b.** George's brother became a war hero.

6. George wouldn't have met Mary if he had left town.

___T___ **a.** George met Mary.

___F___ **b.** George left town.

7. George would have been happy if he had liked his job.

___T___ **a.** George wasn't happy.

___F___ **b.** George liked his job.

8. George says, "I wish I had traveled around the world."

___T___ **a.** George feels sad that he hasn't traveled around the world.

___F___ **b.** George has traveled around the world.

George and Mary

2 | GEORGE'S THOUGHTS

Grammar Notes 1–3, 5

Complete George's thoughts about the past. Use the correct form of the words in parentheses.

1. I didn't go into business with my friend Sam. If I _____*had gone*_____ into business
   (go)
   with him, I _____*might have become*_____ a success.
   (may / become)

2. I couldn't go into the army because I was deaf in one ear. I *would have gone* into
   (go)
   the army if I _____*hadn't lose*_____ the hearing in that ear.
   (not lose)

3. Mary and I weren't able to go on a honeymoon. We *could have gone* away if
   (can / go)
   my father _____*hadn't gotten*_____ sick.
   (not get)

4. My uncle lost $8,000 of the company's money. I *wouldn't have felt* so desperate if
   (not feel)
   he _____*had found*_____ the money.
   (find)

5. I'm so unhappy about losing my father's business. I wish I _____*had*_____
   never _____*been*_____ born.
   (be)

6. Clarence showed me how the world would look without me. I *wouldn't have known*
   (not know)
   that I was so important if Clarence _____*hadn't shown*_____ me.
   (not show)

7. If I _____*hadn't rescued*_____ my brother, he *wouldn't have saved* all those
   (not rescue)   **(not save)**
   lives when he was a soldier.

8. My old boss once almost made a terrible mistake. If I _____*hadn't helped*_____ him, he
   (not help)
   _____*might have gone*_____ to jail.
   (may / go)

9. Mary *wouldn't have been* happy if she _____*hadn't met*_____ me.
   (not be)   **(not meet)**

10. Many people *couldn't have bough* new homes if we _____*hadn't stayed*_____ in
    (can't / buy)   **(not stay)**
    business all these years.

11. Life here really *would have been* worse if I _____*hadn't been*_____ born.
    (be)   **(not be)**

3 | REGRETS AND WISHES

Grammar Note 6

These characters in the movie feel bad about some things. Read their regrets. Then write their wishes.

1. **Clarence (the angel):** I wasn't a first-class angel then. I didn't have much self-confidence.

   I wish I had been a first-class angel then.

   I wish I had had more self-confidence.

2. **Mr. Gower (George's childhood employer):** I hit little George when he was trying to help me. I wasn't nice to him.

   I wish I hadn't hit little George

   I wish I had been nice to him.

3. **George:** My father had a heart attack. I had to stay and run the business.

   I wish my father hadn't had a heart attact.

   I wish I hadn't had to stay and run the business

4. **Mary (George's wife):** We weren't able to go on a honeymoon. We needed the money to save the business.

   I wish we had been able to go on a honeymoon.

   I wish we hadn't needed the money to save the business.

5. **Mr. Potter (the meanest person in town):** I wasn't able to trick George out of his business. He didn't accept my offer to buy his business.

   I wish I had been able to trick George out of his business.

   I wish He had accepted my offer to buy his business.

6. **Billy (George's uncle):** I lost $8,000. George got into trouble with the law because of me.

   I wish I hadn't lost $8000,

   I wish George hadn't gotten into trouble with ~

7. **George's daughter:** Daddy was upset about the business. He yelled at us last night.

   I wish Daddy hadn't been upset.

   I wish he hadn't yelled at us

8. **George's friends:** We didn't know about George's troubles earlier. We didn't help him immediately.

   we wish we had known about ~ ~

   we wish we had helped him immediately.

4 | MICHAEL J. FOX

Grammar Notes 1–4

Actor Michael J. Fox starred in Back to the Future, *another movie that explores what would have happened if something in the past had been different. Read about Fox. Using the words in parentheses, combine each pair of sentences to make one past unreal conditional sentence.*

1. Michael J. Fox wasn't tall as a teenager. He didn't become a professional hockey player. (might)

   If Michael J. Fox had been tall as a teenager, he might have become a professional hockey player.

2. Fox quit high school in order to act. He didn't graduate. (would)

   If Fox hadn't quit highschool in order to act, he would have graduated.

3. Fox moved to Los Angeles. He got several roles on TV. (might)

   If Fox hadn't moved to los Angeles, he might have gotten several ——

4. He met Tracey Pollan on the TV show *Family Ties*. They got married. (might)

   If he hadn't met Tracey —— — They might not have gotten married

5. Fox was very successful on TV. He got the leading role in *Back to the Future*. (would)

   If Fox hadn't been very successful — he wouldn't have gotten —

6. Actor Eric Stolz didn't remain in *Back to the Future*. Fox played the lead. (could)

   If Actor Eric Stolz hadn't remained ——, Fox couldn't played —

7. Fox didn't have free time. He didn't watch old movies and sports on TV. (could)

   If Fox had had free time, he could have watched —

8. He became ill. He didn't stay in his TV series *Spin City*. (would)

   If he hadn't become ill, he would have stayed ——

9. Fox stopped working. He wrote a book called *Lucky Man* about his life and illness. (might)

   If Fox hadn't stopped — he might not have written ——

10. He developed Parkinson's disease. He started an organization to search for a cure. (would)

    If he hadn't developed ——, he wouldn't have started ——

5 | EDITING

Read this journal entry. There are eight mistakes in the use of the past unreal conditional.
The first mistake is already corrected. Find and correct seven more.

Tonight we rented the movie <u>Back to the Future</u>. I thought it was great,

and I usually don't like science fiction movies. I might never ~~had~~ have seen it if I

hadn't ~~read~~ read Fox's autobiography, <u>Lucky Man</u>. His book was so good that I

wanted to see his most famous movie. Now I wish I ~~saw~~ had seen it in the theater

when it first came out. It would have been better if we would ~~have~~ had watched it

on a big screen. Michael J. Fox was very good. He looked really young—just like a

teenager. Of course, he still looks very young—I would have recognized him even

when I hadn't known he was in the film.

In the movie, Marty McFly goes back in time. He wants to change the

past in order to improve his present life as a teenager. It's a funny idea, but

it's very different from Fox's real philosophy. He's had a lot of problems in his

life, but he still calls himself "Lucky Man." As a teenager, he was too small to

become a professional hockey player—but if he hadn't looked so young, he ~~can't~~ couldn't

have gotten his role in the TV hit series <u>Family Ties</u>. In Hollywood, he had ~~to~~

sold sell his furniture to pay his bills, but he kept trying to find acting jobs. If he

hadn't ~~wouldn't have~~ had had, he might never have become a star. Getting Parkinson's disease

was a terrible blow, but he has even turned that into something good. If Fox

hadn't ~~hasn't~~ become sick, he might never ~~had~~ have become so close to his family. And he

wouldn't have started the Michael J. Fox Foundation to help find a cure.

Communication Practice

6 | LISTENING

🎧 *Some friends are discussing a party. Listen to their conversations. Then listen again and circle the letter of the sentence you heard.*

1. **a.** If I had her number, I would call her.
   (b.) If I'd had her number, I would've called her.

2. **a.** I would've invited him if he'd been in town.
   b. I wouldn't have invited him if he'd been in town.

3. **a.** If he'd changed jobs, he would've gotten the same benefits.
   b. If he'd changed jobs, he wouldn't have gotten the same benefits.

4. **a.** I liked it better on a big screen.
   b. I would've liked it better on a big screen.

5. **a.** I wish David had invited her.
   b. I wish David hadn't invited her.

6. **a.** I would have.
   b. I wouldn't have.

7. **a.** If I'd invited Holly, I would've invited Greg.
   b. If I'd invited Holly, I wouldn't have invited Greg.

8. **a.** If the party had been on a Saturday, they could've come.
   b. If the party hadn't been on a Saturday, they could've come.

7 | WHAT WOULD YOU HAVE DONE?

Read the following situations. In small groups, discuss what you would have done in each situation. If I had sold my bussiness I would have been a ~

1. Zeke started his business making and selling energy bars* when he was a teenager. Ten years later, a large company offered to buy the business. Zeke turned the offer down because he wanted to make sure Zeke's Bars were always very high quality. If he had accepted, he could have retired rich by age 35. What would you have done?

   Example: A: I wouldn't have rejected it. I would've sold the business and started a new one.
   B: Not me. I would have . . .

2. A man was walking down the street when he found ten $100 bills lying on the ground. There was no one else around. He picked them up and put them in his pocket.
   If I had found 10 100 bill I would have by a new car and a new house.

3. A woman came home late and found her apartment door unlocked. She was sure she had locked it. No one else had the keys. She went inside.

*Food that gives you energy and that is in the shape of a candy bar.

8 | IF ONLY . . .

With a partner, discuss a situation in your life that you regret. Describe the situation and talk about what you wish had happened and why.

Example: Someone asked me to go to a party the night before a test. I didn't like the course, and I didn't feel like studying, so I decided to go. The next day I failed the test, and I had to repeat the course. I wish I hadn't gone to the party. If I had stayed home, I would have studied for the test. If I had been prepared, I would have passed.

9 | WRITING

If you hadn't been born, what would have been different for your family, friends, teammates, or community? Choose two areas of your life to discuss and write a paragraph about all the things that would have been different. Use past unreal conditionals.

Example: Two important areas of my life are my family and my friends. I am an only child, so if I hadn't been born, my parents would have been sad. They wanted a child very much. If they hadn't had me, they might have . . .

10 | ON THE INTERNET

Do a search on a person who changed the world. Choose a person that you know about or one from the list. How would life have been different if that person hadn't been born? Discuss your findings with a classmate.

Marie Curie

Thomas Edison

Ludwig von Beethoven

Mother Teresa

Johannes Gutenberg

Marco Polo

Princess Diana

El Zahrawi

Rachel Carson

Example: **A:** If Marie Curie hadn't been born, she wouldn't have discovered helpful uses for radioactivity.
B: She wouldn't have worked with Pierre Curie.

From **Grammar** to **Writing**
Showing Cause and Effect

One way to develop a topic is to discuss its causes and effects. To show cause
and effect, you can connect **sentences** with *as a result* and *therefore*. In individual
sentences, you can connect **clauses** with *so*, *because*, or *if*.

Example

CAUSE	EFFECT
I was shy.	*I didn't talk in class.* $\longrightarrow$

I was shy. **As a result**, I didn't talk in class.
I was shy. **Therefore**, I didn't talk in class.
I was shy, **so** I didn't talk in class.
Because I was shy, I didn't talk in class.
If I hadn't been shy, I would have talked in class.

Punctuation Note

Use a comma after *as a result* and *therefore.* Use a comma before *so.* Use a comma after a clause beginning
with *because* or *if* when it comes before the main clause.

1 | *Read this essay. Underline sentences or clauses that show a cause once.
Underline sentences or clauses that show an effect twice. Circle the connecting words.*

> My biggest problem in school is my fear of talking in class. My hands
> always shake (if) I answer a question or present a paper. If it is a big
> assignment, I even feel sick to my stomach.
> There are several reasons for my problem, but my family's attitude is the
> most important. My family motto is, "Children should be seen, but not
> heard." Because my parents never ask for our opinions, we never give them.
> I can feel my mother's disapproval if a talkative friend visits. In addition, my
> parents classify their children. My older brother is the "Smart One." I am the
> "Creative One." I think I would do better in school if they expected more, but
> they don't expect much. Therefore, I have not tried very hard.
> Recently I decided to do something about my problem. I discovered that I
> feel less nervous about giving a speech in class if I role-play my presentation
> with a friend. I have also joined a discussion club. As a result, I get a lot of
> practice talking. My problem has causes, so it must have solutions!

2 Connect the following sentences. Use the word(s) in parentheses.

1. Mr. Stewart didn't help me. I never spoke in class. (if)

If Mr. Stewart hadn't helped me, I never would have spoken in class.

2. He believed in me. I became more courageous. (because)

_____

3. We worked in groups. I got used to talking about ideas with classmates. (so)

_____

4. I have gotten a lot of practice. I feel more confident. (as a result)

_____

5. Sena didn't understand the question. She didn't raise her hand. (therefore)

_____

3 Before you write . . .

1. Work with a partner. Discuss the causes of a strong feeling that you have.

   Example: I usually feel excited at the beginning of the school year.

2. Complete this outline for a cause and effect essay.

Paragraph I   The feeling you are going to write about: _____

   One or two examples: _____

Paragraph II   The causes and effects of the feeling:

   A. _____

   B. _____

   C. _____

Paragraph III How you deal with the feeling:

   A. _____

   B. _____

4 Write a three-paragraph essay about the causes and effects of a feeling that you have. Use your outline to organize your writing.

5 Exchange essays with a different partner. Outline your partner's essay. Write questions about anything that is not clear.

6 Work with your partner. Discuss each other's questions from Exercise 5. Then rewrite your own essay and make any necessary corrections.

Review Test

I   *Circle the letter of the correct word(s) to complete each sentence.*

1. I _____ late for work if the bus doesn't arrive soon.   A B Ⓒ D
   (**A**) am   (**C**) 'll be
   (**B**) was   (**D**) 've been

2. I _____ a flight attendant if I didn't get airsick.   Ⓐ B C D
   (**A**) would become   (**C**) become
   (**B**) became   (**D**) had become

3. What do you do when your bus _____ late?   A Ⓑ C D
   (**A**) were   (**C**) would be
   (**B**) is   (**D**) had been

4. If the teacher cancels class today, I _____ you.   A B Ⓒ D
   (**A**) have joined   (**C**) 'll join
   (**B**) could have joined   (**D**) join

5. This flight is full. _____ someone gives up a seat,   A Ⓑ C D
   you won't get on this flight today.
   (**A**) If   (**C**) When
   (**B**) Unless   (**D**) Where

6. If you _____ early enough, we can't save a seat for you.   A B Ⓒ D
   (**A**) 'll check in   (**C**) don't check in
   (**B**) check in   (**D**) have checked in

7. If I hadn't been fascinated with flying, I _____ a pilot.   A B C Ⓓ
   (**A**) would become   (**C**) won't become
   (**B**) became   (**D**) wouldn't have become

8. I'm going to Gerry's for Thanksgiving, but I can't stand to eat turkey.   Ⓐ B C D
   What _____ if that happened to you?
   (**A**) would you do   (**C**) do you do
   (**B**) did you do   (**D**) will you do

(continued)

9. If I _____ you, I'd just go for dessert.   A B (C) D
   (**A**) am   (**C**) were
   (**B**) was   (**D**) had been

10. I'm so busy these days. I wish I _____ more free time.   (A) B C D
    (**A**) had   (**C**) have
    (**B**) had had   (**D**) would have

11. What _____ if you didn't have to work for six months?   (A) B C D
    (**A**) would you do   (**C**) did you do
    (**B**) will you do   (**D**) have you done

12. If I were free for six months, I _____ around the world.   A (B) C D
    (**A**) traveled   (**C**) travel
    (**B**) 'd travel   (**D**) 'll travel

13. It's very hot. If you drink some water, you _____ better.   A B C (D)
    (**A**) feel   (**C**) have felt
    (**B**) felt   (**D**) might feel

14. I _____ nervous whenever I fly.   A (B) C D
    (**A**) would get   (**C**) 'll get
    (**B**) get   (**D**) had gotten

15. Unless the airlines _____ ticket prices, I'm not going to fly anymore.   A B C (D)
    (**A**) don't lower (**C**) would lower
    (**B**) lowered   (**D**) lower

16. Your roommate is really noisy. If I _____ with him, I'd talk to him   (A) B C D
    about the problem.
    (**A**) lived   (**C**) live
    (**B**) 'll live   (**D**) would live

17. If he _____ soon, I'll probably move.   (A) B C D
    (**A**) doesn't change   (**C**) wouldn't change
    (**B**) wouldn't   (**D**) didn't change

18. What would you have done if you _____ the lottery last week?   A (B) C D
    (**A**) win   (**C**) 'd have won
    (**B**) 'd won   (**D**) 'll win

19. Whenever there's a thunderstorm, the cat _____ under the bed.   A B (C) D
    (**A**) is hiding   (**C**) hides
    (**B**) would hide   (**D**) hid

20. I didn't like the hotel. I wish we _____ to stay there.   **A** Ⓑ **C** **D**
    (**A**) haven't decided   (**C**) didn't decide
    (**B**) hadn't decided   (**D**) won't decide

21. Mary _____ the exam unless she had hired a tutor.   Ⓐ **B** **C** **D**
    (**A**) couldn't have passed   (**C**) couldn't pass
    (**B**) can't pass   (**D**) could pass

22. When Carlos has a headache, he _____ some tea.   **A** **B** **C** Ⓓ
    (**A**) would drink   (**C**) 's drunk
    (**B**) drank   (**D**) drinks

23. If Sami doesn't call soon, we _____ without him.   Ⓐ **B** **C** **D**
    (**A**) 're going to leave   (**C**) 'd leave
    (**B**) left   (**D**) 'd have left

II *Complete this conversation with the correct form of the verbs in parentheses.*

A: We had a great time at Drew's house Sunday. Why didn't you come?

B: I had to study for Spanish.

A: If you ___*had come*___ with us, you ___would have seen___ an
           1. (come)   **2. (see)**
awesome movie.

B: Yeah? What?

A: We rented *Back to the Future*. It's about a kid who time-travels back to his parents'

high-school days. He changes his own future. It's so cool. At the end, his parents . . .

B: Wait—don't tell me. If you ___*Tell*___ me the ending, you
                                    3. (tell)
___*'ll spoil*___ it for me. I want to see it myself.
     4. (spoil)

A: OK. But have you ever thought about that?

B: About what?

A: About how things could be different. You grew up here in Baileyville, and you're almost

an adult now. But what ___*would*___ your childhood ___*have been*___ like if
                                                          5. (be)
you ___*had been born*___ in a different family?
        6. (be born)

(continued)

B: Let's see. If I _____ had had _____ a different family, I
7. (have)

_____ wouldn't have grown up _____ here in Baileyville.
8. (not grow up)

A: And if you _____ hadn't grown up _____ here, I _____ wouldn't have met _____ you.
9. (not grow up)   10. (not meet)

B: That's true. But getting back to the here-and-now, how did you do on the Spanish test?

don't pass

A: I flunked. I wish I _____ hadn't taken _____ that course. I'm going to fail.
11. (not take)

B: You just don't study enough. If you _____ study _____ more, you
12. (study)

_____ will pass _____ this course easily this semester.
13. (pass)

A: That's easy for you to say. You always get A's.

B: Sometimes I don't. It's not automatic. I _____ don't get _____ A's unless I
14. (not get)

_____ study _____ .
15. (study)

A: I suppose you're right.

B: If I _____ were _____ you, I _____ would try _____ to get better
16. (be)   17. (try)

grades. It's important for your future.

III *Complete this news article with the correct form of the verbs in parentheses. Choose the affirmative or the negative.*

WHAT WOULD YOU DO?
By Dewitt Rite

Imagine that you are unemployed and have a family to support. What

_____ would _____ you _____ do _____ if you _____ found _____ a wallet in the
1. (do)   2. (find)

street? _____ Would _____ you _____ keep _____ the money if you _____ Knew _____
3. (keep)   4. (know)

no one would ever find out?

When Lara Williams faced that situation last week, she brought the wallet to the police,

who traced it to Mr. and Mrs. Asuki, tourists from Japan. The Asukis were pleasantly

surprised to see the wallet—and their money—again. "If we _____ hadn't gotten _____ the money
5. (get)

back, we _____ money for the rest of our trip. It _____ a long
6. (borrow)   7. (take)

time to pay back that debt," beamed Mrs. Asuki.

The police officer who handled the situation was not surprised, however. "Most people

are honest," commented Lieutenant Kronsky. "If they _____, our job
                                                        8. (be)

_____ even harder than it is."
    9. (be)

Did Mrs. Williams have a hard time making her decision? "Frankly, yes. We need the

money. I _____ Mr. Asuki's wallet in the gutter unless I _____
          10. (see)   11. (look)

down just at that moment. For a little while, it seemed like fate had sent it to us. But each

time I _____ a difficult decision to make, I always _____ the
        12. (have)   13. (discuss)

problem with my husband. We both knew what was right in this situation. We always tell

our kids, if something _____ to you, _____ it. Our kids
                        14. (belong)   15. (return)

_____ the rules unless we _____ the rules ourselves."
    16. (follow)   17. (obey)

The Asukis have offered the Williamses a reward, and a friendship has sprung up

between the two families. "If the Williams family ever _____ to Japan, they
                                                        18. (come)

_____ our guests," said Mr. and Mrs. Asuki.
    19. (be)

IV *Rewrite each sentence or group of sentences as a wish.*

1. I want spring vacation to last six months.

I wish spring vacation lasted six months.

2. I didn't buy business-class tickets. I'm sorry I didn't.

I wish I bought business-class tickets.

3. Oh, no. The in-flight movie is *Back to the Future IV*. I hate that one.

_____

4. I'm sorry that we went to Disney World on vacation.

_____

5. The beach is a better place to go.

_____

6. Florida's nice. I'd like to live there.

_____

7. Maybe my office can transfer me to Orlando.

_____

V *Each sentence has four underlined words or phrases. The four underlined parts of the sentences are marked A, B, C, or D. Circle the letter of the <u>one</u> underlined part that is NOT CORRECT.*

1. <u>Whenever</u> we <u>will get</u> a long <u>holiday</u>, my family <u>takes</u> a trip.　　A ⓑ C D
    A　　　　B　　　　　C　　　　　　　D

2. We <u>always</u> <u>went</u> camping <u>if</u> we don't <u>get</u> a lot of time off.　　A Ⓑ C D
      A　　B　　　　　C　　　　　D

3. <u>Unless</u> we <u>had</u> <u>gone</u> to Florida last year, I wouldn't <u>had known</u> how　　A B C D
    A　　　　B　　C

    great Disney World was.

4. If I <u>am</u> older, I <u>would</u> <u>try</u> <u>to get</u> a job in Florida.　　A B C D
       A　　　　　B　　　C　　D

5. We <u>could</u> <u>had</u> seen <u>more</u> if the lines <u>had been</u> shorter.　　A B C D
      A　　B　　　　C　　　　　　D

6. I <u>wish</u> my friend <u>could have</u> <u>came</u> with us when we <u>went</u> last year.　　A B C D
     A　　　　　　B　　　C　　　　　　　　D

7. <u>Unless</u> you're interested in the movies, you <u>can</u> <u>visit</u> Universal Studios　　
    A　　　　　　　　　　　　　　　　　B　　C

    and <u>see</u> all the movie sets.　　A B C D
       D

8. <u>If</u> you stay a <u>week</u>, you <u>would</u> <u>have</u> more time to do things.　　A B C D
    A　　　　　B　　　　C　　　D

▶ *To check your answers, go to Answer Key on page RT-5.*

PART
X

Indirect Speech
and Embedded Questions

25 Direct and Indirect Speech

Grammar in Context

BEFORE YOU READ

🎧 *Look at the photo and read what the woman is saying. Is it ever all right to tell a lie? If so, in what situations? Read this magazine article about lying.*

THE TRUTH ABOUT LYING

BY JENNIFER MORALES

At 9:00, a supervisor from Rick Spivak's bank telephoned and **said Rick's credit card payment was late**. **"The check is in the mail,"** Rick **replied** quickly. At 11:45, Rick left for a 12 o'clock meeting across town. Arriving late, Rick **told his client that traffic had been bad**. That evening, Rick's fiancée, Ann, came home with a new haircut. Rick hated it. **"It looks great,"** he **said**.

Three lies in one day! Does Rick have a problem? Or is he just an ordinary guy? Each time, he **told himself that sometimes the truth causes too many problems**. Most of us tell white lies—harmless untruths that help us avoid trouble. These are our four most common reasons:

◆ To get something more quickly or to avoid unpleasant situations: **"I have to have that report by 5:00 today,"** or **"I tried to call you, but your cell phone was turned off."**

◆ To appear nicer or more interesting to a new friend or to feel better about yourself: **"I run a mile every day,"** or **"I'm looking better these days."**

◆ To make a polite excuse: **"I'd love to go to your party, but I have to work."**

◆ To protect someone else's feelings: **"Your hair looks great that way!"**

He **said my hair looked great this way!**

Is telling lies a new trend? In one survey, the majority of people **said that people were more honest in the past**. Nevertheless, lying wasn't really born yesterday. In the 18th century, the French philosopher Vauvenargues told the truth about lying when he **wrote, "All men are born truthful and die liars."**

AFTER YOU READ

Find the situations in the article. Check the person's exact words.

1. The supervisor at Rick's bank (to Rick):
   - ☐ "His credit card payment was late."
   - ☑ "Your credit card payment is late."

2. Rick (to his client):
   - ☐ "Traffic had been bad."
   - ☑ "Traffic was bad."

3. Many people (to a new friend):
   - ☐ "You run a mile every day."
   - ☑ "I run a mile every day."

4. People answering a survey question:
   - ☐ "That people were more honest ten years ago."
   - ☑ "People were more honest ten years ago."

Grammar Presentation

DIRECT AND INDIRECT SPEECH

Direct Speech		
Direct Statement	**Subject**	**Reporting Verb**
"The check **is** in the mail," "The haircut **looks** great," "The traffic **was** bad,"	he	**said**.

Indirect Speech				
Subject	**Reporting Verb**	**Noun/ Pronoun**		**Indirect Statement**
He	**told**	the bank Ann her	**(that)**	the check **was** in the mail. the haircut **looked** great. the traffic **had been** bad.
	said			

GRAMMAR NOTES

EXAMPLES

1. **Direct speech** (also called *quoted speech*) states the <u>exact words</u> that a speaker used. In writing, put <u>quotation marks</u> before and after the speech you are quoting. The quotation can go at the beginning or at the end of the sentence.	• **"The check is in the mail,"** he said. • **"I like that tie,"** she told him. • He said, **"The traffic is bad."** OR • **"The traffic is bad,"** he said.

2. **Indirect speech** (also called *reported speech*) reports what a speaker said <u>without using the exact words</u>. The word ***that*** can introduce indirect speech. ▶ **BE CAREFUL!** Do not use quotation marks when writing indirect speech.	• He said **the check was in the mail**. • She told him **she liked that tie**. • He said ***that*** **the check was in the mail**. • She told him ***that*** **she liked that tie**. • She said **she had to work**. NOT She said ~~"she had to work."~~

3. **Reporting verbs** (such as ***say*** or ***tell***) are usually in the <u>simple past</u> for both direct and indirect speech. USAGE NOTE: When you mention the listener, it is more common to use ***tell*** than ***said***. ▶ **BE CAREFUL!** Do not use ***tell*** when you don't mention the listener.	**DIRECT SPEECH** • "It's a great haircut," he **said**. **INDIRECT SPEECH** • He **said** it was a great haircut. • He **told** her that it was a great haircut. • "I'm sorry to be late," Rick **told *Ann***. • He **said** he had been sick. NOT He ~~told~~ he had been sick.

4. When the reporting verb is in the <u>simple past</u> (*said, told*) in indirect speech, we often **change the verb tense** the speaker used. The <u>simple present</u> becomes the <u>simple past</u>. The <u>simple past</u> becomes the <u>past perfect</u>.	 **DIRECT SPEECH** • "I only ***buy*** shoes on sale," she **said**. **INDIRECT SPEECH** • She **said** she only ***bought*** shoes on sale. **DIRECT SPEECH** • "I ***found*** a great store," she **said**. **INDIRECT SPEECH** • She **said** she ***had found*** a great store.

5. You do not have to change the tense when you report:

a. something that was **just said**.

> **A:** **I'm** tired from all this shopping.
> **B:** What did you say?
> **A:** I **said** I**'m** tired.
> > OR
> I **said** I *was* tired.

b. something that is **still true**.

> • Rick **said** the bank *wants* a check.
> > OR
> • Rick **said** the bank *wanted* a check.

c. a **general truth** or **scientific law**.

> • Mrs. Smith **told** her students that water *freezes* at 0° Celsius.
> > OR
> • Mrs. Smith **told** her students that water *froze* at 0° Celsius.

6. When the reporting verb is in the <u>simple present</u>, **do not change the verb tense** in indirect speech.

USAGE NOTE: In newspapers, magazines, and on the TV and radio news, reporting verbs are often in the simple present.

> **DIRECT SPEECH**
> **Ann:** I *run* a mile every day.
>
> **INDIRECT SPEECH**
> • Ann **says** that she *runs* a mile every day. NOT Ann says that she ~~ran~~ a mile every day.
> • Fifty-seven percent of women **report** that they always *tell* the truth.

7. In **indirect speech**, make changes in **pronouns and possessives** to keep the speaker's <u>original meaning</u>.

> • Rick told Ann, "**I** like **your** haircut."
> • Rick told Ann that *he* liked *her* haircut.

Reference Notes
For the **punctuation rules for direct speech**, see Appendix 26 on page A-13.
For additional **tense changes in indirect speech**, see Unit 26, page 382.
For a list of **reporting verbs**, see Appendix 13 on page A-5.

Focused Practice

1 | DISCOVER THE GRAMMAR

Read this magazine article about lying on the job. Circle the reporting verbs. Underline the examples of direct speech once. Underline the examples of indirect speech twice.

"Lying during a job interview is risky business," (says) Martha Toledo, director of the management consulting firm Maxwell. "The truth has a funny way of coming out." Toledo tells the story of one woman applying for a job as an office manager. The woman told the interviewer that she had a B.A. degree. Actually, she was eight credits short. She also said that she had made $50,000 at her last job. The truth was $10,000 less. "Many firms really do check facts," warns Toledo. In this case, a call to the applicant's company revealed the discrepancies.

Toledo relates a story about another job applicant, George. During an interview, George reported that he had quit his last job. George landed the new job and was doing well until the company hired another employee, Pete. George and Pete had worked at the same company. Pete eventually told his boss that his old company had fired George.

2 | CONFESSIONS

Grammar Notes 3, 6–7

Complete the student's essay with the correct words.

Once when I was a teenager, I went to my Aunt Leah's house. Aunt Leah collected pottery, and as soon as I got there, she _____told_____ me she _____wanted_____ to show me
1. (said / told)   2. (wants / wanted)

_____ new bowl. She _____ she _____ just bought it.
3. (my / her)   4. (said / told)   5. (has / had)

It was beautiful. When Aunt Leah went to answer the door, I picked up the bowl to examine it. It slipped from my hands and smashed to pieces on the floor. As Aunt Leah walked back into the

room, I screamed and _____ that the cat had just broken _____ new
6. (said / told)   7. (her / your)

bowl. Aunt Leah got this funny look on her face and _____ me that it really
8. (said / told)

_____ very important.
9. (isn't / wasn't)

I didn't sleep at all that night, and the next morning I called my aunt and _____
10. (said / told)

her that I had broken _____ bowl. She said _____ 'd known that all
11. (her / your)   12. (I / she)

along. We still laugh about the story today.

3 | TO BE HONEST

Grammar Notes 3, 6–7

Look at the pictures. Rewrite the statements as indirect speech. Use **said** *as the reporting verb and make necessary changes in the verbs and pronouns.*

1.

   She said it was her own recipe.

2.

   that

   He said ~~his~~ car ~~was~~ brok down.
   he said his car had broken down.

3.

   He said ~~that~~ he had to drive his
   aunt to the airport.

4.

   she   *she*
   ~~He~~ said That ~~he~~ exercised every day.
                    or   es

5.

   He said That He just mailed The check
           or
           had just mailed

6.

   He said That she is 35
            or
            was

4 | **THEN SHE SAID**   *Grammar Notes 3–7*

Rewrite Lisa and Ben's conversation using indirect speech. Use the reporting verbs in parentheses. Make necessary changes in the verbs and pronouns.

1. LISA: I just heard about a job at a scientific research company.

(tell) *She told him she had just heard about a job at a scientific research company.*

2. BEN: Oh, I majored in science at Florida State.

(say) *He said that he had majored in science at Florida State.*

3. LISA: The starting salary is good.

(say) She said that the starting salary was (or is) good.

4. BEN: I need more money. *or needs*

(say) He said that he ~~had~~ needed more money.

5. LISA: They want someone with some experience as a programmer.

She said (say) *that* they wanted (want) someone with some ~~

6. BEN: Well, I work as a programmer for Data Systems.

(tell) He told her (that) he worked (works) as a prog ~~

7. LISA: Oh—they need a college graduate.

(say) She said that they ~~had~~ *need* needed a college graduate.

8. BEN: Well, I graduated from Florida State.

(tell) He told her (that) He had graduated ~~

9. LISA: But they don't want a recent graduate.

(say) She said that They didn't (don't) want a ~~

10. BEN: I got my degree four years ago.

(tell) He Told her (that) He had gotten his degree ~~

11. LISA: It sounds like the right job for you.

(tell) She Told him (that) It had sounded like ~~

12. BEN: I think so too.

(say) He said That he had Thought ~~

5 | EDITING

Read this article. There are <u>eight</u> mistakes in the use of direct and indirect speech. The first mistake is already corrected. Find and correct seven more.

WARNING!!!! THIS MESSAGE IS A HOAX!!!!!

Everyone gets urgent e-mail messages. They tell you that Bill
Gates now ~~wanted~~ *wants* to give away his money—to YOU! They say *tell*
you that a popular floor cleaner kills family pets. They report *reported* that
your computer monitor *has* had taken photographs of you. Since I'm
a good-hearted person, I used to forward these e-mails to all my
friends. Not long ago, a very annoyed friend *explained* explains that the
story about killer bananas was a hoax (an untrue story). He told
me about these common telltale signs of hoaxes:

! The e-mail always says that it *is* was very urgent. It has lots of
exclamation points.

! It tells *you* that it is not a hoax and quotes important people.
(The quotations are false.)

! It urges you to send the e-mail to everyone you know.

He also told *said* that *Hoaxbusters* (http://hoaxbusters.org) had lists of
Internet hoaxes. You can avoid the embarrassment of forwarding
all your friends a false warning. So, before *you* announce that
sunscreen *has* had made people blind, check out the story on
Hoaxbusters!

Communication Practice

6 | LISTENING

Read Lisa's weekly planner. Then listen to the conversations. Lisa wasn't always honest. Listen again and notice the differences between what Lisa said and the truth. Then write sentences about Lisa's white lies.

SATURDAY		MONDAY
Morning		Morning
Afternoon		Afternoon
Evening	*6:00 date with Ben!*	*6:00 Vegetarian Society meeting* Evening
		7:30 dinner with Chris
SUNDAY	*sleep late!*	**TUESDAY**
Morning	*9:00 ~~aerobics class~~*	Morning
Afternoon		*4:00 weekly staff* Afternoon
		meeting – present sales report
Evening		Evening

1. _She said her parents were in town, but she has a date with Ben._
2. _She said she had never missed class. - she is going to sleep_
3. _____
4. _____

7 | WHY LIE?

Review the four reasons for lying described in "The Truth About Lying" on page 368. Work in small groups. Is it OK to lie in these four circumstances? Give examples from your own experience to support your ideas.

Example: Once my friend told me that my haircut looked great, but it really looked awful. I think she should have told me the truth. Now it's hard for me to believe anything she says.

8 | HONESTY QUESTIONNAIRE

Complete the questionnaire. Then work in groups. Summarize your group's results and report them to the rest of the class.

	Always	Usually	Sometimes	Rarely	Never
1. I tell the truth to my friends.					
2. I tell the truth to my family.					
3. It's OK to lie on the job.					
4. "White lies" protect people's feelings.					
5. Most people are honest.					
6. It's best to tell the truth.					
7. I tell people my real age.					
8. My friends are honest with me.					
9. It's difficult to tell a convincing lie.					
10. Politicians are honest.					
11. Doctors tell their patients the whole truth.					
12. I answer questionnaires honestly.					

Example: Five of us said that we usually told the truth.
Only one of us said it was always best to tell the truth.

9 | TO TELL THE TRUTH

Play this game as a class. Three "contestants" leave the room. They choose one experience to report to the class. Only one contestant has actually had the experience. The other two must tell convincing lies to make the class believe that they have had the experience.

After the contestants choose the experience, they go back into the room and sit in front of the class. Each contestant states the experience. Then class members ask each contestant detailed questions about it.

Example: CONTESTANT A: Once I climbed a 10,000-meter-high mountain.
CONTESTANT B: Once I climbed a 10,000-meter-high mountain.
CONTESTANT C: Once I climbed a 10,000-meter-high mountain.
CLASS MEMBER: Contestant A, how long did it take you?
Contestant B, how long did it take *you*?
Contestant C, how many people were with you?

After each contestant has answered questions, the class decides which contestant is telling the truth. Class members explain which statements convinced them that a contestant was lying or telling the truth.

Example: I believed Contestant A because she said that it had taken her two days.
I think Contestant C was lying. He said he'd climbed the mountain alone.

10 | QUOTABLE QUOTES

*In groups, discuss these famous quotations about lying. Do you agree with them? Give examples to support your opinion. Use **says** to report the proverbs and **said** to report the ideas of individuals.*

All men are born truthful and die liars.
   —*Vauvenargues (French philosopher, 1715–1747)*

> **Example:** Vauvenargues said that all men are born truthful and die liars.
>   I agree because babies don't lie, but children and adults do.

A half truth is a whole lie.
   —*Jewish proverb*

A little inaccuracy saves tons of explanation.
   —*Saki (British short-story writer, 1870–1916)*

A liar needs a good memory.
   —*Quintilian (first-century Roman orator)*

The man who speaks the truth is always at ease.
   —*Persian proverb*

The cruelest lies are often told in silence.
   —*Robert Louis Stevenson (Scottish novelist, 1850–1894)*

11 | WRITING

Read the conversation between Rick and Ann. Then write a paragraph reporting what they said. Use direct and indirect speech.

RICK: Hi, honey. Sorry I'm late.

ANN: That's all right. I made liver and onions. It's almost ready.

RICK: *(looking upset)* It smells great, honey. It's one of my favorites.

ANN: You look upset!

RICK: I'm OK. I had a rough day at work. Oh, I stopped and bought some frogs' legs for dinner on Wednesday. It's my turn to cook.

ANN: *(looking upset)* That's interesting. I look forward to trying them.

> **Example:** Rick came home and said he was sorry he was late. Ann said that was all right.

12 | ON THE INTERNET

  A hoax *is an untrue story or a trick that makes people believe something that is untrue. There are many e-mail hoaxes on the Internet. Do a search on* **Internet hoaxes** *and find some common hoaxes. Report them to a group.*

> **Example:** One e-mail hoax said that an Internet site had everybody's passport information.
>   Another one said people had caught a terrible disease by breathing fresh air.

Indirect Speech: Tense Changes

Grammar in Context

BEFORE YOU READ

🎧 *Look at the photos on this page and the next. What is happening? What do you think the title of the article means? Read this article from a news magazine.*

THE FLOOD OF THE CENTURY

Central Europe

July was hot and dry. Then, in August, the skies opened. Writing from Berlin on August 13, 2002, journalist John Hooper reported **that it had been raining for more than 24 hours straight**. A huge weather system was dumping rain on eastern and central Europe. Berliners worried not only about their own city but also about Prague and Dresden, the homes of priceless art and architectural treasures. Hooper noted **that evacuations had already started in Prague and were beginning in Dresden**.

As Hooper wrote his story, 50,000 residents were streaming out of Prague, and the 16th century Charles Bridge was in danger of collapsing. Still, Mayor Igor Nemec told reporters **that the historic Old Town should remain safe**. Dr. Irena Kopencova wasn't that optimistic. She was sloshing through the National Library of the Czech Republic in rubber boots, grabbing old manuscripts. She said sadly **that many original copies of the most treasured poems in the Czech language had been lost**.

(continued)

Prague under water

THE FLOOD OF THE CENTURY

A few days later, Dresden was battling its worst flood since 1501. Heiko Ringel stopped stacking sandbags to talk to reporter Julian Coman of the *News Telegraph*. Ringel didn't live in Dresden anymore, but he said **he was back in his hometown that summer to help**. Why? He couldn't stand seeing all that history swept away. He said **it would have been too cruel to bear**. "Dresden and Prague are the twin jewels of Central Europe."

All over Dresden, museum staff rushed items to the top floors. Egyptian stone tablets lay jumbled with Roman statues,

Saving art

and masterpieces by Rembrandt were stacked 10 deep on top of paintings by Rubens. Museum director Martin Rohl still worried. He told Coman **that with another few feet of water, nothing would be safe**.

The danger didn't stop tourism. "Flood tourists" moved from city to city gaping at the flood of the century. One speculated **that it might even be the flood of the millennium**. John Hooper didn't agree. He thought climate change was causing these events, and believed that they would get worse. His headline announced **that summer 2002 would go down in history as the time weather had changed forever**.

Was Hooper right? Were the floods of 2002 just the beginning of worse and worse disasters caused by global warming? Or were they "normal disasters" that we should expect once every 100 years? Right after the floods, statistical studies claimed **that floods were not getting worse, but that flood damage was increasing**. They concluded **that people ought to stop building so close to water**. Then, in 2003, thousands died in Europe in a heat wave that even statistics could not call "normal." By 2004, more and more scientists were warning **that governments had to do something about climate change**. The summers of 2002 and 2003 had already shown us how much we could lose if we don't listen.

AFTER YOU READ

Check the exact words that people in the article said or wrote.

1. John Hooper said:

- ☑ "It had been raining for more than 24 hours."
- ☑ "It has been raining for more than 24 hours."

2. Heiko Ringel said:

- ☑ "I'm back in my hometown this summer to help."
- ☐ "He's back in his hometown this summer to help."

3. Martin Rohl said:

☐ "With another few feet of water, nothing was safe."

☑ "With another few feet of water, nothing will be safe."

4. Scientists said:

☑ "Governments have to do something about climate change."

☐ "Governments had to do something about climate change."

Grammar Presentation

INDIRECT SPEECH: TENSE CHANGES

Direct Speech			Indirect Speech			
Subject	Reporting Verb	Direct Statement	Subject	Reporting Verb	Noun/ Pronoun	Indirect Statement
He	said,	"I **live** in Dresden." "I **moved** here in June." "I'**m looking** for an apartment." "I'**ve started** a new job." "I'**m going to stay** here." "I'**ll invite** you for the holidays." "We **can go** to museums." "I **may look** for a roommate." "I **should get back** to work." "I **have to finish** my report." "You **must come** to visit." "We **ought to see** each other more often."	He	told said	Jim me you him her us them	(that)	he **lived** in Dresden. he **had moved** there in June. he **was looking** for an apartment. he **had started** a new job. he **was going to stay** there. he **would invite** me/us for the holidays. we **could go** to museums. he **might look** for a roommate. he **should get back** to work. he **had to finish** his report. I/we **had to come** to visit. we **ought to see** each other more often.

GRAMMAR NOTES   **EXAMPLES**

---

1. As you learned in Unit 25, when the reporting verb is in the <u>simple past</u>, the **verb tense** in the indirect speech statement often **changes**.

DIRECT SPEECH		INDIRECT SPEECH	DIRECT SPEECH	INDIRECT SPEECH
Simple present	→	Simple past	He said, "It**'s** cloudy."	He said it **was** cloudy.
Present progressive	→	Past progressive	She said, "A storm **is coming**."	She said a storm **was coming**.
Simple past	→	Past perfect	He said, "Klaus **called**."	He said that Klaus **had called**.
Present perfect	→	Past perfect	She told him, "I**'ve heard** the news."	She told him that she**'d heard** the news.

---

2. Modals often change in indirect speech.

DIRECT SPEECH		INDIRECT SPEECH	DIRECT SPEECH	INDIRECT SPEECH
will	→	*would*	I said, "The winds **will be** strong."	I said the winds **would be** strong.
can	→	*could*	"You **can stay** with us," they told us.	They told us we **could stay** with them.
may	→	*might*	He said, "The storm **may last** all night."	He said that the storm **might last** all night.
must	→	*had to*	"You **must leave**," he told us.	He told us that we **had to leave**.

---

3. The following **do not change** in indirect speech:

	DIRECT SPEECH	INDIRECT SPEECH
a. *should*, *could*, *might*, and *ought to*	"You **should listen** to the news," he told us.	He told us that we **should listen** to the news.
b. the past perfect	"I **had moved** here a week before the flood," he said.	He said that he **had moved** here a week before the flood.
c. the present and past unreal conditional	"If I **knew**, I **would tell** you," said Jim.	Jim said if he **knew**, he **would tell** me.
	"If I **had known**, I **would have told** you," said Jim.	He said that if he **had known,** he **would have told** me.
d. past modals	"I **should have left**."	He said that he **should have left**.
	"We **couldn't have known**."	They said they **couldn't have known**.

4. **Change time words** in indirect speech to keep the speaker's <u>original meaning</u>.

DIRECT SPEECH		INDIRECT SPEECH
now	→	**then**
today	→	**that day**
tomorrow	→	**the next day**
yesterday	→	**the day before**
this week / month / year	→	**that week / month / year**
last week / month / year	→	**the week / month / year before**
next week / month / year	→	**the following week / month / year**

Uta to Klaus:
- "I just got home **yesterday**. I'll start cleaning up **tomorrow**."

Klaus to Heiko (a few days later):
- Uta told me she had just gotten home **the day before**. She said she would start cleaning up **the next day**.

Lotte to her mother (right after the storm):
- "Our home won't be repaired until **next month**."

The family newsletter (two months later):
- Lotte reported that their home wouldn't be repaired until **the following month**.

5. **Change *here*** and ***this*** in indirect speech to keep the speaker's <u>original meaning</u>.

DIRECT SPEECH		INDIRECT SPEECH
here	→	**there**
this	→	**that**

Jim (in Athens) to Erica (in Berlin):
- I love it **here**. **This** climate is great.

Erica to Susan (both in Berlin):
- Jim said he loved it **there**. He told me that **that** climate was great.

Reference Note
For a list of **reporting verbs**, see Appendix 13 on page A-5.

Focused Practice

1 | DISCOVER THE GRAMMAR

Read the sentences in indirect speech. Then circle the letter of the direct speech that is being reported.

1. The local weather forecaster said that it was going to be a terrible storm.

   a. "It was going to be a terrible storm."

   b. "It's going to be a terrible storm."

   c. "It was a terrible storm."

2. She said the winds might reach 60 kilometers per hour.

   a. "The winds reached 60 kilometers per hour."

   b. "The winds would reach 60 kilometers per hour."

   c. "The winds may reach 60 kilometers per hour."

(continued)

3. She said there would be more rain the next day.

    a. "There will be more rain the next day."

✓ **b.** "There would be more rain tomorrow."

✓ **c.** "There will be more rain tomorrow."

4. She told people that they should try to leave the area.

✓ **a.** "You should try to leave the area."

    b. "You should have tried to leave the area."

    c. "You would leave the area."

5. She reported that people were leaving the city.

✓ **a.** "People are leaving the city."

    b. "People were leaving the city."

    c. "People left the city."

6. She said that they could expect a lot of damage. *direct speech*

✓ **a.** "We could expect a lot of damage."

    b. "We could have expected a lot of damage."

✓ **c.** "We can expect a lot of damage."

7. She said that the floods were the worst they had had there.

    a. "The floods are the worst we have here."

✓ **b.** "The floods are the worst we have had here."

    c. "The floods are the worst we have had there."

8. She told them that the emergency relief workers had arrived the day before.

    a. "Emergency relief workers arrived the day before."

✓ **b.** "Emergency relief workers arrived yesterday."

    c. "Emergency relief workers arrived today."

9. She reported that the president would be there to inspect the damage.

✓ **a.** "The president will be here to inspect the damage."

    b. "The president will be there to inspect the damage."

    c. "The president would be there to inspect the damage."

10. She said that if they hadn't had time to prepare, the danger would have been even greater.

    a. "If we hadn't had time to prepare, the danger would have been even greater."

    b. "If we don't have time to prepare, the danger will be even greater."

✓ **c.** "If we didn't have time to prepare, the danger would be even greater."

2 | RUMORS

You are in Berlin. Imagine you heard these rumors yesterday, and you are reporting them today. Use **They said** *to report the rumors.*

1. "The storm changed direction last night."

   They said that the storm had changed direction the night before.

2. "It's going to pass north of here."

   They said that it was going to pass north of here

3. "The gas station ran out of gasoline this afternoon."

   They said that the gas station had run out of gasoline that afternoon.

4. "It's not really a hurricane, just a big storm."

   They said that it wasnot really a hurricane, just a big storm.

5. "They've closed the bridge because of rising water."

   They said that they had closed the bridge because of rising water.

6. "They won't restore the electricity until tomorrow."

   They said that they wouldn't restore —— until today.

7. "They can't reopen the schools for at least a week."

   They said that they couldn't reopen the schools ——.

8. "You ought to use bottled water for a few days."

   They said that we ought to use —— .

3 | FIGHTING FLOODS

Read this interview between radio station WWEA and meteorologist Dr. Ronald Myers.

WWEA: Exactly how common are floods?

MYERS: Floods are the most common of all natural disasters except fire. They are also the most widespread.

WWEA: What causes them?

MYERS: Usually they are the result of intense, heavy rainfall. But they can also be caused by melting snow. Another cause is unusually high tides in coastal areas.

WWEA: And what causes these high tides?

MYERS: Severe winds over the ocean surface cause high tides. Often the winds are part of a hurricane.

WWEA: What is a *flash flood*? Is it just a very bad flood?

MYERS: No. A flash flood comes with little or no warning. Because of this, it's the most dangerous type of flood. In fact, flash floods cause almost 75 percent of all flood-related deaths.

(continued)

WWEA: That's terrible. Is there anything that can be done?

MYERS: We've made progress in predicting floods. But we must get better at predicting flash floods.

WWEA: Is there anything that can be done to actually prevent floods?

MYERS: People must improve their protection of the Earth and the environment. When we replace grass and soil with roads and buildings, the ground loses its ability to absorb rainfall. This can lead to flooding. In addition, many scientists believe that global warming is causing an increase in the number of floods.

WWEA: So the answer lies in better prediction and better treatment of the Earth?

MYERS: Exactly. We can't completely stop floods from happening. It's part of nature. But we *can* help to predict them and to prevent their number from increasing.

Now read the following statements. For each statement write **That's right** *or* **That's wrong** *and report what Dr. Myers said.*

1. Floods are not very common.

   That's wrong. He said floods were the most common of all natural disasters except fire.

2. They are very widespread.

   That's right. she said floods were the most widespread.

3. Floods are usually caused by melting snow.

   Thatswrong. He said usually They were the result of intents. heavy rainfall.

4. A flash flood is just a very bad flood.

   Thatswrong sHe said That flash flood came with little or no warning.

5. A flash flood is the most dangerous type of flood.

   ThaTs right. He said flood was The most dangerous Type of flood

6. Flash floods cause 25 percent of all flood-related deaths.

   That's wrong. she said flash floods caused almost 75 percen —

7. We have made progress in predicting floods.

   That's right she said They had made progress in predicting floods.

8. People are doing a good job of protecting the Earth and the environment.

   That's wrong she said people had to improve their protection of the Earth and The Environment

9. Replacing grass and dirt with roads and buildings can lead to flooding.

   ThaTs right He said They

10. Many scientists believe that global warming is causing an increase in the number of floods.

    ThaTs right. He said many scientists believed that warming was causing

11. We can completely stop floods from happening.

    Thats wrong He said we couldn't completely

flesh= meat   flush = Toilet

flash = camera

weather advisery

4 | WEATHER REPORTS

Grammar Notes 1–5

Klaus and Eva live in Germany. Read the information that Klaus got during the day. Then write what people said. Use direct speech.

Klaus's mother called. She told him that she was listening to the weather report. She said that she was worried about Klaus and Eva. She told him that if they weren't so stubborn they'd pack up and leave right then.

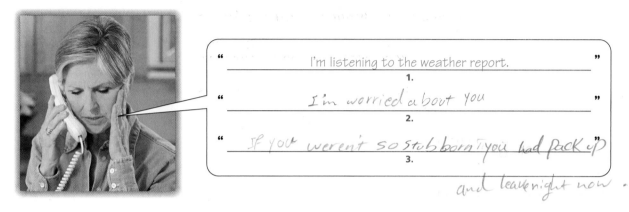

" I'm listening to the weather report. "
1.

" I'm worried about you "
2.

" If you weren't so stubborn you had pack up "
3.

and leave right now .

Klaus's father gave him some good advice. He said he'd had some experience with floods. He said Klaus and Eva had to put sandbags in front of their doors. He also told Klaus that they ought to fill the sinks and bathtubs with clean water. He said they should buy a lot of batteries.

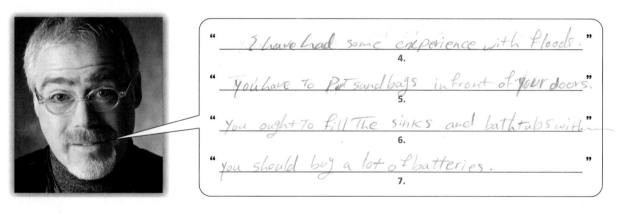

" I have had some experience with floods. "
4.

" You have to put sandbags in front of your doors. "
5.

" You ought to fill the sinks and bathtubs with "
6.

" You should buy a lot of batteries. "
7.

Stefan called. He and Uta are worried. Their place is too close to the river. They said that they couldn't stay there, and they told Klaus that they wanted to stay with him and Eva. They said they were leaving that night. They told Klaus they should have called him and Eva sooner.

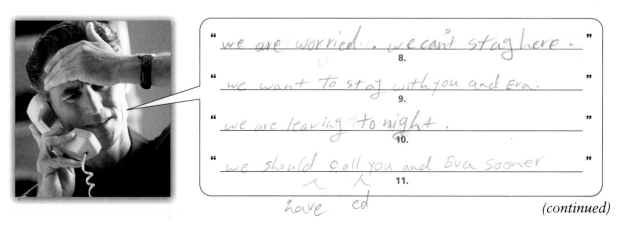

" we are worried. we can't stay here . "
8.

" we want to stay with you and Eva. "
9.

" we are leaving tonight . "
10.

" we should call you and Eva sooner "
11.
have   ed

(continued)

Klaus listened to the weather advisory in the afternoon. The forecaster said the storm would hit that night. She warned that the rainfall was going to be very heavy, and she said that the storm might last for several hours.

" *The storm will hit tonight.* "
          12.

" *The rainfall is going to be very heavy* "
          13.

" *The storm may last for several hours.* "
          14.

---

5 | EDITING

Read this student's report. There are <u>nine</u> mistakes in the use of indirect speech. The first mistake is already corrected. Find and correct eight more.

> What is it like to live through a flood? For my report, I interviewed the
>
> Nemec family, who experienced last month's floods in our city. They reported
>
>   *they*
> that ~~we~~ had experienced fear and sadness. On September 14, the family went to
>   *couldn't*
> a movie. Jerzy, a high school student, said they can't drive the car home
>   *us*
> because their street was flooded. He told it had happened in only three hours.
>   *had*
> Mrs. Nemec said that all their belongings were ruined, but that their cat has
>
> gone to an upstairs bedroom. They were sad about losing so many things, but
>   *would*
> she said she will have been much sadder to lose the family pet. Jerzy's father
>
> also said it had been a complete mess here, and the family had worked all this
>
> week to clean out the house. Anna, who is in junior high school, wanted to keep
>
> her old dollhouse. It had belonged to her mother and her mother's mother. At
>
> first, her father told her that she can't keep it because seeing it would just
>
> make her sad. Anna replied that she saw memories in that dollhouse—not just
>
> broken wood. In the end, they kept it. Mrs. Nemec said that Anna had taught
>
> them something important today.

Communication Practice

6 | LISTENING

∩ *Work in groups of four. Listen to the weather advisory. Listen again and check the correct information. It's all right to leave something blank. After you listen, pool your information.*

Schools

1. Today schools ☑ closed at 10:00. ☐ will close at 1:00.
2. Students and teachers ☐ should stay at school. ☑ should go home immediately.
3. Tomorrow schools ☐ will open. ☑ may stay closed.

Roads

4. Road conditions ☐ are safe. ☑ are dangerous.
5. Drivers must ☑ drive slowly. ☐ pick up passengers.
6. Everyone should ☑ avoid driving. ☐ continue driving.

Public Offices

7. Libraries ☐ will stay open. ☑ will close at 1:00.
8. Post offices ☑ will stay open until 5:00. ☐ will close early.
9. Government offices ☑ will be closed tomorrow. ☐ will remain open tomorrow.

Businesses

10. Banks ☑ will close at noon. ☐ will stay open until 3:00.
11. Gas stations ☐ will close at noon. ☑ will stay open until evening.
12. Supermarkets ☑ are open now. ☐ are closed now.

Now compare your information with what other group members heard. Complete any missing information in your chart. Then listen again and check your answers.

> **Example:** A: She said that schools would close at 1:00.
> B: That's not right. She said that schools had closed at 10:00.

7 | TELEPHONE GAME

Work in groups of six to ten students. Student A whispers something in the ear of Student B. Student B reports (in a whisper) what he or she heard to Student C. Each student reports to the next student in a whisper and may only say the information once. Expect surprises— people often hear things inaccurately or report them differently from what was said. The last student tells the group what he or she heard.

> **Example:** A: There won't be any class tomorrow.
> B: He said that there wouldn't be any class tomorrow.
> C: She said that there'd be a guest in class tomorrow.

8 INTERVIEW

Use the questions below to interview three of your classmates. Report your findings to the class.

Have you ever experienced an extreme weather condition or other natural phenomenon such as the following?

a hurricane or typhoon	a flood
very hot weather	a sandstorm
very cold weather	an earthquake
a drought	other: _____

- How did you feel?
- What did you do to protect yourself?
- What advice would you give to someone in the same situation?

Example: Arielle told me she had experienced a very hot summer when temperatures reached over 40°C. She told me that she had felt sick a lot of the time. She said she had stayed indoors until evening every day. Arielle told me that everyone should move slowly and drink a lot of liquids in hot weather.

9 WRITING

Write a paragraph reporting someone else's experience in an extreme weather condition or natural phenomenon. You can use information from your interview in Exercise 8, or you can interview another person. Use indirect speech.

Example: My friend Julie told me about a dust storm in Australia. She said that one afternoon, the sky had gotten very dark and the wind had started to blow hard. Her mother told her that they all had to go inside right away and close all the windows. Then . . .

10 ON THE INTERNET

Do a search to find tomorrow's weather forecast for your city or town. Take notes. Report to your classmates two days from now. What did the forecast say? Was it accurate?

Example: The forecast said it would be partly cloudy in the morning and that the sun was going to come out in the afternoon. It was cloudy in the morning, but then it rained.

Indirect Instructions, Commands, Requests, and Invitations

Grammar in Context

BEFORE YOU READ

🎧 *Look at the photo. What time is it? Where is the man? How does he feel? Why does he feel that way? Read this transcript of a radio interview with the director of a sleep clinic.*

HERE'S TO YOUR HEALTH

THE SNOOZE NEWS

CONNIE: Good morning! This is Connie Sung, bringing you "Here's to Your Health," a program about today's health issues. This morning, we've invited Dr. Thorton Ray **to talk to us about insomnia**. Dr. Ray is the director of the Sleep Disorders Clinic. Welcome to the show!

DR. RAY: Thanks, Connie. It's great to be here.

CONNIE: Your book *Night Shift* will be coming out soon. In it, you tell people **to pay more attention to sleep disorders**. What's the big deal about losing a little sleep?

DR. RAY: I always tell people **to think of the biggest industrial disaster that they've ever heard about**. Usually it was caused at least in part by sleep deprivation. Then I ask them **to think about what can happen if they drive when they're tired**. Every year, up to 200,000 automobile accidents in this country are caused by drowsy drivers.

CONNIE: Wow! That *is* a big problem.

DR. RAY: And a costly one. We figure that fatigue costs businesses about $70 million a year.

(*continued*)

HERE'S TO YOUR HEALTH

CONNIE: That's astounding! But getting back to the personal level, if I came to your clinic, what would you advise me **to do**?

DR. RAY: First, I would find out about some of your habits. If you drank coffee or cola late in the day, I would tell you **to stop**. Caffeine interferes with sleep.

CONNIE: What about old-fashioned remedies like warm milk?

DR. RAY: Actually, a lot of home remedies do make sense. We tell patients **to have a high-carbohydrate snack like a banana before they go to bed**. Warm milk helps too. But I'd advise you **not to eat a heavy meal before bed**.

CONNIE: My doctor told me **to get more exercise,** but when I run at night, I have a hard time getting to sleep.

DR. RAY: It's true that if you exercise regularly, you'll sleep better. But we always tell patients **not to exercise too close to bedtime**.

CONNIE: My mother always said **to get up and scrub the floor when I couldn't sleep**.

DR. RAY: That works. I advised one patient **to balance his checkbook**. He went right to sleep, just to escape from the task.

CONNIE: Suppose I try these remedies and they don't help?

"I couldn't sleep."

DR. RAY: We often ask patients **to come and spend a night at our sleep clinic**. Our equipment monitors the patient through the night. In fact, if you're interested, we can invite you **to come to the clinic for a night**.

CONNIE: Maybe I should do that.

fatigued=very tired

AFTER YOU READ

Check the things that Dr. Ray suggests for people with insomnia.

☑ **1.** Stop drinking coffee and cola late in the day.

☐ **2.** Eat a heavy meal before going to bed.

☑ **3.** Get more exercise.

☐ **4.** Exercise right before bedtime.

☑ **5.** Get up from bed and balance your checkbook.

☑ **6.** Spend the night at the sleep clinic.

Grammar Presentation

INDIRECT INSTRUCTIONS, COMMANDS, REQUESTS, AND INVITATIONS

Direct Speech		
Subject	Reporting Verb	Direct Speech
He	said,	"**Drink** warm milk." "**Don't drink** coffee." "Can you **turn out** the light, please?" "Why don't you **visit** the clinic?"

Indirect Speech			
Subject	Reporting Verb	Noun/ Pronoun	Indirect Speech
He	told advised asked	Connie her	**to drink** warm milk. **not to drink** coffee. **to turn out** the light.
	said		
	invited	her	**to visit** the clinic.

GRAMMAR NOTES

EXAMPLES

	DIRECT SPEECH	INDIRECT SPEECH
1. In indirect speech, use the **infinitive** (*to* + **base form** of the verb) for:		
a. instructions	"Come early," said the doctor.	The doctor said **to come** early.
b. commands	"Lie down."	The doctor told her **to lie down**.
c. requests	"Could you please arrive by 8:00?"	He asked her **to arrive** by 8:00.
d. invitations	"Could you join us for dinner?"	They invited us **to join** them for dinner.

	DIRECT SPEECH	INDIRECT SPEECH
2. Use a **negative infinitive** (*not* + **infinitive**) for:		
a. negative instructions	"Don't eat after 9:00 P.M."	He told me **not to eat** after 9:00 P.M.
b. negative commands	"Don't wake Cindy!"	Mrs. Bartolotta told me **not to wake** Cindy.
c. negative requests	"Please don't set the alarm."	Jean-Pierre asked me **not to set** the alarm.

Reference Note
For a list of **reporting verbs**, see Appendix 13 on page A-5.

Focused Practice

1 | DISCOVER THE GRAMMAR

Connie Sung decided to write an article about her visit to Dr. Ray's clinic. Read her notes for the article. Underline the indirect instructions, commands, requests, and invitations. Circle the reporting verbs that introduce them.

2/18	11:00 A.M. The clinic called and (asked) me to arrive at 8:30 tonight. They (told) me to bring my nightshirt and toothbrush. They (told) me people also liked to bring their own pillow, but I decided to travel light.
	8:30 P.M. I arrived on schedule. My room was small but cozy. Only the video camera and cable (told) me I was in a sleep clinic. Juan Estrada, the technician on duty, (told) me to relax and watch TV for an hour.
	9:30 P.M. Juan came back and got me ready for the test. He pasted 12 small metal disks to my face, legs, and stomach. I (asked) him to explain, and he (told) me that the disks, called electrodes, would be connected to a machine that records electrical activity in the brain. I felt like a Martian in a science fiction movie.
	11:30 P.M. Juan came back and (asked) me to get into bed. After he hooked me up to the machine, he (instructed) me not to leave the bed that night. I fell asleep easily.
2/19	7:00 A.M. Juan came to awaken me and to disconnect the wires. He (invited) me to join him in the next room, where he had spent the night monitoring the equipment. I looked at the pages of graphs and wondered aloud whether Juan and Dr. Ray would be able to read my weird dream of the night before. Juan laughed and (told) me not to worry. "These just show electrical impulses," he assured me.
	8:00 A.M. Dr. Ray reviewed my data with me. He (told) me I had healthy sleep patterns, except for some leg movements during the night. He (told) me to get more exercise, and I promised I would.

2 | DEAR HELEN

Grammar Notes 1–2

Read the questions to Helen, a newspaper columnist specializing in health matters, and report her instructions. Use the reporting verbs in parentheses.

Q: I have trouble getting to sleep every night.—MIKE LANDERS, DETROIT

A: Don't drink anything with caffeine after 2:00 P.M. Try exercising regularly, early in the day.

1. (tell) *She told him not to drink anything with caffeine after 2:00 P.M.*

2. (say) *She said to try exercising regularly, early in the day.*

Q: What can I do to soothe a sore throat? I never take medicine unless I have to.—ANNE BLY, TROY

A: Sip some hot herbal tea with honey. But don't drink black tea. It will make your throat dry.

3. (say) *She said to sip some hot herbal tea with honey.*

4. (tell) *She told her not to drink black tea. It would make her throat dry.*

Q: I get leg cramps at night. They wake me up, and I can't get back to sleep.—LOU RICH, DALLAS

A: The next time you feel a cramp, do this: Pinch the place between your upper lip and your nose. The cramp should stop right away.

5. (say) *She said to pinch the place between her upper lip and her nose.*

Q: Do you know of an inexpensive way to remove stains on teeth?—PETE LEE, BROOKLYN

A: Make a toothpaste of one tablespoon of baking soda and a little water. Brush as usual.

6. (tell) *She told him to make a toothpaste of one tablespoon of baking soda and a little water*

7. (say) *He said to Brush as usual.*

Q: What can I do to ease an itchy poison ivy rash?—MARVIN SMITH, HARTFORD

A: Spread cool, cooked oatmeal over the rash. Also, try soaking the rash in a cool bath with a quarter cup of baking soda. Don't scratch the rash. That will make it worse.

8. (tell) *She told him to spread cool, cooked oatmeal over the rash.*

9. (say) *She said to try soaking the rash in a cool bath with a quarter cup of baking soda*

10. (tell) *She told her not to scratch the rash that would make it worse.*

Q: Bugs love me. They bite me all the time.—ED SMALL, TULSA

A: There are a few things you can do to keep bugs away. Eat onions or garlic every day. Your skin will have a slight odor that bugs hate. Or ask your doctor about a vitamin B supplement.

11. (say) *She said to*

12. (tell) *She told him to ask his doctor about*

IMPORTANT: CALL YOUR DOCTOR ABOUT ANY CONDITION THAT DOESN'T IMPROVE OR GETS WORSE.

3 | CONNIE'S DREAM

Grammar Notes 1–2

Connie had a dream at the sleep clinic. She wrote about it in her journal. Read her account of the dream and underline the indirect instructions, commands, requests, and invitations. Then complete the cartoon by writing what each character said.

I dreamed that a Martian came into my room. He told me to get up. Then he said to follow him. There was a spaceship outside the clinic. I asked the Martian to show me the ship, so he invited me to come aboard. Juan, the lab technician, was on the ship. Suddenly, Juan told me to pilot the ship. He ordered me not to leave the controls. Then he went to sleep. Next, Dr. Ray was at my side giving me instructions. He told me to slow down. Then he said to point the ship toward the Earth. There was a loud knocking noise as we hit the ground, and I told everyone not to panic. Then I heard Juan tell me to wake up. I opened my eyes and saw him walking into my room at the sleep clinic.

4 | EDITING

Read this entry in Zahra's journal. There are twelve mistakes in the use of indirect instructions, commands, requests, and invitations. The first mistake is already corrected. Find and correct eleven more. Don't forget to check punctuation. Mistakes with quotation marks count as one mistake for the sentence.

In writing class today, the teacher asked Juan ~to~ read one of his stories. It was wonderful and everyone in class enjoyed it a lot. After class, the teacher invited me ~To~ read a story in class next week. I don't feel ready to do this. I asked her ~no~ not to call on me next week because I'm having trouble getting ideas. She told me ~that~ not to worry, and she said to wait for two weeks. I still was worried about coming up with an idea, so I decided to talk to Juan after class. I asked him ~To~ tell me the source for his ideas. He was really helpful. He said that they came from his dreams! I was very surprised. He ~said~ told me to keep a dream journal for ideas. Then he invited me "~to~ read some of his journal." It was very interesting, so I asked him to give me some tips on remembering dreams. (Juan says that everyone dreams, but I usually don't remember my dreams in the morning.) Again, Juan was very helpful. He said ~to get~ getting a good night's sleep because the longer dreams come after a long period of sleep. He also ~tell~ told me to keep my journal by the bed and to write as soon as I wake up. He said to ~no~ not to move from the sleeping position. He also told me not ~to~ think about the day at first. (If you think about your day, you might forget your dreams.) Most important—every night he tells himself ~that~ to remember his dreams. These all sound like great ideas, and I want to try them out right away. The only problem is—I'm so excited about this, I'm not sure I'll be able to fall asleep!

Do you have computer skills?

Communication Practice

5 | LISTENING

🎧 *Juan went to a headache clinic. Listen to the conversation to find out what he learned there. Then listen again and check the correct column to show what they told him to do, what they told him not to do, and what they didn't mention.*

	Do	Don't Do	Not Mentioned
1. Get regular exercise.	☑	☐	☐
2. Get eight hours of sleep.	☐	☐	☐
3. Take painkillers.	☐	☐	☐
4. Use an ice pack.	☐	☐	☐
5. Massage around the eyes.	☐	☐	☐
6. Eat three big meals a day.	☐	☐	☐
7. Eat chocolate.	☐	☐	☐
8. Avoid cheese.	☐	☐	☐

6 | SIMPLE REMEDIES

What advice have you heard for the following problems? Work in pairs and talk about what to do and what not to do for them. Then report to the class.

minor kitchen burns   a cold

insomnia   blisters

insect bites   poison ivy

headaches   a sore throat

snoring   other: _____

hiccups

Example: **A:** My mother always told me to hold a burn under cold water.
B: They say not to put butter on a burn.

7 | HOME ALONE

Jeff's parents went out for the evening and left a list of instructions for him. Work in pairs. Read the list and look at the picture. Talk about which instructions Jeff followed and which ones he didn't follow. Use indirect instructions.

Dear Jeff,

We'll be home late. Here are a few things to remember—

    Don't stay up after 10:00.

    Take the garbage out.

    Wash the dishes.

    Do your homework.

    Let the cat in.

    Don't watch any horror movies. (They give you
      nightmares—remember?)

    Don't invite your friends over tonight.

               Love,
               Mom and Dad

Example: His parents told him not to stay up after 10:00, but it's 11:30 and he's still awake.

8 | WRITING

Write a paragraph about a dream you had or one that someone has told you about. You can even invent a dream. Use the paragraph from Connie's journal in Exercise 3 as a model. Use indirect instructions, commands, requests, and invitations.

Example: One night I dreamed that I was in my grandmother's kitchen. In my dream, I saw a beautiful, carved wooden door. My grandmother invited me to open the door. She said that there were a lot of rooms in the house, and she invited me to explore them with her.

Exchange your paragraph with a partner. Draw a sketch of your partner's dream and write the direct speech in speech bubbles. Discuss your sketch with your partner to make sure you understood the story and the indirect speech in your partner's dream.

9 | ON THE INTERNET

Do a search on a problem or something you need help doing. Choose your own problem or one of the problems listed below. Search for tips on how to solve the problem. For example, type in **tips on losing weight**. *Report your findings to the class.*

losing weight

stopping smoking

making new friends

finding a new job

saving money

Example: I looked up information on losing weight. The website said to exercise regularly. It said not to eat too much bread . . .

Indirect Questions

Grammar in Context

BEFORE YOU READ

🎧 *Look at the photo and the title of the article. What do you think a* stress interview *is?*
Read this excerpt from an article about job interviews.

The **STRESS**
Interview
By Miguel Vega

> Why can't you work under pressure?
> Have you cleaned out your car recently?
> Who wrote your application letter for you?

> Do I really
> want this job?

A few weeks ago, Melissa Morrow had an unusual job interview. First, the interviewer asked **why she couldn't work under pressure**. Before she could answer, he asked **if she had cleaned out her car recently**. Then he wanted to know **who had written her application letter for her**. Melissa was shocked, but she handled herself well. She asked the interviewer **whether he was going to ask her serious questions**. Then she politely ended the interview.

Melissa had had a stress interview, a type of job interview that features tough, tricky questions, long silences, and negative evaluations of the job candidate. To the candidate, this may seem unnecessarily nasty on the interviewer's part. However, some positions require an ability to handle just this kind of pressure. If there is an accident at a nuclear power plant, for example, the plant's public relations officer must remain calm when hostile reporters ask **how the accident could have occurred**.

(continued)

The STRESS Interview

The uncomfortable atmosphere of a stress interview gives the potential employer a chance to watch a candidate react to pressure. In one case, the interviewer ended each interview by saying, "We're really not sure that you're the right person for this job." One excellent candidate asked the interviewer angrily **if he was sure he knew how to conduct an interview**. She clearly could not handle the pressure she would encounter as a television news anchor—the job she was interviewing for.

Stress interviews may be appropriate for some jobs, but they can also work against a company. Some good candidates may refuse the job after a hostile interview. Melissa Morrow handled her interview beautifully, but later asked herself **if she really wanted to work for that company**. Her answer was *no*.

A word of warning to job candidates: Not all tough questioning is legitimate. In some countries, certain questions are illegal unless the answers are directly related to the job. If an interviewer asks **how old you are, whether you are married**, or **how much money you owe**, you can refuse to answer. If you think a question is improper, ask the interviewer **how the answer specifically relates to that job**. If you don't get a satisfactory explanation, you don't have to answer the question. And remember: Whatever happens, don't lose your cool. The interview will be over before you know it!

DID YOU KNOW . . .

In some countries, employers must hire only on the basis of skills and experience. In Canada, most countries in Europe, and in the United States, for example, an interviewer cannot ask an applicant certain questions unless the information is related to the job. Here are some questions an interviewer may NOT ask:

X How old are you?

X What is your religion?

X Are you married?

X What does your husband (or wife) do?

X Have you ever been arrested?

X How many children do you have?

X How tall are you?

X Where were you born?

AFTER YOU READ

Check the questions the interviewer asked Melissa.

☐ 1. "Why can't you work under pressure?"

☐ 2. "Have you cleaned your car out recently?"

☐ 3. "Is he going to ask me serious questions?"

☐ 4. "How can the accident have occurred?"

☐ 5. "Does she really want to work for this company?"

☐ 6. "Are you sure you know how to conduct an interview?"

Grammar Presentation

INDIRECT QUESTIONS

Direct Speech: *Yes / No* Questions		
Subject	**Reporting Verb**	**Direct Question**
He	asked,	**"Do you have** any experience**?"** **"Can you create** spreadsheets**?"** **"Will you stay** for a year**?"**

Indirect Speech: *Yes / No* Questions			
Subject	**Reporting Verb**	**(Noun / Pronoun)**	**Indirect Question**
He	asked	(Melissa) (her)	**if** **whether (or not)** **she had** any experience. **she could create** spreadsheets. **she would stay** for a year.

Direct Speech: *Wh-* Questions About the Subject		
Subject	**Reporting Verb**	**Direct Question**
He	asked,	**"Who told you** about the job**?"** **"What happened** on **your** last job**?"**

Indirect Speech: *Wh-* Questions About the Subject			
Subject	**Reporting Verb**	**(Noun / Pronoun)**	**Indirect Question**
He	asked	(Bob) (him)	**who had told him** about the job. **what had happened** on **his** last job.

(continued)

Direct Speech: *Wh-* Questions About the Predicate		
Subject	**Reporting Verb**	**Direct Question**
He	asked,	"Who(m) **did you work** for**?**" "Where **do you work** now**?**" "How **are you going to get** to work**?**" "Why **have you decided to change** jobs**?**" "How much **are you making?**"

Indirect Speech: *Wh-* Questions About the Predicate			
Subject	**Reporting Verb**	**(Noun / Pronoun)**	**Indirect Question**
He	asked	(Melissa) (her)	**who(m) she had worked** for. **where she worked** now. **how she was going to get** to work. **why she had decided to change** jobs. **how much she was making.**

GRAMMAR NOTES

EXAMPLES

1. Use *if* or *whether* in **indirect *yes/no* questions**. USAGE NOTES *Whether* is more formal than *if*. We often use *whether or not* to report *yes/no* questions.	**DIRECT QUESTION** **INDIRECT QUESTION** "Can you type?" She asked me she asked. *if* **I could type**. "Do you know He wanted to know how to use a *whether* **I knew how** scanner?" he asked. **to use a scanner**. • My boss wants to know *whether* **the report is ready**. • He wanted to know *whether or not* **the report was ready**.

2. Use **question words** in indirect *wh-* questions.	**DIRECT QUESTION**	**INDIRECT QUESTION**
	"Where is your office?" I asked.	I asked *where* **his office was**.
	I asked, "How much is the salary?"	I asked *how much* **the salary was**.

3. Use **statement word order** (subject + verb), not question word order for:	**STATEMENT**	
	subject verb **They hired** Li.	
	DIRECT QUESTION	**INDIRECT QUESTION**
a. indirect *yes/no* questions	Did they hire Li?	I asked **if they had hired** Li.
b. indirect *wh-* questions about the predicate (usually the last part of the sentence)	Who did they hire?	I asked **who they had hired**.
c. indirect *wh-* questions about the subject (usually the first part of the sentence)	Which company hired Li?	I asked **which company had hired** Li.
▶ **BE CAREFUL!** If a direct question about the subject has the form **question word + *be* + noun**, then the indirect question has the form **question word + noun + *be***.	Who is the boss?	I asked **who the boss was**. NOT I asked who ~~was the boss~~.

4. In indirect questions:	**DIRECT QUESTION**	**INDIRECT QUESTION**
	Why did you leave?	She asked me **why I had left**. NOT She asked me why ~~did I leave~~.
a. do not use the auxiliary *do, does,* or *did.*		
b. do not end with a question mark (end with a period).		NOT She asked me why I had left~~?~~

Reference Notes

The same **verb tense changes and other changes** occur in both indirect questions and indirect statements (see Units 25 and 26).

For a list of **reporting verbs** in questions, see Appendix 13 on page A-5.

Focused Practice

1 | DISCOVER THE GRAMMAR

🎧 *Melissa Morrow is telling a friend about her job interview. Underline the indirect questions in the conversation.*

DON: So, how did the interview go?

MELISSA: It was very strange.

DON: What happened?

MELISSA: Well, it started off OK. He asked me <u>how much experience I had had</u>, and I told him I had been a public relations officer for 10 years. Let's see . . . He also asked what I would change about my current job. That was a little tricky.

DON: What did you say?

MELISSA: Well, I didn't want to say anything negative, so I told him that I was ready for more responsibility.

DON: Good. What else did he ask?

MELISSA: Oh, you know, the regular things. He asked what my greatest success had been, and how much money I was making.

DON: Sounds like a normal interview to me. What was so strange about it?

MELISSA: Well, at one point, he just stopped talking for a long time. Then he asked me all these bizarre questions that weren't even related to the job.

DON: Like what?

MELISSA: He asked me if I had cleaned out my car recently.

DON: You're kidding.

MELISSA: No, I'm not. Then he asked me why my employer didn't want me to stay.

DON: That's crazy. I hope you told him that you hadn't been fired.

MELISSA: Of course. Oh, and he asked me if I was good enough to work for his company.

DON: What did you tell him?

MELISSA: I told him that with my skills and experience I was one of the best in my field.

DON: That was a great answer. It sounds like you handled yourself very well.

MELISSA: Thanks. But now I'm asking myself if I really want this job.

DON: Take your time. Don't make any snap decisions.

Now check the direct questions that the interviewer asked Melissa.

☑ **1.** How much experience have you had?

☐ **2.** What would you change about your current job?

☑ **3.** Are you ready for more responsibility?

☐ **4.** What was your greatest success?

☐ **5.** How much are you making now?

☐ 6. Was it a normal interview?

☑ 7. Have you cleaned out your car recently?

☑ 8. Have you been fired?

☑ 9. Are you good enough to work for this company?

☐ 10. Do you ever make snap decisions?

2 | NOSY NEIGHBOR   *Grammar Notes 1–4*

🎧 *Claire has an interview next week. Her neighbor, Jaime, wants to know all about it.*
Report Jaime's questions using the correct order of the words in parentheses.

> **JAIME:** I heard you're going on an interview next week. What kind of job is it?
>
> **CLAIRE:** It's for a job as an office assistant.

1. _He asked what kind of job it was._
   (kind of job / what / was / it)

> **JAIME:** Oh, really? When is the interview?
>
> **CLAIRE:** It's on Tuesday at 9:00.

2. _He asked when the interview was._
   (the interview / was / when)

> **JAIME:** Where's the company?
>
> **CLAIRE:** It's downtown on the west side.

3. _He asked where the company was._
   (was / where / the company)

> **JAIME:** Do you need directions?
>
> **CLAIRE:** No, I know the way.

4. _He asked if she needed directions._
   (her)
   (needed / if / she / directions)

> **JAIME:** How long does it take to get there?
>
> **CLAIRE:** About half an hour.

5. _He asked How long it takes to get there_
   (to get there / it / takes / how long)

> **JAIME:** Are you going to drive?
>
> **CLAIRE:** I think so. It's probably the fastest way.

6. _He asked her if she was going to drive._
   (was going / if / she / to drive)

(continued)

JAIME: Who's going to interview you?

CLAIRE: Uhmmm. I'm not sure. Probably the manager of the department.

7. *He asked her who was going to interview.*

(was going / her / who / to interview)

JAIME: Well, good luck. When will they let you know?

CLAIRE: It will take a while. They have a lot of candidates.

8. *He asked when they would let her know.*

(her / they / would / when / let / know)

3 | WHO'S ASKING?

Grammar Notes 1–4

Read these questions, which were asked during Claire's interview. Claire asked some of the questions, and the manager, Mr. Stollins, asked others. Decide who asked each question. Then rewrite each question as indirect speech.

1. "What type of training is available for the job?"

   Claire asked what type of training was available for the job..

2. "What kind of experience do you have?"

   claire asked what kind of experience I had.

3. "Is there opportunity for promotion?"

   claire asked if There is ~was~ opportunity for promotion.

4. "Are you interviewing with other companies?"

   he asked if I was interviewing with other companies.

5. "What will my responsibilities be?"

   he asked what my responsibilities would be.

6. "How is job performance rewarded?"

   he asked How job performance rewarded was.

7. "What was your starting salary at your last job?"

   he asked what my starting salary at my last job had been.

8. "Did you get along well with your last employer?"

   he asked if I had got along well with my last employer.

9. "Do you hire many women?"

   he asked if I hired many women.

10. "Why did you apply for this position?"

    he asked why I had applied for this position.

11. "Have you had any major layoffs in the past few years?"

    he asked if I had had any

4 | EDITING

Read this memo an interviewer wrote after an interview. There are seven mistakes in the use of indirect questions. The first mistake is already corrected. Find and correct six more. Don't forget to check punctuation. Mistakes with quotation marks count as one mistake for the sentence.

May 15, 2006

TO: Francesca Giuffrida

FROM: Ken Marley

SUBJECT: Interview with Carlos Lopez

This morning I interviewed Carlos Lopez for the administrative
assistant position. Since this job requires a lot of contact with the
public, I did some stress questioning. I asked Mr. Lopez why
~~couldn't he~~ *he couldn't* work under pressure. I also asked him why his
supervisor disliked him. Finally, I inquired when he would quit the
job with our company?

Mr. Lopez kept his poise throughout the interview. He answered all
my questions calmly, and he had some excellent questions of his
own. He asked "if we expected changes in the job." He also wanted
to know how often do we evaluate employees. I was quite
impressed when he asked why did I decide to join this company.

Mr. Lopez is an excellent candidate for the job, and I believe he will
handle the responsibilities well. At the end of the interview, Mr.
Lopez inquired when we could let him know our decision? I asked
him if whether he was considering another job, and he said he
was. I think we should act quickly to hire Mr. Lopez.

Communication Practice

5 | LISTENING

🎧 *You are going to hear a job interview that takes place in Canada. First read the checklist. Then listen to the interview and check the topics the interviewer asks about.*

Possible Job Interview Topics

OK to Ask
- ☐ Name
- ☐ Address
- ☐ Work experience
- ☐ Reason for leaving job
- ☑ Reason for seeking position that is open
- ☐ Salary
- ☐ Education
- ☐ Professional affiliations
- ☐ Convictions for crimes
- ☐ Skills
- ☐ Job performance
- ☐ Permission to work in Canada

Not OK to Ask *
- ☑ Age
- ☑ Race
- ☐ Sex
- ☐ Religion
- ☐ National origin
- ☐ Height or weight
- ☐ Marital status
- ☐ Information about spouse
- ☐ Arrest record
- ☐ Physical disabilities
- ☐ Children
- ☐ Citizenship
- ☐ English language skill
- ☐ Financial situation

*illegal to ask if not related to the job

Listen again and write the illegal questions the interviewer asks.

1. How old are you?
2. How race are you?
3. what religion do yo believe?
4. _____
5. _____
6. _____
7. _____

Now report the illegal questions to the class.

Example: He asked her how old she was.

6 | ROLE PLAY: A JOB INTERVIEW

Work in groups. Using the advertisement and the résumé, develop questions for a job interview. Half of the group should write questions for the interviewer, and the other half should write questions for the candidate. Then select two people to act out the interview for the class.

Pat Rogers
215 West Hill Drive
Baltimore, MD 21233
Telephone: (410) 555-7777
Fax: (410) 555-7932
progers@email.com

MEDICAL RECEPTIONIST for busy doctor's office. Mature individual needed to answer phones, greet patients, make appointments. Some filing and billing. Similar experience preferred. Computer skills a plus.

EDUCATION	**Taylor Community College** Associate's Degree (Business) 2001
	Middlesex High School High school diploma, 1998
EXPERIENCE 2001–Present Patients Plus Baltimore, MD	**Medical receptionist** Responsibilities: Greet patients, make appointments, answer telephones, update computer records
1998–2001 Union Hospital Baltimore, MD	**Admitting clerk, hospital admissions office** Responsibilities: Interviewed patients for admission, input information in computer, answered telephones

Now discuss each group's role-play interview as a class. Use these questions to guide your discussion. Support your ideas by reporting questions that were asked in the interview.

1. Was it a stress interview? Why or why not?

2. Did the interviewer ask any illegal questions? Which ones were illegal?

3. Which of the candidate's questions were the most useful in evaluating the job? Explain your choices.

4. Which of the interviewer's questions gave the clearest picture of the candidate? Explain your choices.

5. If you were the interviewer, would you hire this candidate? Why or why not?

6. If you were the candidate, would you want to work for this company? Why or why not?

Example: I think it was a stress interview because the interviewer asked him why he couldn't find a new job. The interviewer asked two illegal questions. She asked when the candidate was born. She also asked where the candidate was from.

7 | CURIOUS QUESTIONS

Work in pairs. What would you like to know about your partner? Make a list of questions. Ask and answer each other's questions. Then get together with another pair and report your conversations.

> **Example:** She asked me what I was going to do next semester. I told her I was going to take the advanced-level grammar class.

8 | IN YOUR EXPERIENCE

In small groups, discuss a personal experience with a school or job interview. (If you do not have a personal experience, use the experience of someone you know.) Talk about these questions:

- What did the interviewer want to find out?

- What was the most difficult question to answer? Why?

- Were there any questions that you didn't want to answer? What did you say?

- What did you ask the interviewer?

9 | WRITING

Before you look for work, it's a good idea to talk to people who are already working in jobs that might interest you. In these kinds of "informational interviews" you can ask what the tasks in that job are, why people like or dislike the work, or how much you can expect to be paid. Write a list of questions to ask in an informational interview about a job.

> **Example:** Do you like your job?
> How much vacation time do you get?

Now interview someone and write a report about the interview. Use indirect questions.

> **Example:** I interviewed Pete Ortiz, who is an assistant in the computer lab. I wanted to talk to him because I'm interested in applying for a job in the lab. I asked Pete if he liked working there, and he told me he liked it most of the time . . .

10 | ON THE INTERNET

🌐 *Do a search to find an interview with a famous person. Choose two or three interesting questions that the interviewer asked. Report the questions and the answers to the class.*

> **Example:** I read an interview with Turkish movie director Ferzan Ozpetek. The interviewer asked him where he got the idea for his movie *Facing Windows*. He said that he had gotten the idea from a real-life experience.

Embedded Questions

Grammar in Context

BEFORE YOU READ

Look at the cartoon. What is the man worried about? Read this interview about tipping.

THE TIP

In China it used to be illegal, in New Zealand it's uncommon, but in Germany it's included in the bill. In the United States and Canada it's common but illogical: You tip the person who delivers flowers, but not the person who delivers a package.

Do *you* often wonder **what to do** about tipping?

Our correspondent, Marjorie S. Fuchs, interviewed Irene Frankel, author of *Tips on Tipping*, to help us through the tipping maze.

MSF: Tell me **why you decided to write a book about tipping**.

IF: I began writing it for people from cultures where tipping wasn't a custom. But when I started researching, I found that Americans, too, often weren't sure **how to tip**, so *Tips* became a book for anybody living in the United States.

"I wonder **how much we should give**."

MSF: Does your book explain **who to tip**?

IF: Oh, absolutely. It tells you **who to tip, how much to tip, and when to tip**. Equally important, it tells you **when not to tip**.

MSF: That *is* important. Suppose I don't know **whether to tip someone**, and I left your book at home. Is it OK to ask?

(continued)

413

THE TIP

IF: Sure. If you don't know **whether to leave a tip**, the best thing to do is ask. People usually won't tell you **what to do**, but they *will* tell you **what most customers do**.

MSF: I always wonder **what to do when I get bad service**. Should I still tip?

IF: Don't tip the ordinary amount, but tip *something* so that the service person doesn't think that you just forgot to leave a tip.

MSF: Is there any reason **why we tip a restaurant server but not a flight attendant**?

IF: Not that I know. The rules for tipping in the United States are very illogical, and there are often contradictions in who we tip. That's why I wrote this book.

MSF: Another thing—I've never understood **why a restaurant tip depends on the amount of the bill rather than on the amount of work involved in serving the meal**. After all, bringing out a $20 dish of food involves the same amount of work as carrying out a $5 plate.

IF: You're right. It makes no sense. That's just the way it is.

MSF: One last question. Suppose I'm planning a trip to Egypt. Tell me **how I can learn about tipping customs in that country**.

IF: Usually travel agents know **what the rules are for tipping in each country**. Look up the information on the Internet if you can't find out from a travel agent or a book.

MSF: Well, thanks for all the good tips. I know our readers will find them very helpful. *I* certainly did.

IF: Thank *you*.

AFTER YOU READ

Circle the correct words to complete these embedded questions from the interview.

1. Tell me why <u>did you decide / you decided</u> to write a book about tipping.

2. It tells you when <u>no / not</u> to tip.

3. I always wonder what <u>do I do / to do</u> when I get bad service.

4. Is there any reason why <u>do we tip / we tip</u> a restaurant server but not a flight attendant?

5. Tell me how <u>I can / can I</u> learn about tipping customs in that country.

Grammar Presentation

EMBEDDED QUESTIONS

Main Clause	Embedded Question
I'm not sure He wondered	**if I left the right tip.** **whether (or not) five dollars was enough.**
Can you remember	**how much our bill was?**

Wh- Word + Infinitive	
I don't know	**how much to tip.**
Do you know	**where to leave the tip?**

GRAMMAR NOTES

EXAMPLES

1. Embedded questions are questions that are inside another sentence. An embedded question can be:	
a. inside a statement	• I don't know **who our server is.**
b. inside another question	• Do you remember **who our server is?**
▶ **BE CAREFUL!** If the embedded question is inside a <u>statement</u>, use a **period** at the end of the sentence.	• I wonder **if that's our server.** NOT I wonder if that's our server?
If the embedded question is inside a <u>question</u>, use a **question mark** at the end of the sentence.	• Do you know **if that's our server?**

2. Use embedded questions to:	**DIRECT QUESTION**	**EMBEDDED QUESTION**
a. express something you do not know	Why didn't he tip the mechanic?	I don't know **why he didn't tip the mechanic.**
b. ask politely for information	Is the tip included?	Can you tell me **if the tip is included**?
USAGE NOTE: Embedded questions are <u>more polite</u> than direct questions.	*Less formal:* Does our bill include a service charge?	*More polite:* Can you tell me **if our bill includes a service charge**?

(continued)

3. Begin **embedded** *yes/no* **questions** with *if*, *whether*, or *whether or not*.

USAGE NOTE: **Whether** is more formal than *if*.

- Do you know *if they delivered the pizza*?

  OR

- Do you know *whether* they delivered the **pizza**?

  OR

- Do you know *whether or not* they **delivered the pizza**?

Begin **embedded** *wh-* **questions** with a **question word**.

- Many tourists wonder *how much* to tip their restaurant server.

---

4. Use **statement word order** (subject + verb), not question word order in:

a. embedded *yes/no questions*

Do not leave out *if* or *whether* in embedded *yes/no* questions.

b. embedded *wh-* questions about the predicate (usually the last part of the sentence)

Do not use the auxiliary verbs *do*, *does*, or *did* in embedded questions.

c. embedded *wh-* questions about the subject (usually the first part of the sentence)

▶ **BE CAREFUL!** If a direct question about the subject has the form **question word + *be* + noun**, then the indirect question has the form **question word + noun + *be***.

DIRECT QUESTION	EMBEDDED QUESTION
Is it 6:00 yet?	Could you tell me **if it is** 6:00 yet? NOT Could you tell me ~~is it~~ 6:00 yet?
Why did they order pizza?	I wondered why **they ordered** pizza. NOT I wondered why ~~did they order~~ pizza.
Who ordered pizza?	I can't remember **who ordered** pizza.
Who is our waiter?	Do you know **who** our waiter **is**? NOT Do you know ~~who is our waiter~~?

<table>
<tr><td>

5. In embedded questions, you can also use:

    a. question word + infinitive

    b. *whether* **+ infinitive**

▶ **BE CAREFUL!** Do not use the infinitive after *if* or *why*.

</td><td>

- Let's ask where we should leave the tip.

      OR

- Let's ask *where* **to leave** the tip.

- I wonder whether I should leave a tip.

      OR

- I wonder *whether* **to leave** a tip.

- I don't understand *why* **I should tip.** NOT I don't understand why ~~to tip~~.

</td></tr>
</table>

<table>
<tr><td>

6. Embedded questions often follow these phrases:

    I don't know . . .

    I'd like to know . . .

    Do you know . . . ?

    Can you tell me . . . ?

    I can't remember . . .

    Can you remember . . . ?

    Let's ask . . .

    We need to find out . . .

    I'd like to find out . . .

    I wonder . . .

    I'm not sure . . .

    It doesn't say . . .

    Could you explain . . . ?

    I can't imagine . . .

</td><td>

- ***I don't know*** what the name of the restaurant is.
- ***Can you remember*** how much the shrimp costs?
- ***Let's ask*** what today's specials are.
- ***I wonder*** what time the restaurant closes.
- ***Could you explain*** what that sign means?
- ***I can't imagine*** why this restaurant isn't more popular.

</td></tr>
</table>

Focused Practice

1 | DISCOVER THE GRAMMAR

Read the advertisement for Tips on Tipping. *Underline the embedded questions.*

Tips on Tipping

This book is for you if . . .

you've ever avoided a situation just because you didn't know how much to tip.
you've ever realized (too late) that you were supposed to offer a tip.
you've ever given a huge tip and then wondered if a tip was necessary at all.
you've ever needed to know how to calculate the right tip instantly.
you're new to the United States and you're not sure who you should tip here.
you'd like to learn how tipping properly can get you the best service for your money.

What readers are saying . . .

"I can't imagine how I got along without it."
   —*Chris Sarton, Minneapolis, Minnesota*
"Take *Tips* along if you want a stress-free vacation."
   —*Midori Otaka, Osaka, Japan*
"I took my fiancée to dinner at Deux Saisons and knew exactly how to tip everyone!"
   —*S. Prasad, San Francisco, California*
"You need this book—whether you stay in hostels or five-star hotels."
   —*Cuno Pumpin, Bern, Switzerland*

Send for the ultimate guide to tipping and get all the answers to your tipping questions.

Yes! I want to learn who to tip, when to tip, and how much to tip. Please send me additional information on *Tips on Tipping.* I understand that the book will be $4.95 plus $2.00 postage and handling for each copy. (New York residents: Add sales tax.) Contact Martin Unlimited, Inc. at dmifdmif@yahoo.com.

2 | SERVICE CHARGES

Grammar Notes 1–4, 6

Complete this travel column about tipping customs around the world. Change the direct questions in parentheses to embedded questions. Use correct punctuation.

Tipping customs vary, so travelers should find out who, where, and how much to tip. Here are some frequently asked questions.

Q: Can you tell me whether _I should tip in Canada?_
1. **(Should I tip in Canada?)**

A: Yes. Tipping practices in Canada are similar to those in the United States.

Q: I know that some places in France include a service charge. Could you explain

_____
2. **(How can I tell if the tip is included in the bill?)**

A: Look for the phrase *service compris* (service included) on the bill.

Q: I'm going to China next month. I understand that tipping used to be illegal. Do you know

_____
3. **(Will restaurant servers accept tips now?)**

A: Yes. You should leave 3 percent in a restaurant.

Q: On a recent trip to Iceland, I found that service people refused tips. Could you explain

_____
4. **(Why did this happen?)**

A: In Iceland, people often feel insulted by tips. Just say thank you—that's enough.

Q: Our family is planning a trip to Norway to visit my in-laws. My daughter doesn't know how to ski and wants to take some lessons while we're there. I'd like to know

_____
5. **(Should I tip her instructor?)**

A: Tipping is rare all over Scandinavia. Take the instructor to lunch instead.

Q: I'm going to work in Japan for a year. I'm bringing a lot of luggage. Could you tell me

_____
6. **(How much should I tip the airport and train porters?)**

A: There's a fixed fee per bag for airport porters. No tipping is expected on trains.

Q: My husband and I are planning a trip to several cities in Australia. Please tell us

_____
7. **(Who expects a tip and who doesn't?)**

A: Restaurant servers expect a tip of 10 percent, but you don't need to tip taxi drivers.

3 | WHEN IN ROME . . .

Grammar Notes 1–4, 6

Two foreign exchange students are visiting Rome, Italy. Complete their conversations. Choose the appropriate questions from the list and change them to embedded questions. Use correct punctuation.

- How much are we supposed to tip the taxi driver?
- Could we rent a car and drive there?
- Do they have tour buses that go there?
- How much does the subway cost?
- How far are you going?
- How are we going to choose?
- How much does a bus tour cost?
- What did they put in the sauce?
- Where is the Forum?
- ~~Where is it?~~
- Where do they sell them?

A. **DRIVER:** Where do you want to go? The airport?

MARTINA: The Hotel Forte. Do you know _where it is?_____
1.

DRIVER: Sure. Get in and I'll take you there.

MARTINA: *(whispering to Miuki)* Do you know _____
2.

MIUKI: According to the book, we're supposed to leave 10–15 percent. I've got it.

B. **MARTINA:** There's so much to see in Rome. I don't know _____
1.

MIUKI: We could take a bus tour of the city first, and then decide.

MARTINA: Does the guidebook say _____
2.

MIUKI: Yeah. About $15 per person, plus tips for the guide and the driver.

C. **MARTINA:** That was delicious.

MIUKI: Let's try to find out _____
1.

MARTINA: It tasted like it had a lot of garlic and basil. I'll ask the waiter.

D. **MARTINA:** Excuse me. Can you tell me _____
1.

OFFICER: Sure. Just turn right and go straight.

E.   MIUKI: Let's take the subway. Do you know _____

_____
1.

MARTINA: It's not expensive. I don't think it depends on _____

_____
2.

But we have to get tickets, and I'm not sure _____
3.

MIUKI: Oh. Probably right in the station or at a newsstand.

F. MARTINA: I'd like to visit Ostia Antica. It's supposed to be like the ruins at Pompeii.

MIUKI: I wonder _____
1.

MARTINA: I really don't want to go with a big group of people. What about you? Do you think

_____
2.

MIUKI: Good idea! It'll be nice to drive around and see some of the countryside too.

4 | ASKING FOR ADVICE   *Grammar Note 5*

Complete the conversation between Martina and Miuki. Use a question word and the infinitive form of the verbs in the box.

figure out	get	go	invite	leave	~~wear~~

MARTINA: I can't decide _____*what to wear*_____ Friday night.
1.

MIUKI: Your red dress. You always look great in it. By the way, where are you going?

MARTINA: Trattoria da Luigi with Janek. We're meeting there at 8:00.

MIUKI: Great! You know _____ there, don't you?
2.

MARTINA: Yes, but I'm not sure _____.
3.

MIUKI: Leave at 7:30. That'll give you enough time.

MARTINA: I'd like to take Janek someplace for dessert afterward, but I don't know

_____.
4.

MIUKI: The desserts at da Luigi's are supposed to be pretty good.

MARTINA: Oh. By the way, it's Janek's birthday, so I'm paying. But I'm still not quite sure

_____ the tip.
5.

MIUKI: Service is usually included in Italy. The menu should tell you. So, who else is going?

MARTINA: Well, I thought about asking a few people to join us, but I really didn't know

_____.
6.

MIUKI: Don't worry. I'm sure it will be fine with just the two of you.

5 | EDITING

Read this post to a travelers' website. There are ten mistakes in the use of embedded questions. The first mistake is already corrected. Find and correct nine more. Don't forget to check punctuation.

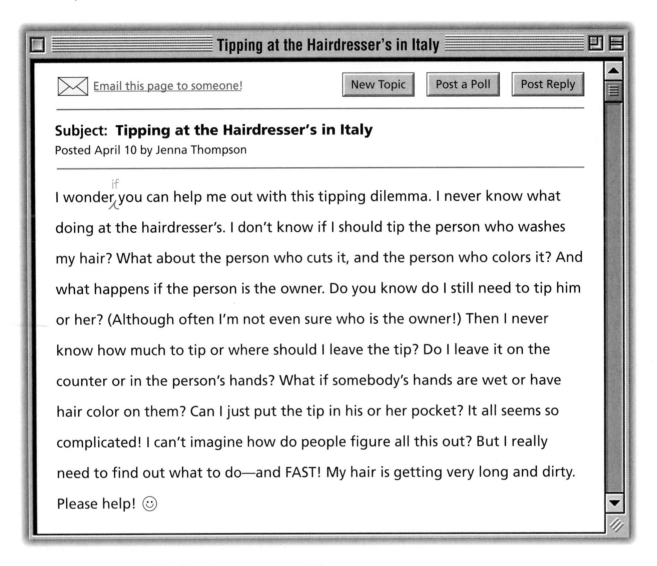

Tipping at the Hairdresser's in Italy

✉ Email this page to someone!   New Topic   Post a Poll   Post Reply

Subject: Tipping at the Hairdresser's in Italy
Posted April 10 by Jenna Thompson

I wonder *if* ‸ you can help me out with this tipping dilemma. I never know what doing at the hairdresser's. I don't know if I should tip the person who washes my hair? What about the person who cuts it, and the person who colors it? And what happens if the person is the owner. Do you know do I still need to tip him or her? (Although often I'm not even sure who is the owner!) Then I never know how much to tip or where should I leave the tip? Do I leave it on the counter or in the person's hands? What if somebody's hands are wet or have hair color on them? Can I just put the tip in his or her pocket? It all seems so complicated! I can't imagine how do people figure all this out? But I really need to find out what to do—and FAST! My hair is getting very long and dirty. Please help! ☺

Communication Practice

6 | LISTENING

🎧 *A travel agent is being interviewed on a call-in radio show. The topic is tipping. Listen to the callers' questions. Then listen again, and circle the letter of the correct response to each caller's question.*

1. Caller One
   a. Between 15 and 20 percent of the total bill.
   b. The waiter.

2. Caller Two

    a. About 15 percent of the fare.

    b. Only if you are happy with the ride.

3. Caller Three

    a. Before you leave.

    b. On the table.

4. Caller Four

    a. The person who takes you to your seat.

    b. One euro for one person. Two euros for two or more people.

5. Caller Five

    a. The manager.

    b. Don't leave a tip.

6. Caller Six

    a. $1.00.

    b. At the cashier.

7. Caller Seven

    a. Look it up on the Internet.

    b. It's included in the bill.

8. Caller Eight

    a. $1.00.

    b. The person who delivers your food.

7 | TIPPING

Work in small groups. Discuss these questions.

1. Do you think tipping is a good system? Why or why not?

2. Were you ever in a situation where you didn't know what to do about a tip? What did you do?

3. How do people tip in your country and in other countries you know?

    Example: **A:** I'm not sure whether tipping is good or not. I think people should get paid enough so that they don't have to depend on tips.

             B: I wonder if you would still get good service if the tip were included.

             C: Sure you would. A service charge is included in a lot of countries, and the service is still good.

8 | INFORMATION GAP: EATING OUT

Work in groups of three. Students A and B are customers in a restaurant. Student C is the server. Students A and B, look at the menu below. Student C, turn to page 426 and follow the instructions there.

Trattoria da Luigi

English version

Appetizers

Bruschetta	1.25
Roasted vegetables	3.25

FIRST COURSE

Soup of the day (*please ask*)	2.95
Caesar salad	3.25
Luigi's salad	2.95
Linguine with clam sauce	10.80
Spaghetti da Luigi	12.90

SECOND COURSE
Chicken

Chicken da Luigi	7.95
Half roasted chicken	6.95

Beef

Veal parmigiano	15.90
Steak frites	12.90

Fish

Catch of the day (*please ask*)	price varies
Shrimp marinara	15.80
Filet of sole with sauce Dijon	13.90

Side Dishes

Vegetable of the day	2.50
Roasted potatoes	2.50

Desserts

Fruit tart (in season)	4.30
Ice cream	3.40
Chocolate cake	2.50
Fresh fruit	2.95
Dessert of the day (*please ask*)	price varies

Service Charge Not Included

Student A, you are allergic to tomatoes and dairy products. Student B, you don't eat meat or chicken. Discuss the menu with your partner. Then ask your server about items on the menu and order a meal. When you get the check, figure out a 15 percent tip.

Example: A: Do you know what's in a Caesar salad?

B: Not really. We'll have to ask the server.
Excuse me. Can you tell us what's in the Caesar salad?

C: Sure. It has lettuce, parmesan cheese, and croutons.

9 | THE FIRST TIME IS ALWAYS THE HARDEST

Think about the first time you did something—for example, the first time you:

drove a car

traveled to a foreign country

went on a job interview

became a parent

Work in pairs. Discuss what problems you had.

Example: I remember the first time I drove a car. I didn't know how to start it. I didn't know which gear to use. I even had to ask how to turn the wipers on . . .

10 | ROLE PLAY: INFORMATION PLEASE!

Work in pairs (A and B). Student A, you are a desk clerk at a hotel. Student B, you are a guest at the hotel. Use embedded questions to find out information about the following:

restaurants

banks

interesting sights

shopping

transportation

tipping

entertainment

laundry

Example: A: Can I help you?
B: Yes. Could you tell me where to find a good, inexpensive restaurant around here?
A: There are some nice restaurants around the university.

11 | WRITING

Think about a time you were traveling. Write a paragraph about a situation that confused or surprised you. Use embedded questions.

Example: When I was an exchange student in China, my Chinese friends always wanted to know how old I was. I couldn't understand why new friends needed to know my age. I wasn't sure whether to tell the truth, because I was younger than them . . .

12 | ON THE INTERNET

Ⓒ *Do a search on tipping customs in a country you are interested in. Report your findings to the class.*

Example: I wanted to know if you should tip a taxi driver in Russia. I'm confused. One site said that taxi drivers do not expect tips. Another site said they expect a tip of 10 percent. I really don't know what to do!

INFORMATION GAP FOR STUDENT C

Student C, read these notes about today's menu. Answer your customers' questions. When they are done ordering, look at the menu on page 424 and write up the order and figure out the check.

Trattoria da Luigi

Appetizers
Bruschetta (toasted bread with chopped tomatoes, garlic, olive oil)
Roasted vegetables (onions, red pepper, zucchini, eggplant)

FIRST COURSE
Soup of the day
Monday: vegetable soup (carrots, peas, string beans in a tomato broth)
Tuesday: tomato soup
Wednesday: pea soup
Thursday: onion soup
Friday: fish soup
Saturday: potato soup (includes cream)

Caesar salad (lettuce, parmesan cheese,
croutons—cubes of bread toasted in olive oil and garlic)
Luigi's salad (spinach, mushrooms, tomatoes, onions)
Spaghetti da Luigi (spaghetti with spinach, fresh
tomatoes, and mushrooms in a light cream sauce)

SECOND COURSE
Chicken da Luigi (chicken baked in a tomato sauce
with olives and basil)
Steak frites (steak cooked in pan with butter,
served with french fried potatoes)
Catch of the day: grilled flounder—6.95 euros
Shrimp marinara (shrimp in tomato sauce)
Filet of sole with sauce Dijon (mustard sauce)

Side Dishes
Vegetable of the day: broccoli

Desserts
Fruit tart (cherry, apple, blueberry)
Ice cream (chocolate, strawberry, vanilla)
Fresh fruit (apples, bananas, strawberries)
Dessert of the day: strawberry shortcake (yellow cake
with fresh strawberries and whipped cream—3.25 euros)

Example: A: Do you know what's in a Caesar salad?
  B: Not really. We'll have to ask the server.
      Excuse me. Can you tell us what's in the Caesar salad?
  C: Sure. It has lettuce, parmesan cheese, and croutons.

From **Grammar** to **Writing**
Using Direct and Indirect Speech

A letter of complaint often includes both direct and indirect speech to describe a problem. We use direct speech only when it is important (for 100 percent accuracy) to report someone's exact words or to communicate a speaker's attitude. Otherwise, we use indirect speech.

1 | *Read this letter of complaint. Underline all the examples of indirect speech once. Underline all the examples of direct speech twice.*

Computer Town, Inc.
Customer Service Department
One Swell Way
Dallas, TX 75201

Dear Customer Service Manager:

In September 2004, I purchased a computer from your company. After the one-year warranty expired, I bought an extended service contract every year. I always received a renewal notice in the mail that told me <u>that my policy was going to expire in a few weeks</u>. This year, however, I did not receive the notice, and, as a result, I missed the deadline.

Upon realizing this mistake, I immediately called your company and asked if I could renew the service contract. The representative said, <u>"It's too late, Miss."</u> He said that if I wanted to extend my contract, they would have to send someone to my home to inspect my computer. He also told me I would have to pay $160 for this visit. He said that my only other option was to ship my computer back to the company for inspection. I told him that neither of these options was acceptable.

When I asked him why I hadn't been notified that my contract was going to expire, he said, "We don't send notices out anymore." I said that I wanted to make a complaint. He said, "Don't complain to me. I don't even park the cars of the people who make these decisions."

I think that your representatives should be more polite when speaking to customers. I also think that your customers should have

(continued)

been told that they would no longer receive renewal notices in the mail. That way, I would not have missed the deadline. I would, therefore, greatly appreciate it if I could have my service contract renewed without having to go through the inconvenience and expense of having my computer inspected.

Thank you for your attention.

Sincerely yours,

Anne Marie Clarke

Anne Marie Clarke
Customer No. 5378593

2 | Look at the letter in Exercise 1. Circle the correct words to complete these sentences. Give an example of each item.

1. The word *that* often introduces direct / (indirect) speech.

   He told me that I would have to pay $160 for this visit.

2. Use quotation marks for direct / indirect speech.

   _____

3. Put final punctuation inside / outside the quotation marks.

   _____

4. Don't use a comma before direct / indirect speech.

   _____

5. Capitalize the first word of direct / indirect speech.

   _____

6. You can leave out the word *that* / question word when it introduces a reported statement / question.

   _____

7. The writer used direct / indirect speech to show that the representative on the phone was rude.

   _____

3 | *Before you write . . .*

1. Think of an incident you would like to complain about, or make one up.

2. Work with a partner. Discuss each other's incidents and ask questions. Talk about where to use direct speech most effectively.

4 | *Write your letter of complaint. Remember to use indirect speech, and, if appropriate, direct speech. Be sure to capitalize and punctuate correctly.*

5 | *Exchange letters with a different partner. Then answer the following questions.*

	Yes	**No**
1. Do you understand the writer's complaint?	☐	☐
2. Did the writer choose direct speech to show the other person's attitude?	☐	☐
3. Did the writer choose direct speech for 100 percent accuracy?	☐	☐
4. Did the writer use quotation marks for direct speech only?	☐	☐
5. Is the direct speech punctuated correctly?	☐	☐

6 | *Work with your partner. Discuss each other's editing questions from Exercise 5. Then rewrite your own letter and make any necessary corrections.*

Review Test

I *Karen and Jon had a party a week ago. Karen is telling a friend about the conversations she had before the party. Read what people actually said. Then circle the correct word(s) to complete each reported sentence.*

1. "We'd like you and Bill to come to a party at our apartment this Friday."

   I invited Maria and Bill <u>came /</u> <u>(to come)</u> to a party at our apartment <u>last / this</u> Friday.
           a.   **b.**

2. "It'll be a housewarming for our new apartment."

   I told them it <u>would be / will be</u> a housewarming for <u>our / their</u> new apartment.
               a.   **b.**

3. "We'll be a little late."

   Maria <u>said / told</u> me that <u>they / we</u> would be a little late.
         a.   **b.**

4. "What time is your party going to start?"

   Sheila <u>said / asked</u> what time our party <u>is / was</u> going to start.
           a.   **b.**

5. "Should I bring something?"

   She asked if <u>I / she</u> <u>should bring / should have brought</u> something.
               a.   **b.**

6. "Thanks, Sheila, but that's OK. Don't bring anything."

   I thanked her, but I <u>told / said</u> her <u>not to bring / didn't bring</u> anything.
                    a.   **b.**

7. "Hi, Karen. I've been planning to call you and Jon for a long time."

   Tory told me he <u>'s been planning / 'd been planning</u> to call <u>us / you</u> for a long time.
                    a.   **b.**

8. "I don't know how to get to your place."

   He said he <u>didn't know how / doesn't know how</u> to get to <u>your / our</u> place.
               a.   **b.**

9. "Is there a bus stop nearby?"

   He <u>said / asked</u> <u>was there / if there was</u> a bus stop nearby.
     a.   **b.**

(continued)

10. "Don't be afraid of getting lost."

I told Tory <u>not to be / be</u> afraid of getting lost.

a.

11. "Take the Woodmere Avenue bus."

I <u>invited / told</u> him <u>take / to take</u> the Woodmere Avenue bus.

a.   b.

12. "I'm sorry, Karen. I can't come tomorrow night."

Nita said that she <u>can't / couldn't</u> come <u>the following night / tomorrow night</u>.

a.   b.

13. "My cousin from Detroit is arriving today."

She told me her cousin from Detroit <u>is / was</u> arriving <u>today / that day</u>.

a.   b.

14. "Bring your cousin along."

I <u>said / told</u> Nita to bring <u>her / your</u> cousin along.

a.   b.

15. "The weather bureau has issued a storm warning for tonight."

Jon told me that the weather bureau <u>has issued / had issued</u> a storm warning for <u>tonight / that night</u>.

a.   b.

16. "Schools will close early today."

The forecaster said that schools <u>would /will</u> close early <u>today / that day</u>.

a.   b.

17. "Motorists must drive with extreme caution."

She said that motorists <u>must have driven / had to drive</u> with extreme caution.

a.

18. "I love snow."

Jon always <u>tells / says</u> that he <u>loves / loved</u> snow.

a.   b.

19. "Would you please shovel the driveway?"

The next morning I asked <u>you / him</u> <u>to shovel / if he had shoveled</u> the driveway.

a.   b.

20. "Where are my boots?"

He <u>told / asked</u> me where <u>were his boots / his boots were</u>.

a.   b.

II *Each sentence has four underlined words or phrases. The four underlined parts of the sentences are marked A, B, C, or D. Circle the letter of the <u>one</u> underlined part that is NOT CORRECT.*

1. I <u>wonder</u> <u>how much</u> <u>should I</u> <u>tip</u> the driver for a trip to the airport.
      A   B   C   D
         A B Ⓒ D

2. Bob <u>said</u> <u>don't</u> forget <u>to bring</u> my bathing suit <u>because</u> they have a pool.
       A   B   C   D
         A B C D

3. The <u>forecaster</u> <u>said</u>, "<u>The</u> weather <u>was going</u> to be great tomorrow."
        A   B   C   D
         A B C D

4. <u>Cindy asked</u> Paz <u>if he knew</u> the phone number of the restaurant or
       A   B
         A B C D

   <u>if</u> <u>should she</u> look it up.
   C   D

5. She <u>wasn't sure</u> <u>if</u> or not <u>she</u> <u>needed</u> an umbrella.
        A   B   C   D
         A B C D

6. The bus driver <u>said</u> me I <u>should</u> <u>get off</u> at Pine Street and <u>walk</u> to Oak.
            A   B   C   D
         A B C D

7. Juan <u>said</u> that <u>if</u> he <u>had known</u>, he <u>would</u> told me the way.
       A   B   C   D
         A B C D

8. <u>When</u> I <u>talked</u> to Pat last month, she <u>told</u> she <u>was leaving</u>.
      A   B   C   D
         A B C D

9. It <u>was snowing</u> last night when Vick <u>called</u> me from Florida and <u>told</u>
      A   B   C

   me he loved the warm weather down <u>here</u>.
                                   D
         A B C D

10. My doctor <u>told me</u> <u>to</u> <u>wearing</u> a hat whenever I <u>go</u> into the sun.
           A   B   C   D
         A B C D

III *Read the direct speech. Circle the letter of the correct word(s) to complete the same speech reported the following day.*

1. "You look beautiful in that dress."
                                               A B C Ⓓ
   She told me _____ beautiful in that dress.
   (**A**) you look   (**C**) I'll look
   (**B**) you looked   (**D**) I looked

2. "Have you met Bill and Maria yet?"
                                               A B C D
   Harry asked me _____ Bill and Maria yet.
   (**A**) if I met   (**C**) did I meet
   (**B**) have I met   (**D**) if I had met

(continued)

3. "Is Tory coming tonight?"

    I asked Jon _____ Tory was coming that night.

    (**A**) whether   (**C**) when

    (**B**) did   (**D**) is

      A B C D

4. "I'm not sure."

    He told me _____ sure.

    (**A**) I wasn't   (**C**) he isn't

    (**B**) he wasn't   (**D**) I'm not

      A B C D

5. "Why don't you ride home with us?"

    Bill invited me _____ home with them.

    (**A**) why I didn't ride   (**C**) to ride

    (**B**) not to ride   (**D**) riding

      A B C D

6. "It may snow tonight."

    He said it might snow _____.

    (**A**) tomorrow night   (**C**) at night

    (**B**) that night   (**D**) tonight

      A B C D

7. "Call me tomorrow."

    Karen said _____ her the next day.

    (**A**) to call   (**C**) call

    (**B**) me to call   (**D**) I will call

      A B C D

8. "We ought to get together more often."

    We all said that we _____ together more often.

    (**A**) had better get   (**C**) ought to get

    (**B**) ought to have gotten (**D**) should have gotten

      A B C D

9. "Don't drive fast."

    Jon told Maria _____ fast.

    (**A**) to not drive   (**C**) they don't drive

    (**B**) don't drive   (**D**) not to drive

      A B C D

10. "I had a great time."

    Bill told Jon _____ had had a great time.

    (**A**) I   (**C**) you

    (**B**) he   (**D**) Jon

      A B C D

IV *Report the conversation that Nita and Jon had at the party last week. Use the verbs in parentheses.*

1. **NITA:** How long have you and Karen been living here?

   (ask) *Nita asked how long Jon and Karen had been living there.*

2. **JON:** We moved in three weeks ago.

   (tell) *Jon Told her*

3. **NITA:** Do you like this place better than your old apartment?

   (ask) _____

4. **JON:** We like it a lot more.

   (say) _____

5. **JON:** When did your cousin arrive from Detroit?

   (ask) _____

6. **NITA:** He just came yesterday.

   (tell) _____

7. **JON:** It's been an incredible winter.

   (say) _____

8. **NITA:** The roads may close again with this storm.

   (say) _____

9. **JON:** Don't drive tonight.

   (say) _____

10. **JON:** Stay here with your cousin.

    (say) _____

11. **NITA:** We should try to make it home.

    (tell) _____

12. **NITA:** I have to walk my dog early tomorrow morning.

    (say) _____

V *Read this draft of a news story. There are nine mistakes in the use of direct and indirect speech and embedded questions. The first mistake is already corrected. Find and correct eight more. Don't forget to check punctuation. Mistakes with quotation marks count as one mistake for the sentence.*

Motorists returning home during last night's snow storm were pleasantly surprised. Early yesterday afternoon, forecasters had predicted that Route 10 ~~will~~ *would* close because of high winds. However, all major highways remained open last night. One woman, stopping for a newspaper on Woodmere Avenue at about midnight, told this reporter that she and her cousin have almost decided to stay with a friend tonight, rather than drive home. Her cousin told me that I had just arrived from Detroit, where the storm hit first. He said "that it had been a big one." School children seemed especially pleased. Yesterday morning, most schools announced that they will close at 1:00 P.M. Several kids at James Fox Elementary reported that they are planning to spend that afternoon sledding and having snowball fights.

Many people are wondering how could weather forecasters have made such a big *could* mistake. Carla Donati, the weather reporter for WCSX, said that they really were not sure why this had happened? The National Weather Service has not commented.

▶ *To check your answers, go to the Answer Key on page RT-6.*

APPENDICES

1 | Irregular Verbs

Base Form	Simple Past	Past Participle	Base Form	Simple Past	Past Participle
arise	arose	arisen	give	gave	given
awake	awoke	awoken	go	went	gone
be	was/were	been	grind	ground	ground
beat	beat	beaten/beat	grow	grew	grown
become	became	become	hang	hung	hung
begin	began	begun	have	had	had
bend	bent	bent	hear	heard	heard
bet	bet	bet	hide	hid	hidden
bite	bit	bitten	hit	hit	hit
bleed	bled	bled	hold	held	held
blow	blew	blown	hurt	hurt	hurt
break	broke	broken	keep	kept	kept
bring	brought	brought	kneel	knelt/kneeled	knelt/kneeled
build	built	built	knit	knit/knitted	knit/knitted
burn	burned/burnt	burned/burnt	know	knew	known
burst	burst	burst	lay	laid	laid
buy	bought	bought	lead	led	led
catch	caught	caught	leap	leaped/leapt	leaped/leapt
choose	chose	chosen	leave	left	left
cling	clung	clung	lend	lent	lent
come	came	come	let	let	let
cost	cost	cost	lie (lie down)	lay	lain
creep	crept	crept	light	lit/lighted	lit/lighted
cut	cut	cut	lose	lost	lost
deal	dealt	dealt	make	made	made
dig	dug	dug	mean	meant	meant
dive	dived/dove	dived	meet	met	met
do	did	done	pay	paid	paid
draw	drew	drawn	prove	proved	proved/proven
dream	dreamed/dreamt	dreamed/dreamt	put	put	put
drink	drank	drunk	quit	quit	quit
drive	drove	driven	read /rid/	read /rɛd/	read /rɛd/
eat	ate	eaten	ride	rode	ridden
fall	fell	fallen	ring	rang	rung
feed	fed	fed	rise	rose	risen
feel	felt	felt	run	ran	run
fight	fought	fought	say	said	said
find	found	found	see	saw	seen
fit	fit/fitted	fit	seek	sought	sought
flee	fled	fled	sell	sold	sold
fling	flung	flung	send	sent	sent
fly	flew	flown	set	set	set
forbid	forbade/forbid	forbidden	sew	sewed	sewn/sewed
forget	forgot	forgotten	shake	shook	shaken
forgive	forgave	forgiven	shave	shaved	shaved/shaven
freeze	froze	frozen	shine (intransitive)	shone/shined	shone/shined
get	got	gotten/got	shoot	shot	shot

(continued)

BASE FORM	SIMPLE PAST	PAST PARTICIPLE	BASE FORM	SIMPLE PAST	PAST PARTICIPLE
show	showed	shown	strike	struck	struck/stricken
shrink	shrank/shrunk	shrunk/shrunken	swear	swore	sworn
shut	shut	shut	sweep	swept	swept
sing	sang	sung	swim	swam	swum
sink	sank/sunk	sunk	swing	swung	swung
sit	sat	sat	take	took	taken
sleep	slept	slept	teach	taught	taught
slide	slid	slid	tear	tore	torn
speak	spoke	spoken	tell	told	told
speed	sped/speeded	sped/speeded	think	thought	thought
spend	spent	spent	throw	threw	thrown
spill	spilled/spilt	spilled/spilt	understand	understood	understood
spin	spun	spun	upset	upset	upset
spit	spit/spat	spat	wake	woke	woken
split	split	split	wear	wore	worn
spread	spread	spread	weave	wove/weaved	woven/weaved
spring	sprang	sprung	weep	wept	wept
stand	stood	stood	win	won	won
steal	stole	stolen	wind	wound	wound
stick	stuck	stuck	withdraw	withdrew	withdrawn
sting	stung	stung	wring	wrung	wrung
stink	stank/stunk	stunk	write	wrote	written

2 | Non-Action Verbs

EMOTIONS
admire
adore
appreciate
care
detest
dislike
doubt
envy
fear
hate
like
love
regret
respect
trust

MENTAL STATES
agree
assume
believe
consider
disagree
disbelieve
estimate
expect
feel (believe)
find (believe)
guess
hesitate
hope
imagine

know
mean
mind
presume
realize
recognize
remember
see (understand)
suppose
suspect
think (believe)
understand
wonder

WANTS AND PREFERENCES
desire
hope
need
prefer
want
wish

PERCEPTION AND THE SENSES
feel
hear
notice
observe
perceive
see
smell
sound
taste

APPEARANCE AND VALUE
appear
be
cost
equal
look (seem)
matter
represent
resemble
seem
signify
weigh

POSSESSION AND RELATIONSHIP
belong
contain
have
own
possess

3 | Verbs Followed by the Gerund (Base Form of Verb + -ing)

acknowledge
admit
advise
appreciate
avoid
can't help
celebrate

consider
delay
deny
detest
discontinue
discuss
dislike

endure
enjoy
escape
explain
feel like
finish
forgive

give up (stop)
imagine
justify
keep (continue)
mention
mind (object to)
miss

postpone
practice
prevent
prohibit
propose
quit

recall
recommend
regret
report
resent
resist

risk
suggest
support
tolerate
understand

4 | Verbs Followed by the Infinitive (*To* + Base Form of Verb)

afford	can('t) afford	expect	hurry	neglect	promise	volunteer
agree	can('t) wait	fail	intend	offer	refuse	wait
appear	choose	grow	learn	pay	request	want
arrange	consent	help	manage	plan	seem	wish
ask	decide	hesitate	mean *(intend)*	prepare	struggle	would like
attempt	deserve	hope	need	pretend	swear	yearn

5 | Verbs Followed by Objects and the Infinitive

advise	choose*	forbid	invite	persuade	require	want*
allow	convince	force	need*	promise*	teach	warn
ask*	enable	get*	order	remind	tell	wish*
cause	encourage	help*	pay*	request	urge	would like*
challenge	expect*	hire	permit			

*These verbs can also be followed by the infinitive without an object (EXAMPLE: *ask to leave* or *ask someone to leave*).

6 | Verbs Followed by the Gerund or the Infinitive

begin	continue	hate	love	remember*	stop*
can't stand	forget*	like	prefer	start	try

*These verbs can be followed by either the gerund or the infinitive but there is a big difference in meaning.

7 | Verb + Preposition Combinations

admit to	choose between /	dream about/of	look forward to	resort to
advise against	among	feel like/about	object to	succeed in
apologize for	complain about	go along with	pay for	talk about
approve of	count on	insist on	plan on	think about
believe in	deal with	keep on	rely on	wonder about

8 | Adjective + Preposition Expressions

accustomed to	awful at	content with	fond of	opposed to	satisfied with	terrible at
afraid of	bad at	curious about	glad about	pleased about	shocked at/by	tired of
amazed at/by	bored with/by	different from	good at	ready for	sick of	used to
angry at	capable of	excited about	happy about	responsible for	slow at	worried about
ashamed of	careful of	famous for	interested in	sad about	sorry for/about	
aware of	concerned about	fed up with	nervous about	safe from	surprised at/about/by	

9 | Adjectives Followed by the Infinitive

EXAMPLE: *I'm **happy to hear** that.*

afraid	anxious	depressed	disturbed	encouraged	happy	pleased	reluctant	surprised
alarmed	ashamed	determined	eager	excited	hesitant	proud	sad	touched
amazed	curious	disappointed	easy	fortunate	likely	ready	shocked	upset
angry	delighted	distressed	embarrassed	glad	lucky	relieved	sorry	willing

10 | Irregular Comparisons of Adjectives, Adverbs, and Quantifiers

ADJECTIVE	ADVERB	COMPARATIVE	SUPERLATIVE
bad	badly	worse	worst
far	far	farther/further	farthest/furthest
good	well	better	best
little	little	less	least
many/a lot of	—	more	most
much*/a lot of	much*/a lot	more	most

Much is usually only used in questions and negative statements.

11 | Adjectives That Form the Comparative and Superlative in Two Ways

ADJECTIVE	COMPARATIVE	SUPERLATIVE
common	commoner/more common	commonest/most common
cruel	crueler/more cruel	cruelest/most cruel
deadly	deadlier/more deadly	deadliest/most deadly
friendly	friendlier/more friendly	friendliest/most friendly
handsome	handsomer/more handsome	handsomest/most handsome
happy	happier/more happy	happiest/most happy
likely	likelier/more likely	likeliest/most likely
lively	livelier/more lively	liveliest/most lively
lonely	lonelier/more lonely	loneliest/most lonely
lovely	lovelier/more lovely	loveliest/most lovely
narrow	narrower/more narrow	narrowest/most narrow
pleasant	pleasanter/more pleasant	pleasantest/most pleasant
polite	politer/more polite	politest/most polite
quiet	quieter/more quiet	quietest/most quiet
shallow	shallower/more shallow	shallowest/most shallow
sincere	sincerer/more sincere	sincerest/most sincere
stupid	stupider/more stupid	stupidest/most stupid
true	truer/more true	truest/most true

12 | Participial Adjectives

-ed	-ing	-ed	-ing	-ed	-ing
alarmed	alarming	disturbed	disturbing	moved	moving
amazed	amazing	embarrassed	embarrassing	paralyzed	paralyzing
amused	amusing	entertained	entertaining	pleased	pleasing
annoyed	annoying	excited	exciting	relaxed	relaxing
astonished	astonishing	exhausted	exhausting	satisfied	satisfying
bored	boring	fascinated	fascinating	shocked	shocking
confused	confusing	frightened	frightening	surprised	suprising
depressed	depressing	horrified	horrifying	terrified	terrifying
disappointed	disappointing	inspired	inspiring	tired	tiring
disgusted	disgusting	interested	interesting	touched	touching
distressed	distressing	irritated	irritating	troubled	troubling

13 | Reporting Verbs

STATEMENTS

acknowledge	complain	note	state
add	conclude	observe	suggest
admit	confess	promise	tell
announce	declare	remark	warn
answer	deny	repeat	whisper
argue	exclaim	reply	write
assert	explain	report	yell
believe	indicate	respond	
claim	maintain	say	
comment	mean	shout	

INSTRUCTIONS, COMMANDS, REQUESTS, AND INVITATIONS

advise	invite
ask	order
caution	say
command	tell
demand	urge
instruct	warn

QUESTIONS

ask
inquire
question
want to know
wonder

14 | Time Word Changes in Indirect Speech

DIRECT SPEECH		INDIRECT SPEECH
now	→	then
today	→	that day
tomorrow	→	the next day OR the following day OR the day after
yesterday	→	the day before OR the previous day
this week/month/year	→	that week/month/year
last week/month/year	→	the week/month/year before
next week/month/year	→	the following week/month/year

15 | Phrases Introducing Embedded Questions

I don't know . . .
I don't understand . . .
I wonder . . .
I'm not sure . . .
I can't remember . . .
I can't imagine . . .
It doesn't say . . .

I'd like to know . . .
I want to understand . . .
I'd like to find out . . .
We need to find out . . .
Let's ask . . .

Do you know . . . ?
Do you understand . . . ?
Can you tell me . . . ?
Could you explain . . . ?
Can you remember . . . ?
Would you show me . . . ?
Who knows . . . ?

allow oneself	be proud of oneself	enjoy oneself	keep oneself (busy)	remind oneself
amuse oneself	behave oneself	feel sorry for oneself	kill oneself	see oneself
ask oneself	believe in oneself	forgive oneself	look after oneself	take care of oneself
avail oneself of	blame oneself	help oneself	look at oneself	talk to oneself
be hard on oneself	cut oneself	hurt oneself	prepare oneself	teach oneself
be oneself	deprive oneself of	imagine oneself	pride oneself on	tell oneself
be pleased with oneself	dry oneself	introduce oneself	push oneself	treat oneself

17 | **Transitive Phrasal Verbs**

(s.o. = someone   s.t. = something)
- **separable phrasal verbs** show the object between the verb and the particle: *call s.o. up.*
- **verbs which must be separated** have an asterisk (*): *do s.t. over**
- **inseparable phrasal verbs** show the object after the particle: carry on s.t.

Remember: You can put a **noun object** between the verb and the particle of **separable** two-word verbs (**call** *Jan* **up** OR ***call up*** *Jan*). You <u>must</u> put a **pronoun object** between the verb and the particle of separable verbs (***call her up*** NOT ~~call up~~ her).

PHRASAL VERB	MEANING	PHRASAL VERB	MEANING
ask s.o. **over***	*invite to one's home*	**cut** s.t. **off**	1. *stop the supply of*
block s.t. **out**	*stop from passing through (light/ noise)*		2. *remove by cutting*
		cut s.t. **out**	*remove by cutting*
blow s.t. **out**	*stop burning by blowing air on it*	**cut** s.t. **up**	*cut into small pieces*
blow s.t. **up**	1. *make explode*	**do** s.t. **over***	*do again*
	2. *fill with air (a balloon)*	**do** s.o. or s.t. **up**	*make more beautiful*
	3. *make something larger (a photo)*	**draw** s.t. **together**	*unite*
bring s.t. **about**	*make happen*	**dream** s.t. **up**	*invent*
bring s.o. or s.t. **back**	*return*	**drink** s.t. **up**	*drink completely*
bring s.o. **down***	*depress*	**drop** s.o. or s.t. **off**	*take someplace*
bring s.t. **out**	*introduce (a new product/book)*	**drop out of** s.t.	*quit*
bring s.o. **up**	*raise (children)*	**empty** s.t. **out**	*empty completely*
bring s.t. **up**	*bring attention to*	**end up with** s.t.	*have an unexpected result*
build s.t **up**	*increase*	**fall for** s.o.	*feel romantic love for*
burn s.t. **down**	*burn completely*	**fall for** s.t.	*be tricked by, believe*
call s.o. **back***	*return a phone call*	**figure** s.o. or s.t. **out**	*understand (after thinking about)*
call s.o. **in**	*ask for help with a problem*	**fill** s.t. **in**	*complete with information*
call s.t. **off**	*cancel*	**fill** s.t. **out**	*complete (a form)*
call s.o. **up**	*contact by phone*	**fill** s.t. **up**	*fill completely*
carry on s.t.	*continue*	**find** s.t. **out**	*learn information*
carry s.t. **out**	*conduct (an experiment/a plan)*	**fix** s.t. **up**	*redecorate (a home)*
cash in on s.t.	*profit from*	**follow through with** s.t.	*complete*
charge s.t. **up**	*charge with electricity*	**get** s.t. **across**	*get people to understand an idea*
check s.t. **out**	*examine*	**get off** s.t.	*leave (a bus/a train/a phone call)*
cheer s.o. **up**	*cause to feel happier*	**get on** s.t.	*board (a bus/a train/a phone call)*
clean s.o. or s.t. **up**	*cleam completely*	**get out of** s.t.	*leave (a car/taxi)*
clear s.t. **up**	*explain*	**get** s.t. **out of** s.t.*	*benefit from*
close s.t. **down**	*close by force*	**get through with** s.t.	*finish*
come off s.t.	*become unattached*	**get to** s.o. or s.t.	1. *reach s.o. or s.t.*
come up with s.t.	*invent*		2. *upset s.o.*
count on s.o. or s.t.	*depend on*	**get together with** s.o.	*meet*
cover s.o. or s.t. **up**	*cover completely*	**give** s.t. **away**	*give without charging money*
cross s.t. **out**	*draw a line through*	**give** s.t. **back**	*return*
cut s.t. **down**	1. *bring down by cutting (a tree)*	**give** s.t. **out**	*distribute*
	2. *reduce*		

PHRASAL VERB	MEANING
give s.t. **up**	*quit, abandon*
go after s.o. or s.t.	*try to get or win, pursue*
go along with s.t.	*support*
go over s.t.	*review*
hand s.t. **in**	*submit, give work (to a boss/ teacher)*
hand s.t. **out**	*distribute*
hang s.t. **up**	*put on a hook or hanger*
help s.o. **out**	*assist*
hold s.t. **on**	*keep attached*
keep s.o. or s.t. **away**	*cause to stay at a distance*
keep s.t. **on***	*not remove (a piece of clothing/jewelry)*
keep s.o. or s.t. **out**	*prevent from entering*
keep up with s.o. or s.t.	*go as fast as*
lay s.o. **off**	*end employment*
lay s.t. **out**	1. *arrange according to a plan*
	2. *spend money*
leave s.t. **on**	1. *not turn off (a light/radio)*
	2. *not remove (a piece of clothing/jewelry)*
leave s.t. **out**	*omit, not include*
let s.o. **down**	*disappoint*
let s.o. or s.t. **in**	*allow to enter*
let s.o. **off**	1. *allow to leave (a bus/car)*
	2. *not punish*
let s.o. or s.t. **out**	*allow to leave*
light s.t. **up**	*illuminate*
look after s.o. or s.t.	*take care of*
look into s.t.	*research*
look s.o. or s.t. **over**	*examine*
look s.t. **up**	*try to find (in a book/on the Internet)*
make s.t. **up**	*create*
miss out on s.t.	*lose the chance for something good*
move s.t. **around***	*change the location*
pass s.t. **out**	*distribute*
pass s.o. or s.t. **up**	*decide not to use*
pay s.o. or s.t. **back**	*repay*
pick s.o. or s.t. **out**	1. *choose*
	2. *identify*
pick s.o. or s.t. **up**	*lift*
pick s.t. **up**	1. *buy, purchase*
	2. *get (an idea/an interest)*
	3. *answer the phone*
point s.o. or s.t. **out**	*indicate*
put s.t. **away**	*put in an appropriate place*
put s.t. **back**	*return to its original place*
put s.o. or s.t. **down**	*stop holding*
put s.o. **off**	*discourage*
put s.t. **off**	*delay*
put s.t. **on**	*cover the body (with clothes or jewelry)*
put s.t. **together**	*assemble*
put s.t. **up**	*erect*
run into s.o.	*meet accidentally*
see s.t. **through***	*complete*
send s.t. **back**	*return*
send s.t. **out**	*mail*
set s.t. **off**	*cause to explode*

PHRASAL VERB	MEANING
set s.t. **up**	1. *prepare for use*
	2. *establish (a business/an organization)*
settle on s.t.	*choose s.t. after thinking about many possibilities*
show s.o. or s.t. **off**	*display the best qualities*
show up on s.t.	*appear*
shut s.t. **off**	*stop (a machine/light)*
sign s.o. **up** (for s.t.)	*register*
start s.t. **over***	*start again*
stick with/to s.o. or s.t.	*not quit, not leave, persevere*
straighten s.t. **up**	*make neat*
switch s.t. **on**	*start (a machine/light)*
take s.t. **away**	*remove*
take s.o. or s.t. **back**	*return*
take s.t. **down**	*remove*
take s.t. **in**	1. *notice, understand, and remember*
	2. *earn (money)*
take s.t. **off**	*remove*
take s.o. **on**	*hire*
take s.t. **on**	*agree to do*
take s.t. **out**	*borrow from a library*
take s.t. **up**	*begin a job or activity*
talk s.o. **into***	*persuade*
talk s.t. **over**	*discuss*
team up with s.o.	*start to work with*
tear s.t. **down**	*destroy*
tear s.t. **up**	*tear into small pieces*
think back on s.o. or s.t.	*remember*
think s.t. **over**	*consider*
think s.t. **up**	*invent*
throw s.t. **away/out**	*discard, put in the trash*
touch s.t. **up**	*improve by making small changes*
try s.t. **on**	*put clothing on to see if it fits*
try s.t. **out**	*use to see if it works*
turn s.t. **around***	*change the direction so the front is at the back*
turn s.o. **down**	*reject*
turn s.t. **down**	1. *lower the volume (a TV/radio)*
	2. *reject (a job/an idea)*
turn s.t. **in**	*submit, give work (to a boss/ teacher)*
turn s.o. or s.t. **into***	*change from one form to another*
turn s.o. **off***	*[slang] destroy interest*
turn s.t. **off**	*stop (a machine), extinguish (a light)*
turn s.t. **on**	*start (a machine/light)*
turn s.t. **over**	*turn something so the top side is at the bottom*
turn s.t. **up**	*make louder (a TV/radio)*
use s.t. **up**	*use completely, consume*
wake s.o. **up**	*awaken*
watch out for s.o. or s.t.	*be careful about*
work s.t. **off**	*remove by work or activity*
work s.t. **out**	*solve, understand*
write s.t. **down**	*write on a piece of paper*
write s.t. **up**	*write in a finished form*

PHRASAL VERB	MEANING
act up	cause problems
blow up	explode
break down	stop working (a machine)
break out	happen suddenly
burn down	burn completely
call back	return a phone call
catch on	become popular
cheer up	make happier
clean up	clean completely
clear up	become clear
close down	stop operating
come about	happen
come along	come with, accompany
come around	happen
come back	return
come down	become less (price)
come in	enter
come off	become unattached
come out	appear
come up	arise
dress up	wear special clothes
drop in	visit by surprise
drop out	quit
eat out	eat in a restaurant
empty out	empty completely
end up	1. do something unexpected or unintended
	2. reach a final place or condition
fall off	become detached
find out	learn information
follow through	complete
fool around	act playful
get ahead	make progress, succeed
get along	have a good relationship
get back	return
get by	survive
get off	1. leave (a bus, the Internet)
	2. end a phone conversation
get on	enter, board (a bus, a train)
get through	finish
get together	meet
get up	rise from bed, arise
give up	quit
go away	leave a place or person

PHRASAL VERB	MEANING
go back	return
go down	become less (price, number), decrease
go off	explode (a gun/fireworks)
go on	continue
go out	leave
go over	succeed with an audience
go up	1. be built
	2. become more (price, number), increase
grow up	become an adult
hang up	end a phone call
hold on	1. wait
	2. not hang up the phone
keep away	stay at a distance
keep on	continue
keep out	not enter
keep up	go as fast as
lie down	recline
light up	illuminate
look out	be careful
make up	end a disagreement, reconcile
miss out	lose the chance for something good
pay off	be worthwhile
pick up	improve
play around	have fun
run out	not have enough of
show up	appear
sign up	register
sit down	take a seat
slip up	make a mistake
stand up	rise
start over	start again
stay up	remain awake
straighten up	make neat
take off	depart (a plane)
turn out	have a particular result
turn up	appear
wake up	stop sleeping
watch out	be careful
work out	1. be resolved
	2. exercise

A. SOCIAL MODALS AND EXPRESSIONS

FUNCTION	MODAL OR EXPRESSION*	TIME	EXAMPLES
Ability	can can't	Present	• Sam **can swim**. • He **can't skate**.
	could could not	Past	• We **could swim** last year. • We **couldn't skate**.
	be able to* not be able to*	All verb forms	• Lea **is able to run** fast. • She **wasn't able to run** fast last year.
Advice	should shouldn't ought to** had better** had better not**	Present or Future	• You **should study** more. • You **shouldn't miss** class. • We **ought to leave**. • We**'d better go**. • We**'d better not stay**.
Advisability in the Past and **Regret or Blame**	should have should not have ought to have could have might have	Past	• I **should have become** a doctor. • I **shouldn't have wasted** time. • He **ought to have told** me. • She **could have gone** to college. • You **might have called**. I waited for hours.
Necessity	have to* not have to*	All verb forms	• He **has to go** now. • He **doesn't have to go** yet. • I **had to go** yesterday. • I **will have to go** soon.
	have got to* must	Present or Future	• He**'s got** to leave! • You **must use** a pen for the test.
Permission	can	Present or Future	• **Can** I **sit** here? • **Can** I **call** tomorrow? • Yes, you **can**.
	can't could may		• No, you **can't**. Sorry. • **Could** he **leave** now? • **May** I **borrow** your pen? • Yes, you **may**.
	may not		• No, you **may not**. Sorry.
Prohibition	must not can't	Present or Future	• You **must not drive** without a license. • You **can't drive** without a license.
Requests	can	Present or Future	• **Can** you **close** the door, please? • Sure, I **can**.
	can't could will would		• Sorry, I **can't**. • **Could** you please **answer** the phone? • **Will** you **wash** the dishes, please? • **Would** you please **mail** this letter?

*The meaning of this expression is similar to the meaning of a modal. Unlike a modal, it has -s for third person singular.

**The meaning of this expression is similar to the meaning of a modal. Like a modal, it has no -s for third person singular.

B. LOGICAL MODALS AND EXPRESSIONS

FUNCTION	LOGICAL MODAL OR EXPRESSION	TIME	EXAMPLES
Impossibility	can't couldn't	Present or Future	• That **can't be** Ana. She left for France yesterday. • It **can't snow** tomorrow. It's going to be too warm. • He **couldn't be** guilty. He wasn't in town when the crime occurred. • The teacher **couldn't give** the test tomorrow. Tomorrow's Saturday.
	couldn't have	Past	• You **couldn't have failed**. You studied so hard.
Possibility	must must not have to* have got to* may	Present	• This **must be** her house. Her name is on the door. • She **must not be** home. I don't see her car. • She **has to know** him. They went to school together. • He**'s got to be** guilty. We saw him do it. • She **may be** home now.
	may not might might not could	Present or Future	• It **may not rain** tomorrow. • Lee **might be sick** today. • He **might not come** to class. • They **could be** at the library. • It **could rain** tomorrow.
	may have may not have might have might not have could have	Past	• They **may have left** already. I don't see them. • They **may not have arrived** yet. • He **might have called**. I'll check my phone messages. • He **might not have left** a message. • She **could have forgotten** to mail the letter.

*The meaning of this expression is similar to the meaning of a modal. Unlike a modal, it has -s for third person singular.

20 | Irregular Plural Nouns

SINGULAR	PLURAL	SINGULAR	PLURAL	SINGULAR	PLURAL	SINGULAR	PLURAL
analysis	analyses	half	halves	person	people	deer	deer
basis	bases	knife	knives	man	men	fish	fish
crisis	crises	leaf	leaves	woman	women	sheep	sheep
hypothesis	hypotheses	life	lives	child	children		
		loaf	loaves	foot	feet		
		shelf	shelves	tooth	teeth		
		wife	wives	goose	geese		
				mouse	mice		

21 | Spelling Rules for the Simple Present: Third-Person Singular (*he, she, it*)

1. Add **-s** for most verbs.

work	work**s**
buy	buy**s**
ride	ride**s**
return	return**s**

2. Add **-es** for verbs that end in **-ch**, **-s**, **-sh**, **-x**, or **-z**.

watch	watch**es**
pass	pass**es**
rush	rush**es**
relax	relax**es**
buzz	buzz**es**

3. Change the **y** to **i** and add **-es** when the base form ends in a consonant + **y**.

study	stud**ies**
hurry	hurr**ies**
dry	dr**ies**

   Do not change the **y** when the base form ends in a vowel + **y**. Add **-s**.

play	play**s**
enjoy	enjoy**s**

4. A few verbs are irregular.

be	**is**
do	**does**
go	**goes**
have	**has**

22 | Spelling Rules for Base Form of Verb + *-ing* (Progressive and Gerund)

1. Add **-ing** to the base form of the verb.

read	read**ing**
stand	stand**ing**

2. If a verb ends in a silent **-e**, drop the final **-e** and add **-ing**.

leave	leav**ing**
take	tak**ing**

3. In one-syllable words, if the last three letters are a consonant-vowel-consonant combination (CVC), double the last consonant before adding **-ing**.

C V C	
↓ ↓ ↓	
s i t	sit**ting**

C V C	
↓ ↓ ↓	
p l a n	plan**ning**

   Do not double the last consonant in words that end in **-w**, **-x**, or **-y**.

sew	sew**ing**
fix	fix**ing**
play	play**ing**

4. In words of two or more syllables that end in a consonant-vowel-consonant combination, double the last consonant only if the last syllable is stressed.*

admít	admit**ting**	(The last syllable is stressed.)
whísper	whisper**ing**	(The last syllable is not stressed, so don't double the **-r**.)

5. If a verb ends in **-ie**, change the **ie** to **y** before adding **-ing**.

die	d**ying**

   *The symbol ´ shows main stress.

23 | Spelling Rules for the Simple Past of Regular Verbs

1. If the verb ends in a consonant, add **-ed**.

return	return**ed**
help	help**ed**

2. If the verb ends in **-e**, add **-d**.

live	live**d**
create	create**d**
die	die**d**

3. In one-syllable words, if the last three letters are a consonant-vowel-consonant combination (CVC), double the last consonant before adding **-ed**.

C V C
↓ ↓ ↓
h o p   hop**ped**

C V C
↓ ↓ ↓
p l a n   plan**ned**

Do not double the last consonant of one-syllable words ending in **-w**, **-x**, or **-y**.

bow	bow**ed**
mix	mix**ed**
play	play**ed**

4. In words of two or more syllables that end in a consonant-vowel-consonant combination, double the last consonant only if the last syllable is stressed.*

prefér	prefer**red** (The last syllable is stressed, so double the **r**.)
vísit	visit**ed** (The last syllable is not stressed, so don't double the **t**.)

5. If the verb ends in a consonant + **y**, change the **y** to **i** and add **-ed**.

worry	worr**ied**
cry	cr**ied**

6. If the verb ends in a vowel + **y**, add **-ed**. (Do not change the **y** to **i**.)

play	play**ed**
annoy	annoy**ed**
Exceptions:	pay—paid, lay—laid, say—said

*The symbol ′ shows main stress.

24 | Spelling Rules for the Comparative (-er) and Superlative (-est) of Adjectives

1. Add **-er** to one-syllable adjectives to form the comparative. Add **-est** to one-syllable adjectives to form the superlative.

cheap	cheap**er**	cheap**est**
bright	bright**er**	bright**est**

2. If the adjective ends in **-e**, add **-r** or **-st**.

nice	nice**r**	nice**st**

3. If the adjective ends in a consonant + **y**, change **y** to **i** before you add **-er** or **-est**.

pretty	prett**ier**	prett**iest**
Exception:	shy	shy**er** shy**est**

4. In one-syllable words, if the last three letters are a consonant-vowel-consonant combination (CVC), double the last consonant before adding **-er** or **-est**.

C V C
↓ ↓ ↓
b i g   big**ger**   big**gest**

Do not double the consonant in words ending in **-w** or **-y**.

slow	slow**er**	slow**est**
gray	gray**er**	gray**est**

25 | Spelling Rules for Adverbs Ending in -ly

1. Add **-ly** to the corresponding adjective.

nice	nice**ly**
quiet	quiet**ly**
beautiful	beautiful**ly**

2. If the adjective ends in a consonant + **y**, change the **y** to **i** before adding **-ly**.

easy	eas**ily**

3. If the adjective ends in **-le**, drop the **e** and add **-y**.

possible	possib**ly**

Do not drop the **e** for other adjectives ending in **-e**.

extreme	extreme**ly**
Exception:	true tru**ly**

4. If the adjective ends in **-ic**, add **-ally**.

basic	basic**ally**
fantastic	fantastic**ally**

26 | Direct Speech: Punctuation Rules

Direct speech may either follow or come before the reporting verb. When direct speech follows the reporting verb:

  a. Put a comma after the reporting verb.

  b. Use opening quotation marks (") before the first word of the direct speech.

  c. Begin the quotation with a capital letter.

  d. Use the appropriate end punctuation for the direct speech. It may be a period (.), a question mark (?), or an exclamation point (!).

  e. Put closing quotation marks (") after the end punctuation of the quotation.

Examples: He said, "I had a good time."
She asked, "Where's the party?"
They shouted, "Be careful!"

When direct speech comes before the reporting verb:

  a. Begin the sentence with opening quotation marks (").

  b. Use the appropriate end punctuation for the direct speech. If the direct speech is a statement, use a comma (,). If the direct speech is a question, use a question mark (?). If the direct speech is an exclamation, use an exclamation point (!).

  c. Use closing quotation marks after the end punctuation for the direct speech (").

  d. Begin the reporting clause with a lowercase letter.

  e. Use a period at the end of the main sentence (.).

Examples: "I had a good time," he said.
"Where's the party?" she asked.
"Be careful!" they shouted.

27 | Pronunciation Table

These are the pronunciation symbols used in this text. Listen to the pronunciation of the key words.

VOWELS				**CONSONANTS**			
Symbol	Key Word	Symbol	Key Word	Symbol	Key Word	Symbol	Key Word
i	beat, feed	ə	banana, among	p	pack, happy	ʃ	ship, machine, station, special, discussion
ɪ	bit, did	ɚ	shirt, murder	b	back, rubber		
eɪ	date, paid	aɪ	bite, cry, buy, eye	t	tie	ʒ	measure, vision
ɛ	bet, bed	aʊ	about, how	d	die	h	hot, who
æ	bat, bad	ɔɪ	voice, boy	k	came, key, quick	m	men
ɑ	box, odd, father	ɪr	beer	g	game, guest	n	sun, know, pneumonia
ɔ	bought, dog	ɛr	bare	tʃ	church, nature, watch		
oʊ	boat, road	ɑr	bar	dʒ	judge, general, major	ŋ	sung, ringing
ʊ	book, good	ɔr	door	f	fan, photograph	w	wet, white
u	boot, food, student	ʊr	tour	v	van	l	light, long
ʌ	but, mud, mother			θ	thing, breath	r	right, wrong
				ð	then, breathe	y	yes, use, music
				s	sip, city, psychology	t̪	butter, bottle
				z	zip, please, goes		

28 | Pronunciation Rules for the Simple Present: Third-Person Singular (*he, she, it*)

1. The third person singular in the simple present always ends in the letter **-s**. There are three different pronunciations for the final sound of the third person singular.

/**s**/	/**z**/	/**ɪz**/
talk**s**	love**s**	danc**es**

2. The final sound is pronounced /**s**/ after the voiceless sounds /**p**/, /**t**/, /**k**/, and /**f**/.

top	to**ps**
get	ge**ts**
take	take**s**
laugh	lau**ghs**

3. The final sound is pronounced /**z**/ after the voiced sounds /**b**/, /**d**/, /**g**/, /**v**/, /**ð**/, /**m**/, /**n**/, /**ŋ**/, /**l**/, and /**r**/.

describe	descri**bes**
spend	spen**ds**
hug	hu**gs**
live	live**s**
bathe	ba**thes**
seem	see**ms**
remain	remai**ns**
sing	si**ngs**
tell	te**lls**
lower	lowe**rs**

4. The final sound is pronounced /**z**/ after all vowel sounds.

agree	agr**ees**
try	tr**ies**
stay	st**ays**
know	kn**ows**

5. The final sound is pronounced /**ɪz**/ after the sounds /**s**/, /**z**/, /**ʃ**/, /**ʒ**/, /**ʧ**/, and /**ʤ**/. /**ɪz**/ adds a syllable to the verb.

relax	rela**xes**
freeze	free**zes**
rush	ru**shes**
massage	massa**ges**
watch	wa**tches**
judge	ju**dges**

6. **Do** and **say** have a change in vowel sound.

do	/**du**/	does	/**dʌz**/
say	/**sɛɪ**/	says	/**sɛz**/

29 | Pronunciation Rules for the Simple Past of Regular Verbs

1. The regular simple past always ends in the letter **-d**. There are three different pronunciations for the final sound of the regular simple past.

/**t**/	/**d**/	/**ɪd**/
race**d**	live**d**	attend**ed**

2. The final sound is pronounced /**t**/ after the voiceless sounds /**p**/, /**k**/, /**f**/, /**s**/, /**ʃ**/, and /**ʧ**/.

hop	ho**pped**
work	wor**ked**
laugh	lau**ghed**
address	addre**ssed**
publish	publi**shed**
watch	wa**tched**

3. The final sound is pronounced /**d**/ after the voiced sounds /**b**/, /**g**/, /**v**/, /**z**/, /**ʒ**/, /**ʤ**/, /**m**/, /**n**/, /**ŋ**/, /**l**/, /**r**/, and /**ð**/.

rub	ru**bbed**
hug	hu**gged**
live	li**ved**
surprise	surpri**sed**
massage	massa**ged**
change	chan**ged**
rhyme	rhy**med**
return	retur**ned**
bang	ba**nged**
enroll	enro**lled**
appear	appea**red**
bathe	ba**thed**

4. The final sound is pronounced /**d**/ after all vowel sounds.

agree	agr**eed**
play	pla**yed**
die	d**ied**
enjoy	enj**oyed**
row	r**owed**

5. The final sound is pronounced /**ɪd**/ after /**t**/ and /**d**/. /**ɪd**/ adds a syllable to the verb.

start	star**ted**
decide	deci**ded**

	USE FOR . . .	EXAMPLE
capital letter	• the pronoun *I*	Tomorrow **I** will be here at 2:00.
	• proper nouns	His name is **Karl**. He lives in **Germany**.
	• the first word of a sentence.	**When** does the train leave? **At** 2:00.
apostrophe (')	• possessive nouns	Is that **Marta's** coat?
	• contractions	**That's** not hers. **It's** mine.
comma (,)	• after items in a list	He bought **apples, pears, oranges,** and **bananas**.
	• before sentence connectors ***and***, ***but***, ***or***, and ***so***	They watched TV, **and** she played video games.
	• after the first part of a sentence that begins with ***because***	***Because*** **it's raining,** we're not walking to work.
	• after the first part of a sentence that begins with a preposition	***Across from*** **the post office,** there's a good restaurant.
	• after the first part of a sentence that begins with a time clause or an *if* clause	***After*** **he arrived,** we ate dinner. ***If*** **it rains,** we won't go.
	• before and after a non-identifying adjective clause in the middle of a sentence	Tony, **who lives in Paris,** e-mails me every day.
	• before a non-identifying adjective clause at the end of a sentence	I get e-mails every day from Tony, **who lives in Paris**.
exclamation mark (!)	• at the end of a sentence to show surprise or a strong feeling	You're here! That's great! Stop! A car is coming!
period (.)	• at the end of a statement	Today is Wednesday.
question mark (?)	• at the end of a question	What day is today?

GLOSSARY OF GRAMMAR TERMS

action verb a verb that describes an action.
- *Alicia **ran** home.*

active sentence a sentence that focuses on the agent (the person or thing doing the action).
- ***Ari kicked** the ball.*

addition a clause or a short sentence that follows a statement and expresses similarity to or contrast with the information in the statement.
- *Pedro is tall, **and so is Alex**.*
- *Trish doesn't like sports. **Neither does her sister**.*

adjective a word that describes a noun or pronoun.
- *It's a **good** plan, and it's not **difficult**.*

adjective clause a clause that identifies or gives additional information about a noun.
- *The woman **who called you** didn't leave her name.*
- *Samir, **who you met yesterday,** works in the lab.*

adverb a word that describes a verb, an adjective, or another adverb.
- *She drives **carefully**.*
- *She's a **very** good driver.*
- *She drives **really** well.*

affirmative a statement or answer meaning ***yes***.
- *He **works**. (affirmative statement)*
- ***Yes**, he **does**. (affirmative short answer)*

agent the person or thing doing the action in a sentence. In passive sentences, the word ***by*** is used before the agent.
- *This magazine is published **by National Geographic**.*

article a word that goes before a noun. The **indefinite** articles are ***a*** and ***an***.
- *I ate **a** sandwich and **an** apple.*

The **definite** article is ***the***.
- *I didn't like **the** sandwich. **The** apple was good.*

auxiliary verb (also called **helping verb**) a verb used with a main verb. ***Be, do***, and ***have*** are often auxiliary verbs. Modals (***can, should, may, must*** . . .) are also auxiliary verbs.
- *I **am** exercising right now.*
- *I **should** exercise every day.*
- ***Do** you like to exercise?*

base form the simple form of a verb without any endings (*-s, -ed, -ing*) or other changes.
- ***be, have, go, drive***

clause a group of words that has a subject and a verb. A sentence can have one or more clauses.
- *We are leaving now. (one clause)*
- *If it rains, we won't go. (two clauses)*

common noun a word for a person, place, or thing (but not the name of the person, place, or thing).
- *Teresa lives in a **house** near the **beach**.*

comparative the form of an adjective or adverb that shows the difference between two people, places, or things.
- *Alain is **shorter** than Brendan. (adjective)*
- *Brendan runs **faster** than Alain. (adverb)*

conditional sentence a sentence that describes a condition and its result. The sentence can be about the past, the present, or the future. The condition and result can be real or unreal.
- *If it **rains**, I **won't go**. (future, real)*
- *If it **had rained**, I **wouldn't have gone**. (past, unreal)*

continuous See **progressive**.

contraction a short form of a word or words. An apostrophe (') replaces the letter or letters.
- ***she's*** = *she is*
- ***can't*** = *cannot*

count noun a noun you can count. It has a singular and a plural form.

- one **book**, two **books**

definite article *the*. This article goes before a noun that refers to a specific person, place, or thing.

- *Please bring me **the book** on **the table**. I'm almost finished reading it.*

dependent clause (also called **subordinate clause**) a clause that needs a main clause for its meaning.

- ***If I get home early**, I'll call you.*

direct object a noun or pronoun that receives the action of a verb.

- *Marta kicked **the ball**. I saw **her**.*

direct speech language that gives the exact words a speaker used. In writing, quotation marks come before and after the speaker's words.

- ***"I saw Bob yesterday,"** she said.*
- ***"Is he in school?"***

embedded question a question that is inside another sentence.

- *I don't know **where the restaurant is**.*
- *Do you know **if it's on Tenth Street**?*

formal language used in business situations or with adults you do not know.

- *Good afternoon, Mr. Rivera. Please have a seat.*

gerund a word formed with **verb + -ing** that can be used as a subject or an object.

- ***Swimming** is great exercise.*
- *I enjoy **swimming**.*

helping verb See **auxiliary verb**.

identifying adjective clause a clause that identifies which member of a group the sentence is about.

- *There are ten students in the class. The student **who sits in front of me** is from Russia.*

if clause the clause that states the condition in a conditional sentence.

- ***If I had known you were here**, I would have called you.*

imperative a sentence that gives a command or instructions.

- ***Hurry!***
- ***Don't touch that!***

indefinite article *a* or *an*. These articles go before a noun that does not refer to a specific person, place, or thing.

- *Can you bring me **a book**? I'm looking for something to read.*

indefinite pronoun a pronoun such as **someone**, **something**, **anyone**, **anything**, **anywhere**, **no one**, **nothing**, **everyone**, and **everything**. An indefinite pronoun does not refer to a specific person, place, or thing.

- ***Someone** called you last night.*
- *Did **anything** happen?*

indirect object a noun or pronoun (often a person) that receives something as the result of the action of the verb.

- *I told **John** the story.*
- *He gave **me** some good advice.*

indirect speech language that reports what a speaker said without using the exact words.

- *Ann said **she had seen Bob the day before**.*
- *She asked **if he was in school**.*

infinitive *to* + **base form** of the verb.

- *I want **to leave** now.*

infinitive of purpose *(in order) to* + **base form** of the verb. This form gives the reason for an action.

- *I go to school **in order to learn** English.*

informal language used with family, friends, and children.

- *Hi, Pete. Sit down.*

information question See *wh-* **question**.

inseparable phrasal verb a phrasal verb whose parts must stay together.

- *We **ran into** Tomás at the supermarket. (NOT: We ~~ran Tomás into~~ . . .)*

intransitive verb a verb that does not have an object.

- *She **paints**.*
- *We **fell**.*

irregular a word that does not change its form in the usual way.

- **Go** *is an* **irregular** *verb. Its simple past* **(went)** *does not end in* -ed.

main clause a clause that can stand alone as a sentence.

- **I called my friend Tom,** *who lives in Chicago.*

main verb a verb that describes an action or state. It is often used with an auxiliary verb.

- *Jared is* **calling**.
- *Does he* **call** *every day?*

modal a type of auxiliary verb. It goes before a main verb and expresses ideas such as ability, advice, permission, and possibility. **Can, could, will, would, may, might, should,** and **must** are modals.

- **Can** *you swim?*
- *You really* **should** *learn to swim.*

negative a statement or answer meaning **no**.

- *He* **doesn't** *work.* (negative statement)
- **No,** *he* **doesn't**. (negative short answer)

non-action verb a verb that does not describe an action. It describes such things as thoughts, feelings, and senses.

- *I* **remember** *that word.*
- *Chris* **loves** *ice cream.*
- *It* **tastes** *great.*

non-count noun a noun you usually do not count (**air, water, rice, love** . . .). It has only a singular form.

- *The* **rice** *is delicious.*

nonidentifying adjective clause (also called **nonrestrictive adjective clause**) a clause that gives additional information about the noun it refers to. The information is not necessary to identify the noun.

- *My sister Diana,* **who usually hates sports,** *recently started tennis lessons.*

nonrestrictive adjective clause See **nonidentifying adjective clause**.

noun a word for a person, place, or thing.

- *My* **sister, Anne,** *works in an* **office**.
- *She uses a* **computer**.

object a noun or a pronoun that receives the action of a verb.

- *Layla threw* **the ball**.
- *She threw* **it** *to* **Tom**.

object pronoun a pronoun (**me, you, him, her, it, us, them**) that receives the action of the verb.

- *I gave* **her** *a book.*
- *I gave* **it** *to* **her**.

object relative pronoun a relative pronoun that is an object in an adjective clause.

- *I'm reading a book* **that** *I really like.*

paragraph a group of sentences, usually about one topic.

particle a word that looks like a preposition and combines with a main verb to form a phrasal verb. It often changes the meaning of the main verb.

- *He looked the word* **up**. (He looked for the meaning of the word in the dictionary.)

passive causative a sentence formed with **have** or **get + object + past participle**. It is used to talk about services that you arrange for someone to do for you.

- *She* **had the car checked** *at the service station.*
- *He's going to* **get his hair cut** *by André.*

passive sentence a sentence that focuses on the object (the person or thing receiving the action). The passive is formed with **be** + **past participle**.

- **The ball was kicked** *by Ari.*

past participle a verb form (**verb + -ed**). It can also be irregular. It is used to form the present perfect, past perfect, and future perfect. It can also be an adjective.

- *We've* **lived** *here since April.*
- *They had* **spoken** *before.*
- *She's* **interested** *in math.*

phrasal verb (also called **two-word verb**) a verb that has two parts (**verb + particle**). The meaning is often different from the meaning of its separate parts.

- *He* **grew up** *in Texas.* (became an adult)
- *His parents* **brought** *him* **up** *to be honest.* (raised)

phrase   a group of words that forms a unit but does not have a main verb. Many phrases give information about time or place.

- *Last year, we were living in Canada.*

plural   two or more.

- *There **are** three **people** in the restaurant.*
- ***They are** eating dinner.*
- ***We** saw **them**.*

possessive   nouns, pronouns, or adjectives that show a relationship or show that someone owns something.

- *Zach is **Megan's** brother.* (possessive noun)
- *Is that car **his**?* (possessive pronoun)
- *That's **his** car.* (possessive adjective)

predicate   the part of a sentence that has the main verb. It tells what the subject is doing or describes the subject.

- *My sister **works for a travel agency**.*

preposition   a word that goes before nouns and pronouns to show time, place, or direction.

- *I went **to** the bank **on** Monday. It's **next to** my office.*

A preposition also goes before nouns, pronouns, and gerunds in expressions with verbs and adjectives.

- *We rely **on** him.*
- *She's accustomed **to** getting up early*

progressive   (also called **continuous**) the verb form ***be* + verb + *-ing***. It focuses on the continuation (not the completion) of an action.

- *She**'s reading** the paper.*
- *We **were watching** TV when you called.*

pronoun   a word used in place of a noun.

- *That's my brother. You met **him** at my party.*

proper noun   a noun that is the name of a person, place, or thing. It begins with a capital letter.

- ***Maria** goes to **Central High School**.*
- *It's on **High Street**.*

punctuation   marks used in writing (period, comma, . . .) that make the meaning clear. For example, a period (.) shows the end of a sentence. It also shows that the sentence is a statement, not a question.

quantifier   a word or phrase that shows an amount (but not an exact amount). It often comes before a noun.

- *Josh bought **a lot of** books last year.*
- *He doesn't have **much** money.*

question   See ***yes / no* question** and ***wh-* question**.

question word   See ***wh-* word**.

quoted speech   See **direct speech**.

real conditional sentence   a sentence that talks about general truths, habits, or things that happen again and again. It can also talk about things that will happen in the future under certain circumstances.

- *If it rains, he takes the bus.*
- *If it rains tomorrow, we'll take the bus with him.*

regular   a word that changes its form in the usual way.

- ***Play** is a **regular** verb. Its simple past form **(played)** ends in -**ed**.*

relative pronoun   a word that connects an adjective clause to a noun in the main clause.

- *He's the man **who** lives next door.*
- *I'm reading a book **that** I really like.*

reported speech   See **indirect speech**.

reporting verb   a verb such as ***said*, *told*,** or ***asked***. It introduces direct and indirect speech. It can also come after the quotation in direct speech.

- *She **said**, "I'm going to be late."*   OR   *"I'm going to be late," she **said**.*
- *She **told** me that she was going to be late.*

restrictive adjective clause   See **identifying adjective clause**.

result clause   the clause in a conditional sentence that talks about what happens if the condition occurs.

- *If it rains, **I'll stay home**.*
- *If I had a million dollars, **I would travel**.*
- *If I had had your phone number, **I would have called you**.*

sentence   a group of words that has a subject and a main verb.

- ***Computers are** very useful.*

separable phrasal verb a phrasal verb whose parts can separate.

- *Tom **looked** the word **up** in a dictionary.*
- *He **looked** it **up**.*

short answer an answer to a *yes / no* question.
A: *Did you call me last night?*
B: ***No, I didn't.*** OR ***No.***

singular one.

- *They have a **sister**.*
- ***She** works in a **hospital**.*

statement a sentence that gives information. In writing, it ends in a period.

- *Today is Monday.*

stative verb See **non-action verb**.

subject the person, place, or thing that the sentence is about.

- ***Ms. Chen** teaches English.*
- ***Her class** is interesting.*

subject pronoun a pronoun that shows the person (***I**, **you**, **he**, **she**, **it**, **we**, **they***) that the sentence is about.

- ***I** read a lot.*
- ***She** reads a lot too.*

subject relative pronoun a relative pronoun that is the subject of an adjective clause.

- *He's the man **who** lives next door.*

subordinate clause See **dependent clause**.

superlative the form of an adjective or adverb that is used to compare a person, place, or thing to a group of people, places, or things.

- *Cindi is **the shortest** player on the team.* (adjective)
- *She dances **the most gracefully**.* (adverb)

tag question a statement + tag. The **tag** is a short question at the end of the statement. Tag questions check information or comment on a situation.

- *You're Jack Thompson, **aren't you?***
- *It's a nice day, **isn't it?***

tense the form of a verb that shows the time of the action.

- **simple present**: *Fabio **talks** to his friend every day.*
- **simple past**: *Fabio **talked** to his teacher yesterday.*

third-person singular the pronouns *he*, *she*, and *it* or a singular noun. In the simple present, the third-person-singular verb ends in *-s* or *-es*.

- *Tomás **works** in an office.* (Tomás = he)

three-word verb a phrasal verb + preposition.

- *Slow down! I can't **keep up with** you.*

time clause a clause that begins with a time word such as **when**, **before**, **after**, **while**, or **as soon as**.

- *I'll call you **when** I get home.*

transitive verb a verb that has an object.

- *She **likes** apples.*

two-word verb See **phrasal verb**.

unreal conditional sentence a sentence that talks about unreal conditions and their unreal results. The condition and its result can be untrue, imagined, or impossible.

- *If I were a bird, I would fly around the world.*
- *If you had called, I would have invited you to the party.*

verb a word that describes what the subject of the sentence does, thinks, feels, senses, or owns.

- *They **run** two miles every day.*
- *She **loved** that movie.*
- *He **has** a new camera.*

wh- question (also called **information question**) a question that begins with a *wh-* word. You answer a *wh-* question with information.
A: ***Where** are you going?*
B: *To the store.*

wh- word a question word such as ***who**, **what**, **when**, **where**, **which**, **why**, **how***, and ***how much***. It can begin a *wh-* question or an embedded question.

- ***Who** is that?*
- ***What** did you see?*
- ***When** does the movie usually start?*
- *I don't know **how much** it costs.*

yes / no question a question that begins with a form of ***be*** or an auxiliary verb. You can answer a *yes / no* question with *yes* or *no*.
A: ***Are** you a student?*
B: ***Yes**, I am.* OR ***No**, I'm not.*

REVIEW TESTS ANSWER KEY

Note: In this answer key, where the contracted verb form is given, it is the preferred form, though the full form is also acceptable. Where the full verb form is given, it is the preferred form, though the contracted form is also acceptable.

PART I

I (Units 1–4)

2. are discussing
3. Are you thinking
4. wondered
5. love
6. agree
7. argue
8. claim
9. has
10. used
11. called
12. sounds
13. has accepted
14. think
15. means
16. roasted
17. had become
18. stood
19. talked
20. was
21. seems
22. is

II (Units 1–4)

1. b. 's been happening
   c. have
   d. moved
   e. bought
   f. had been looking
   g. had been planning
   h. decided
   i. is
   j. Have you ever been
   k. have
2. a. tried
   b. 've already eaten
   c. smell
   d. 'm thinking
   e. saw
   f. looked
3. a. Have you met
   b. calls
   c. What does she do
   d. was working
   e. laid off
   f. lost
   g. have been cutting
   h. liked
   i. 's trying
4. a. Have Al and Jack
   b. got
   c. 're staying
   d. sounds

e. need
f. have been
g. met
h. are they doing
i. 're taking
j. have been learning

III (Units 1–4)

2. A	6. D	9. C	12. C
3. C	7. B	10. D	13. A
4. A	8. C	11. C	14. D
5. B			

IV (Units 1–4)

2. mentioned
3. don't look
4. guess
5. did . . . decide
6. was
7. loved
8. was
9. had read
10. knew
11. wanted
12. 're attending OR 've been attending
13. got
14. didn't mind
15. was
16. met
17. 've wanted OR 've been wanting
18. understand
19. have . . . had
20. 've been following
21. haven't been able to
22. worry

V (Units 1–4)

Jack and I ~~are staying~~ *have been staying* at the Splendor for almost a week already. We've been spending a lot of time at the beach swimming and water-skiing, and I ~~was taking~~ *'ve been taking* scuba lessons in the hotel pool for several days now. Yesterday, ~~I've been planning~~ *I was planning* OR *I'd been planning* OR *I planned* to take my first dive from a boat. Unfortunately, by the time we left shore, the weather ~~has changed~~ *had changed*. We had to cancel the dive. This morning it was still a little cloudy, so we did something different. We ~~were deciding~~ *decided* to visit the Castle, an old pirate stronghold in Hideaway Bay. We had both read a little about it before we left, and it really sounded fascinating. So ~~we've rented~~ *we rented* a motorbike and took off. They ~~aren't having~~ *don't have* any road signs here outside of town, so by the time we found the Castle, ~~we've been driving for about~~ *we'd been driving* an hour. It was fun, though. When we were ~~seeing~~ *saw* the Castle, dark clouds were drifting over it. It really looked spooky and beautiful.

Well, the weather has cleared, and Jack ~~gets~~ *is getting* ready to go for a dive. I think I'll join him.

PART II

I (Unit 5)
2. I'll mail
3. We're going to go
4. They're going to crash
5. I'm graduating
6. I get
7. I'll see
8. I finish, I start
9. I won't be, I'll take
10. you do

II (Units 5–6)
2. you'll have been studying
3. I'll have graduated
4. what'll you be doing
5. I'll be looking
6. I won't have graduated
7. I'm going to be getting ready
8. you'll be sitting
9. I go
10. I get
11. you'll have found
12. I'm learning
13. you'll be starting

III (Units 5–6)
2. A	5. A	8. C
3. D	6. B	9. A
4. B	7. D	10. C

IV (Units 5–6)
2. won't be driving OR aren't going to be driving
3. 'll have driven
4. won't be polluting OR aren't going to be polluting
5. won't be spending OR aren't going to be spending
6. will . . . be taking OR are . . . going to be taking
7. 'll be working OR 's going to be working

8. 'll have completed
9. 'll have been teaching OR 'll have taught
10. won't have graded

V (Units 5–6)
2. A	4. B	6. D
3. C	5. A	7. B

PART III

I (Unit 7)
2. is
3. Doesn't . . . produce
4. Aren't . . . planting OR Don't . . . plant
5. exports
6. hasn't . . . been
7. visited
8. Didn't . . . name
9. doesn't use
10. Don't . . . speak

II (Unit 7)
2. hasn't he	7. Aren't
3. have they	8. shouldn't we
4. Didn't	9. Won't
5. had they	10. won't we
6. do they	11. Isn't

III (Units 7–8)
2. A	4. B	6. A	8. B	10. A
3. C	5. D	7. A	9. C	

IV (Unit 8)
2. Neither does	7. am too
3. So does	8. doesn't either
4. did too	9. Neither should
5. was too	10. So am
6. So would	

V (Units 7–8)
I'm a pretty bad letter writer, ~~amn't~~ *aren't* I? How are you? You didn't mention Marta in your last letter. ~~Don't~~ *Aren't* you roommates anymore? My new roommate's name is Rafaella. We have a lot in common. She's 18, and so ~~I am~~ *am I*. She lived in Chicago, and, of course, I did too. We have the same study habits too. She doesn't stay up late, and neither ~~don't~~ *do* I.

Luckily, there are some important differences too. You remember what my room looked like at home, ~~didn't~~ *don't* you? Well, I'm not very neat, but Rafaella is. I can't cook, but she can ~~too~~. So life is improving. You have a break soon, ~~do~~ *don't* you? Why don't you come for a visit? I know the three of us would have a good time.

PART IV

I (Units 9–10)

2. C	**6.** D	**10.** C	**14.** D
3. A	**7.** B	**11.** B	**15.** A
4. D	**8.** A	**12.** B	
5. C	**9.** D	**13.** C	

II (Units 9–10)

2. driving	**13.** having to
3. suspending	**14.** feeling OR to feel
4. to drive	**15.** to prevent OR
5. to drive	prevent
6. being	**16.** not to use
7. passing	**17.** to buckle up
8. not to take	**18.** ride
9. to give	**19.** driving
10. pay	**20.** behave
11. to be	**21.** saving
12. obeying	**22.** to make

III (Units 9–10)

2. A	**4.** C	**6.** A	**8.** A
3. D	**5.** B	**7.** D	

IV (Units 9–10)

2. urges Alicia to ask
3. lets students stay
4. doesn't mind my daughter's (OR daughter) recording
5. appreciates the teacher's (OR teacher) being
6. are used to Ms. Allen's (OR Ms. Allen) demanding
7. makes them take
8. gets them to help
9. wants them to do
10. are happy with her teaching

V (Units 9–10)

2. is letting OR is going to let OR will let Caryn use
3. afford to buy
4. persuaded Caryn to take
5. invited Jason to join
6. quit eating OR has quit eating
7. offered to lift
8. suggested turning on
9. made Dan show him OR her
10. denied calling Caryn

PART V

I (Units 11–12)

2. out	**7.** with
3. up	**8.** out
4. over	**9.** out
5. over	**10.** over
6. in	**11.** up

12. down, up	**18.** off
13. up	**19.** through with
14. in	**20.** away
15. up with	**21.** off
16. out	**22.** up, back
17. back	

II (Units 11–12)

2. C	**6.** D	**10.** D	**14.** B
3. D	**7.** B	**11.** D	**15.** B
4. A	**8.** C	**12.** C	
5. B	**9.** C	**13.** A	

III (Units 11–12)

2. call it off
3. carry it out
4. switched it on
5. get along with John OR him
6. keep away from them
7. put it back
8. taken them off
9. wake her up
10. work them out

IV (Units 11–12)

2. A	**5.** D	**8.** D	**11.** D
3. D	**6.** D	**9.** D	**12.** D
4. A	**7.** A	**10.** B	

V (Units 11–12)

2. Please don't throw them away.
3. The teacher turned down my topic proposal (OR turned my topic proposal down).
4. All forms must be turned in by April 8.
5. They could blow up.
6. Don't give up hope.
7. You left it out.
8. The students didn't let me down.
9. Can someone point out what the mistake is?
10. Don't just show up without one.

PART VI

I (Units 13–14)

2. who	**8.** who
3. who	**9.** that
4. where	**10.** which
5. whose	**11.** when
6. which	**12.** when
7. which	

II (Units 13–14)

2. She lives in the house which (OR that) is across the street.
3. This is the time of year when (OR that) she always goes away.

4. She travels with her older sister, who lives in Connecticut.

5. This year they're taking a trip with the car that (OR which) she just bought.

6. They're going to Miami, where they grew up.

7. They have a lot of relatives in Florida, who(m) they haven't seen in years.

8. The family is going to have a reunion, which they've been planning all year.

9. They'll be staying with their Aunt Sonya, whose house is right on a canal.

10. They really need this vacation, which they've been looking forward to all year.

III (Units 13–14)

2. C	6. B	10. C
3. C	7. A	11. C
4. C	8. B	
5. B	9. C	

IV (Units 13–14)

2. D	5. B	8. C
3. B	6. C	9. B
4. C	7. D	10. C

V (Units 13–14)

There is an old German proverb that says,
which OR *that* OR no relative pronoun
"Friendship is a plant ~~who~~ we must often water." This means that we have to nurture our relationships to make them grow and flourish. A relationship that you neglect will wilt and die.

   When I was ten, my family moved from Germany to the United States. There I had a "friend" (whom I will call Jack) who ~~he~~ never invited me to do things with him. Jack lived in a
which OR *that* OR no relative pronoun
house ~~where~~ I never got to see even though it was just a few blocks away from mine. He had family and friends whom I never met. Of course, today I realize that Jack really wasn't a friend at all. He was what in Germany is called a *Bekannter*—
know
someone who you ~~knows~~—an acquaintance. And for an acquaintance, his behavior was fine. I got
when OR no relative pronoun
confused on the day ~~where~~ Jack referred to me as his friend.

   "Friend" is a word that has a different set of expectations for me. In Germany, that word is
whom
reserved for people with ~~that~~ one is really close. I learned through the experience with Jack that although you can translate a word from one language to another, the meaning can still be different. Today I have friends from many
whose
countries. I also have many acquaintances ~~who~~ friendships I have learned to value too.

PART VII

I (Units 15–17)

2. couldn't	9. might have
3. could have	10. must have
4. can't	11. must not have
5. must not	12. could have
6. 's got to	13. shouldn't have
7. has to	14. shouldn't have
8. should	15. 'd better not

II (Units 15–17)

2. may not have been
3. could have been
4. couldn't have been
5. should have studied
6. could . . . have done
7. shouldn't have missed
8. ought to have copied
9. must have come

III (Units 15–17)

2. I should've watched the show about Easter Island.
3. It must've been very interesting.
4. The local library ought to have bought books about Easter Island.
5. Sara should've reminded me about it.
6. John could've told me about it.
7. He must not have remembered our conversation about it.
8. My roommate might've invited me to the party.
9. John might not have gotten an invitation.
10. He couldn't have forgotten our date.

IV (Units 15–17)

2. B	5. D	8. B
3. A	6. B	9. C
4. C	7. C	10. A

V (Units 15–17)

better not
What a day! I guess I'd ~~not better~~ stay up so late
have
anymore. This morning I should ~~of~~ gotten up much earlier. When I got to the post office, the lines were
waited
already long. I must have ~~wait~~ at least half an hour.
fire
My boss was furious that I was late. He might ~~fires~~ me for lateness—even though I couldn't have worked during that time anyway. The computers

have
were down again! We must ~~had~~ lost four hours because of that. While the system was down, some

_to_
of us were able ∧ go out to lunch. Later, we all felt

have
sick. It had to ~~has~~ been the food—we all ate the same thing. On the way home, I got stuck in

have
traffic. A trip that should ∧ taken twenty minutes took forty-five. Tomorrow's Saturday. I just might

sleep
~~sleeping~~ until noon.

PART VIII

I (Units 18–19)
2. leave
3. were mailed
4. have
5. were made
6. were confirmed
7. need
8. be met
9. rent
10. just handed
11. were sent
12. was done

II (Unit 19)
2. might be delivered
3. 'll be read
4. 'll be satisfied
5. have to be packed OR will have to be packed
6. ought to be told
7. could be extended
8. should be painted
9. has to be serviced
10. can be arranged

III (Units 18–20)
2. C	6. D	10. A
3. A	7. B	11. D
4. B	8. A	
5. A	9. C	

IV (Unit 20)
2. have OR get . . . cleaned
3. have OR get . . . looked at
4. have OR get . . . painted
5. had OR got . . . designed
6. have OR get . . . delivered
7. have OR get . . . made up
8. have OR get . . . catered
9. Have OR Get . . . sent

V (Units 18–20)
2. is grown
3. are employed by the sugar industry
4. is exported
5. is struck by hurricanes
6. was popularized by Bob Marley
7. 's listened to (by people)

VI (Units 18–20)
2. C	4. A	6. A
3. D	5. D	7. D

PART IX

I (Units 21–24)
2. A	8. A	14. B	20. B
3. B	9. C	15. D	21. A
4. C	10. A	16. A	22. D
5. B	11. A	17. A	23. A
6. C	12. B	18. B	
7. D	13. D	19. C	

II (Units 21–24)
2. would have seen
3. tell
4. 'll spoil
5. would . . . have been
6. 'd been born
7. 'd had
8. wouldn't have grown up
9. hadn't grown up
10. wouldn't have met
11. hadn't taken
12. studied OR study
13. 'd pass OR 'll pass
14. don't get OR wouldn't get
15. study OR studied
16. were
17. 'd try

III (Units 21–24)
2. found
3. Would . . . keep
4. knew
5. hadn't gotten
6. would've borrowed
7. would've taken
8. weren't
9. would be
10. wouldn't have seen
11. had looked
12. have
13. discuss
14. doesn't belong
15. return

16. won't follow
17. obey
18. comes
19. 'll be

IV (Units 23–24)

2. I wish I had bought business-class tickets.
3. I wish the in-flight movie weren't *Back to the Future IV*.
4. I wish we hadn't gone to Disney World on vacation.
5. I wish we had gone (OR could have gone) to the beach.
6. I wish I (OR we lived) in Florida.
7. I wish my office could transfer me to Orlando.

V (Units 21–24)

2. B	5. B	7. A
3. D	6. C	8. C
4. A		

PART X

I (Units 25–28)

1. **b.** last
2. **a.** would be   **b.** our
3. **a.** told   **b.** they
4. **a.** asked   **b.** was
5. **a.** she   **b.** should bring
6. **a.** told   **b.** not to bring
7. **a.** 'd been planning   **b.** us
8. **a.** didn't know how   **b.** our
9. **a.** asked   **b.** if there was
10. **a.** not to be
11. **a.** told   **b.** to take
12. **a.** couldn't   **b.** the following night
13. **a.** was   **b.** that day
14. **a.** told   **b.** her
15. **a.** had issued   **b.** that night
16. **a.** would   **b.** that day
17. **a.** had to drive
18. **a.** says   **b.** loves
19. **a.** him   **b.** to shovel
20. **a.** asked   **b.** his boots were

II (Units 25–29)

2. B	5. B	8. C
3. D	6. A	9. D
4. D	7. D	10. C

III (Units 25–28)

2. D	5. C	8. C
3. A	6. B	9. D
4. B	7. A	10. B

IV (Units 25–28)

2. Jon told her (that) they had moved in three weeks before.
3. Nita asked if (OR whether) they liked (OR like) that place better than their old apartment.
4. Jon said (that) they liked (OR like) it a lot more.
5. Jon asked (her) when her cousin had arrived from Detroit.
6. Nita told him (that) he had just come the day before.
7. Jon said (that) it had been (OR has been) an incredible winter.
8. Nita said (that) the roads might close again with that storm.
9. Jon said not to drive that night.
10. Jon said to stay there with her cousin.
11. Nita told him (that) they should try to make it home.
12. Nita said (that) she had to walk her dog early the next morning.

V (Units 25–29)

Motorists returning home during last night's snow storm were pleasantly surprised. Early yesterday afternoon, forecasters had predicted that Route 10 *would* ~~will~~ close because of high winds. However, all major highways remained open last night. One woman, stopping for a newspaper on Woodmere Avenue at about midnight, told this reporter that she and her cousin *had* ~~have~~ almost decided to stay with a friend *that night* OR *last night* ~~tonight~~, rather than drive home.

Her cousin told me that *he* ~~I~~ had just arrived from Detroit, where the storm hit first. He said ~~"that it had been a big one."~~ *that it had been a big one.* School children seemed especially pleased. Yesterday morning, most schools announced that they *would* ~~will~~ close at 1:00 P.M. Several kids at James Fox Elementary reported that they *were* ~~are~~ planning to spend that afternoon sledding and having snowball fights.

Many people are wondering how ~~could~~ weather forecasters *could* have made such a big mistake. Carla Donati, the weather reporter for WCSX, said that they were not sure why this had happened~~?~~. The National Weather Service has not commented.

INDEX

This Index is for the full and split editions. All entries are in the full book. Entries for Volume A of the split edition are in black. Entries for Volume B are in color.

Notes

Notes